Helion & Company Limited
Unit 8 Amherst Business Centre
Budbrooke Road
Warwick
CV34 5WE
England
Tel. 01926 499 619
Email: info@helion.co.uk
Website: www.helion.co.uk
Twitter: @helionbooks
Visit our blog http://blog.helion.co.uk/

Designed and typeset by Farr out Publications, Wokingham, Berkshire
Cover design by Paul Hewitt, Battlefield Design (www.battlefield-design.co.uk)

ISBN 978-1-915070-63-0

British Library Cataloguing-in-Publication Data
A catalogue record for this book is available from the British Library

We always welcome receiving book proposals from prospective authors.

CONTENTS

Abbreviations 2
Introduction 2

1 'Cutting Up' the Viet Cong 7
2 The Insurgents Respond 34
3 The X-Factor 50

Conclusion 66
Bibliography 67
Notes 76
About the Author 86

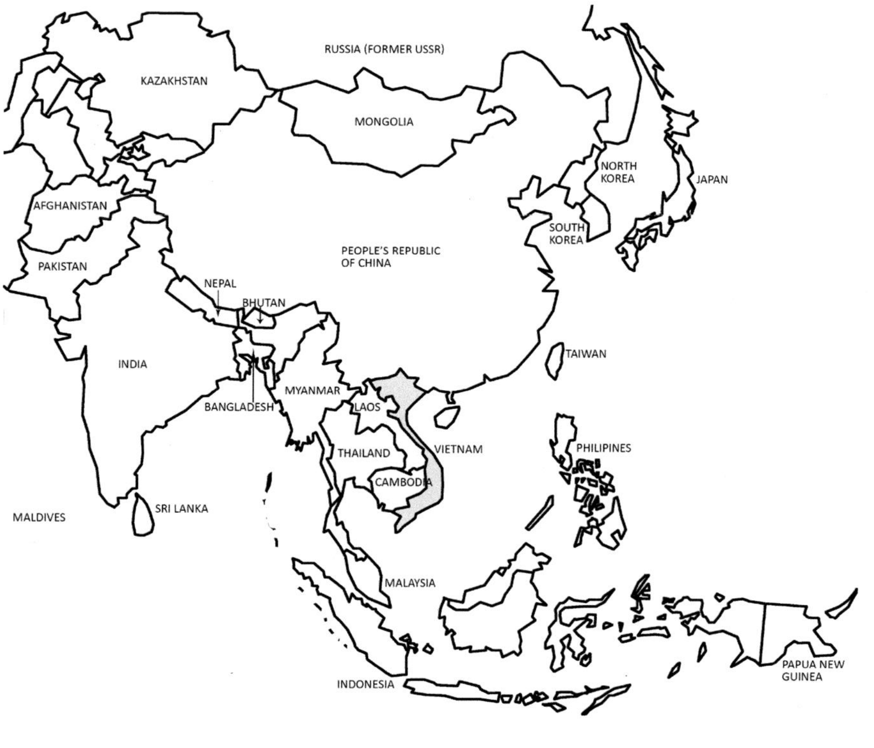

Note: In order to simplify the use of this book, all names, locations and geographic designations are as provided in *The Times World Atlas*, or other traditionally accepted major sources of reference, as of the time of described events.

Dedication

For my family who have helped me throughout this process: My parents for all their love, wisdom and guidance; my brother for his care, encouragement and IT support and my partner for her help, investment and tour guide skills around Boston, MA. I'd also like to acknowledge a 'man from Kent or a Kentish-man' who is no longer with us but who was eager to read this completed book. Perhaps a Heavenly library will obtain a copy? Saying 'Thank You' to all will never be enough.

ABBREVIATIONS

ARVN Army of the Republic of South Vietnam
CIA Central Intelligence Agency
GVN Government of (South) Vietnam
NLF National Liberation Front
NSAM National Security Action Memorandum
NVA North Vietnamese Army
SEATO South East Asia Treaty Organisation
US United States
USOM United States Operations Mission (local office of USAID)
VC Viet Cong

Please Note: Many of the sources used in this research were translated from original Vietnamese documentation. As such, spelling and grammatical errors are left unaltered unless they significantly hinder the reader's understanding. In addition, several captured documents are identified by their date of capture rather than publication.

INTRODUCTION

What of the enemy? The VC know they have an adversary who, for the first time, is capable of defeating him. They have become the hunted instead of the hunter.

—General Paul D. Harkins in a letter to President Diem, 23 February, 1963[1]

A Viet Cong suspect, looking the worse for wear, is arrested and taken for interrogation. Many suspects were beaten before interrogation and US advisors were only allowed to interview them in the final stages of the Diem regime. (Albert Grandolini Collection)

In the early months of 1963, American advisors and analysts in South Vietnam were growing increasingly confident that their counterinsurgency strategy was bearing fruit. The Viet Cong were being killed or captured in large numbers, many parts of South Vietnam were considered to be under government control and even the Viet Cong themselves admitted that they were being 'cut up'. The Counterinsurgency Plan and Strategic Hamlet Programme adopted by the Ngo Diem regime was isolating the VC from their peasant supporters, limiting their access to medicine and weapons and ARVN was pursuing them across the jungles and paddy fields of the South.

ARVN, Self-Defense Corps and Militia-based patrol units are seen in the South Vietnamese countryside. Many village militia units were poorly equipped or were loaned weapons until they could capture their own equipment from the Viet Cong. (Albert Grandolini Collection)

The symbol of the Strategic Hamlet Programme – showing the 'Flaming Torch of Freedom'. (John F. Kennedy Presidential Library, with permission)

ARVN on patrol in the South Vietnamese countryside with an interesting mix of head cover. Notice that the roadside has been cleared to limit the potential for an ambush. (Albert Grandolini Collection)

The British Advisory Mission even suggested that in March 1963, the VC were getting close to eventual collapse.[2] Whilst the 'World' may have sensed imminent US–Diem defeat as they witnessed the assassination of President Diem, escalating American aid and burnt-out homes, the Americans operating in South Vietnam (between 1961 and 1963) believed that the counterinsurgency campaign conducted against the Viet Cong was seriously hurting the 'revolution'. This book presents new research that supports the latter view and reveals how the counterinsurgency strategy of 1961–63 'hunted' the Viet Cong and nearly brought them to their knees.

This book (the first of two) examines events in South Vietnam between 1961 and 1963 and reassesses the historical record. It will show how the Viet Cong were being hunted and starved into submission, insurgent recruitment was adversely affected and, in many parts of the country, government support increased. It looks at how the South Vietnamese government policy damaged insurgent activity and, in particular, examines the centrepiece of the government counterinsurgency strategy: The Strategic Hamlet Programme.

It also examines the wider 'Counterinsurgency Plan' introduced into South Vietnam at this time.[3] The contention of this book is that conventional historical accounts of this period do not tell the full story: a much subtler appreciation and analysis of the counterinsurgency strategy is needed. Whilst it is true that there were massive failures in policy implementation, there were also areas of real success: the VC were being hunted and hurt.

Why is this book needed?

The historian Andrew Preston has argued that much of the historical record surrounding this time period in South Vietnam is not so much 'incorrect as incomplete' and this book will apply Preston's assessment to the counterinsurgency strategy and show that a re-evaluation of this time period is long overdue.[4] Far too often in the history of the Vietnam War, accounts tell a story of inevitable defeat. This book suggests defeat was not preordained and a re-assessment of events is needed. To help in this re-evaluation, the book combines the views of the Vietnamese people, the South Vietnamese Government, the American Military and the Vietnamese guerrilla fighters into a coherent, evaluative whole.[5] A particular feature of the book is the way it uses captured guerrilla documentation to present the argument. The views of the Vietnamese fighting on the ground are vital because they are rarely included in Western accounts of the war. In fact, the focus on insurgent documentation and on interviews with the Vietnamese guerrillas provides a new, 'Ground Up' perspective on this time period. As Davison notes, these are the people who 'bore the brunt of the fighting' and whose 'voices have all too seldom been heard.'[6]

Special Advisors from the Civilian Irregular Defense Group advising and training ARVN during a jungle patrol. The CIA expanded the programme in 1961 with the aim of training not only ARVN but ethnic minority groups in the Central Highlands too. (Albert Grandolini Collection)

ARVN Units patrolling the South Vietnamese countryside. The empty fields were not only used for growing crops but could also be used to provide clear 'fields of fire' in the event of an insurgent attack. The advantage worked both ways and the unit crossed the field quickly. (Albert Grandolini Collection)

Another aim of this book is to give voice to the many brave people in South Vietnam working for the greater good: the Vietnamese and their American allies who were working at considerable risk to their own lives in aid missions or as doctors, teachers and advisors in rural communities. These people often bore the brunt of Viet Cong violence and their sacrifice and determination to build a better nation can often be lost amongst military and political accounts of the war. Why listen to these people? Well, these views are particularly important because, as one of the key actors in the aid mission in South Vietnam at this time (Rufus Phillips) notes:

> If you want to understand what is happening in a particular country you cannot just rely on the higher echelons in Washington, you really need to have somebody come in from the field and give you information directly.[7]

This book gives these people a chance to be heard.

Why focus on 1961–1963?

It is important to focus on the years 1961–63 because although the Vietnam War has been studied and written about extensively by historians, comparatively little has been written about the years 1961 to 1963. In addition, perspectives are often distorted by an overreliance on American documentation or a rather general, vague evaluation of the time period.[8] Whilst writers such as Philip Catton, David Elliott, Edward Miller and Rufus Phillips have attempted to present a more in-depth, detailed analysis of the early years of the war, they are frequently voices in the wilderness.[9] Similarly, whilst David Hunt has produced an excellent account of Vietnamese perceptions in *Vietnam's Southern Revolution: From Peasant Insurrection to Total War*, it examines a later time in the conflict.[10] Too often, the writing about the Vietnam War in 1961–63 has dismissed this time period in one or two sentences: a far more detailed, in-depth analysis is required. As Ang Chen Guan has argued, this time period was when 'key attitudes were formed and vital commitments made' and this book will seek to contribute to the understanding of the Vietnam War in its infancy.[11]

Also, a study of preliminary strategy and tactical approaches will help the understanding of the wider war and the subsequent conflict that cost so many Vietnamese and American lives. As Frank Kitson says, 'people seldom write about their doings in the preparatory stages of subversion, which is unfortunate because a clear understanding of their problems at that time would be of great value': this book aims to fulfil that role.[12]

Structure

In terms of structure, the first two chapters of the book will show how the counterinsurgents' planning and the insurgents' response were interlinked. For example, Chapter One relies heavily on American government documentation and will demonstrate that the military successes of the Diem regime hurt the insurgency. It outlines the counterinsurgency strategy, details the Strategic Hamlet Programme and examines the effectiveness of the strategies on Viet Cong activities. Chapter Two will then explain how this success in damaging the insurgency led to the guerrillas drawing up an 'Anti-Strategic Hamlet Programme' to combat the counterinsurgency initiative. This chapter looks at the VC Anti-Strategic Hamlet Programme and the measures the insurgents undertook to try and undermine government attacks on them.

Finally, Chapter Three demonstrates that increased American involvement in terms of aid and socio-political reform gave the insurgents propaganda to add impetus to their Revolution. In fact, government actions were often counterproductive and made the situation worse. This helped to undermine the counterinsurgency effort and would lead to eventual government defeat later in the war. The second volume in the series examines in greater detail the undermining of government strategy and the way in which the insurgents began to fight back against the counterinsurgency methods employed by the Ngo Diem regime.

ARVN unit/Self-Defense Corps returning to base after a patrol. Note that the lead individual is barefoot. (Albert Grandolini Collection)

ARVN patrol units crossing a bridge and returning to their base – notice the bamboo defences around the bridge in the bottom of the picture. (Albert Grandolini Collection)

Patrols were stepped up throughout South Vietnam. 'Spear and Net' tactics were used to try and corner Viet Cong and drive them out of villages and hamlets where they could be hiding. (Albert Grandolini Collection)

Units awaiting orders before undertaking a jungle patrol in the Central Highlands. Uniform insignia was meagre at this point in the military's history. (Albert Grandolini Collection)

Father Hoa's militia in training; many Catholic priests helped set up and guide local militia groups to counter the Viet Cong and its competing ideology. These militia groups were a substantial back-up force that the South Vietnamese government could use against the insurgents. (Albert Grandolini Collection)

The Montagnards were recruited and trained by the South Vietnamese government – in particular to try and stop infiltration and violence in the Central Highlands region. Here a group receives weapons training, their motley appearance belying the fierce reputation they would earn. (Albert Grandolini Collection)

Communist insurgents infiltrating South Vietnam. Notice how well-equipped these insurgents are – even in the early 1960s – compared with the earlier images of government troops. (Communist Archive/ Albert Grandolini Collection)

Special Advisors from the Civilian Irregular Defense Group training ARVN in the field. This photograph is from later in the conflict – as suggested by the M-16s rifles being carried – but reveals the close working links between both organisations. (Albert Grandolini Collection)

Key Terms

When discussing counterinsurgency, one problem is that there are no agreed set of terms or definitions surrounding counterinsurgency practice and as a result, defining insurgents and counterinsurgents can often be a vague and inexact process.[13] Therefore, any definition needs to consider who the insurgents were, what they did and what they wanted to achieve.

One of the first issues is that the definition of insurgent in this study is complicated by the groups that were operating in South Vietnam at this time; although essentially working for the same goals and often being made up of the same people, the North Vietnamese and the Viet Cong were often described in literature and news reports as being detached from each other. Whilst agreeing with David Kilcullen that any identity in an insurgency is fluid, for the purpose of this study, an insurgent will be a person or persons who was trying to undermine or overthrow the Diem regime.[14]

This will include peasants involved either voluntarily or forcibly in anti-government activity, Viet Cong forces, ex-Viet Minh fighters returning from North Vietnam and North Vietnamese agents and soldiers.

Insurgents can also be defined by their actions: an insurgent will use a combination of political and military methods to achieve their goal. For example, historians such as Bernard Fall

ARVN machine gun post has an M-1919 .30-cal emplaced on high ground and the barrel in a wooden support despite the tripod. Notice the fences in the distance – these were built with the aim of slowing down advancing attackers. (Albert Grandolini Collection)

consider the political process to be a vital part of any insurgency or counterinsurgency campaign and this can encompass the development of political parties but also ideological and administrative action.[15] This is illustrated by the use of Viet Cong propaganda. This propaganda helped to turn the war in South Vietnam into an anti-imperialist, ideological struggle and Viet Cong shadow government networks ran in parallel to the administrative structures of the South Vietnamese regime. This use of political action also means that village cadres and those involved in shadow government structures will be considered insurgents. However, political action is not the only feature of an insurgency: insurgents also use violence and intimidation. This can include methods such as guerrilla warfare, assassination, mutilation, urban unrest, torture and kidnapping.[16]

Those who used such violence or who issued threats of violence on behalf of or in the name of the insurgency will also be classed as insurgents. Therefore, the term insurgent, when used here, will be all-encompassing of both North and South Vietnamese guerrilla forces active in or around South Vietnam at this time and will include those involved (willingly or unwillingly) in using asymmetrical warfare as a central tool in undermining the government of President Diem.

In contrast, the counterinsurgents will be defined as people who were attacking the insurgent network and protecting government structures, buildings and people. This includes ARVN (Army of the Republic of South Vietnam), American personnel in South Vietnam, the Diem regime and American government advisors outside of the country. Essentially, these groups were trying to disrupt insurgent forces, guerrilla leadership and the various factions considered to be supporting the insurgency. As with the insurgents, the counterinsurgents also used a variety of techniques to try and achieve their goals. These included military force, political and economic reform and psychological propaganda to try and undermine the insurgency itself. Specific methods used ranged from relatively benign control measures such as roadblocks and identification cards to censorship, detention without trial, mass arrest and forcible population resettlement. The fundamental aim here was to allow the state to continue to function, disrupt and eventually destroy insurgent networks and arrest the insurgents and their supporters. Ultimately, these approaches were designed to show the power of the government to control the lives of ordinary citizens and combat the fear of the insurgency.[17] Therefore, when discussing counterinsurgents, the definition is also wide-ranging. It will consider those involved in combating the insurgents in South Vietnam through military, political, economic, psychological and social means to be the counterinsurgents in this campaign.

An ARVN Lieutenant leads a patrol through the South Vietnamese countryside armed with an M1928 Thompson sub machine gun. (Albert Grandolini Collection)

Robert McNamara briefs the media on the 'Gulf of Tonkin incident' in 1964. McNamara has received constant criticism for his conduct of the war and his refusal to listen to advice. (Albert Grandolini Collection)

Finally, when judging the success of the counterinsurgency strategy and the Strategic Hamlet Programme, the book will use a wide-ranging criteria based upon the views of those working in South Vietnam at this time.[18] This includes: limiting Viet Cong access to food, medicines and military supplies, providing protection for the general population, building strategic hamlets and forcing the insurgents to attack their own support.[19] Success would also be achieved where the insurgents could be attacked without warning and were unable to gather reinforcements.[20]

Overview

Ultimately, this book will show that the situation in South Vietnam between 1961 and 1963 was incredibly complex, often contradictory and it was possible – as Sir Robert Thompson argued – to find information to prove any point of view that you wished to support:

> In assessing the situation in Vietnam, we had learnt three rules: nothing is what it seems; every statement or comment can be supported by evidence and is therefore true; and, as an extension of Murphy's Law, if the roof can fall in it will.[21]

The books in this series will illustrate that no one single element was responsible for the overthrow of the Diem government and the collapse of the Strategic Hamlet Programme and that success and failure could occur simultaneously.

In fact, there were many parts of the country where the Viet Cong were being destroyed, the counterinsurgency policy was successful and the government of South Vietnam could claim they were – if not 'winning' the conflict – certainly not 'losing' it either. Indeed, had the counterinsurgency policy been examined more accurately, events may have unfolded in a different way. In the end though, as Robert McNamara noted, failure in Vietnam was caused by many factors and issues that although discrete, were 'all in some way linked: failure in one area contributed to or compounded failure in another. Each became a turn in a terrible knot.'[22]

A combination of events, personalities and planning all merged into – to use a cliché – a 'Perfect Storm' to create an unstable situation in South Vietnam. These undermined any successes gained by the Strategic Hamlet Programme and resulted in the strategic hamlet strategy being abandoned. It was replaced by the New Rural Life Hamlets after the American-backed Diem regime was toppled. This book will show that these events were not inevitable.

1
'CUTTING UP' THE VIET CONG

Presenting the Counterinsurgency Plan and the Strategic Hamlet Programme

I think if Diem would have settled with the Buddhists, then the war as we know it would have been over by the end of 1963. It is a historical might-have-been. Nobody can say for sure. But from what I was able to learn afterwards – I do not think any of us knew this at the time, but in talking to Viet Cong defectors and so on in the subsequent years – they told us, "you were really cutting us up".

—Douglas Pike Oral History Interview, 2 June 1981[1]

In order to fight the Viet Cong, President Diem and his brother – with American support – drew up a Counterinsurgency Plan that aimed to isolate the Viet Cong and hunt them down. Many people working in South Vietnam believed this counterinsurgency campaign was seriously hurting the Viet Cong. Indeed, Douglas Pike claimed that VC defectors had told him that the strategy was 'cutting up' the insurgents.

Pike's assertion provides an interesting contrast to much of the historical writing surrounding this time period.[2] A great deal of this academic writing asserts that both the 'Counterinsurgency Plan' and the Strategic Hamlet Programme that supported it, failed.[3] The evidence does not support this view. The following chapter will

President Diem inspecting a guard in the late 1950s/early 1960s. (Albert Grandolini Collection)

Vietnamese villagers are seen being relocated to a strategic hamlet via US Army H-21 helicopters. (Albert Grandolini Collection)

show that – when implemented correctly – the counterinsurgency programme was effective. It will also show that the nature of the threat was clearly understood, the programme was well planned and it was based around sound counterinsurgency theory. The programme was also useful in attacking the base of support for the insurgents and it was beginning to turn some of the rural population against the Viet Cong.

The Problem?

What Did the Americans Know?

The first point to discuss here is that many reports recognised the challenges that the Americans and the Diem regime faced in South Vietnam. For example, there was an appreciation that intelligence gathering was an issue and that the counterinsurgents needed to rectify this as soon as possible. This was documented in a letter to President Kennedy in 1961 in which Maxwell Taylor wrote that there was a 'lack of firm and well organised operational intelligence' which meant 'initiative has been conceded to the enemy.'[4]

ARVN operational briefing – possibly in relation to convoy protection and Viet Cong ambush tactics. (Albert Grandolini Collection)

The 'Counterinsurgency Plan' of 1961 also recorded that 'no adequate operations control or overall planning system presently exists' and this was a problem that needed to be addressed.[5] It was also acknowledged that this lack of useful intelligence created a vicious circle whereby 'poor intelligence, poor command and control arrangements, and poor mobility reinforce each other' and this negatively impacted on strategy and tactics.[6]

Despite these misgivings, intelligence reports that were produced at the time did identify some of the problems faced in the country. For example, a National Intelligence Estimate of March 1961, described how the situation in Vietnam 'continued to deteriorate and has now reached serious proportions' and the Diem government faced a 'Communist internal threat' which was being directed from Hanoi.[7]

Intelligence Estimates went on to describe how this threat was via 'covert direction and support of the Viet Cong' and had intensified

Violence erupts in Saigon in 1960 as a coup attempts to overthrow President Diem. An army M8 Greyhound armoured car has been set ablaze, likely by a Molotov cocktail. (Albert Grandolini Collection)

A US Army helicopter, likely a UH-1A, patrols the Saigon perimeter. (Albert Grandolini Collection)

ARVN troops patrolling the streets in an effort to suppress violence in 1960 – indicating that internal unrest would be the primary problem that the government faced. The M8 armoured car provided transport, protection, and firepower. (Albert Grandolini Collection)

An ARVN patrol hunting the Viet Cong in the Mekong Delta, the open canoe offering no protection from sniper fire from the shoreline. (Albert Grandolini Collection)

'political and propaganda pressures on South Vietnam.'[8] There was an acceptance too that the immediate danger to South Vietnam was 'not from overt invasion.'[9]

This suggests an understanding of the nature of the conflict and indicates that the military planners did not anticipate an immediate conventional war.[10] It was also recognised that the conflict would last a long time and the CIA believed that the war would take 'at least 12 to 18 months of effort' before much improvement occurred.[11] In the meantime, South Vietnam faced a 'prolonged and difficult struggle with the Viet Cong insurgents' before victory could be achieved.[12]

A communist using a light mortar to attack a government outpost – again revealing the level of equipment that the insurgents possessed. (Communist Archive/Albert Grandolini Collection)

Finally, the Americans understood the basic Viet Cong strategy. This is again in contrast to much of the body of literature around the Vietnam War which is often unfairly over-critical of the American understanding of the insurgents' approach to the conflict. For example, Thomas Hammes noted that Mao had outlined the insurgents' methodology in a 'People's War' as early as 1951 and consequently the counterinsurgents should have been aware of the strategy they were facing.[13] Yet again though, the sources shed light on the fact that the Viet Cong approach was understood by the American military.

For example, there was a clear understanding that they were pursuing a strategy to 'bypass US nuclear strength, US conventional naval, air, and ground forces, and the conventional strength of indigenous forces in the area' and that this would be done through 'a variant on Mao's classic three-stage offensive.'[14] Indeed, in a letter to President Kennedy in 1961, Maxwell Taylor revealed that the military strategy being pursued was understood in some detail:

> First, a political base for guerrilla war, subversion, and dissidence is established in each country in the area, exploiting its unique vulnerabilities via trained local or introduced cadres. Second, guerrilla war is begun. Third, a maximum effort is made to translate the Communist position achieved on the ground, plus the weakness and cross-purposes in the non-Communist camp, to induce a neutralist interim solution, blocking the US military presence, as with the proposed renunciation by Laos of SEATO protection. Complete Communist take-over, by whatever means may appear feasible, is the evident ultimate objective.[15]

Communist infiltrators carrying weapons and camouflage on their way to ambush an ARVN unit. (Communist Archive/Albert Grandolini Collection)

Intelligence reports also showed that the insurgent forces were 'in a transitional stage from a guerrilla to a conventional type of warfare' and a CIA report of 1962 noted that 'we do not believe however, that the Communist powers intend to attempt to achieve their objectives in Southeast Asia by large-scale military aggression.'[16] To claim, therefore, that the overall insurgent strategy was misunderstood as being conventionally military in nature appears not to be the case.

In addition to grasping the overall strategic concept of the insurgents, it was also clear that the specific tactical approaches used by the guerrillas were understood by the American intelligence operatives. For example, the CIA noted that the insurgents were achieving maximum effectiveness by 'relying on tactics of surprise, concentration for attack and dispersal upon withdrawal.'[17] This was done to create a sense of unease and uncertainty amongst the rural population by using methods that aimed to neuter ARVN and force the army to remain in their own bases. The Taylor Mission described the strategy:

> To pin down ARVN on defensive missions; to create a pervasive sense of insecurity and frustration by hit-and-run raids on self-defence corps and militia units, ambushing the reserve forces if possible as they come up to defend; and to dramatise the inability of the GVN to govern or to build, by the assassination of officials and the sabotage of public works.[18]

These tactics would feed into the wider conflict and were designed to minimise the risk of American involvement. They were supplemented through activities such as 'subversion, political action, and support of "national liberation" struggles.'[19] This would 'greatly reduce the risk to North Vietnam' of a US military attack and, at the same time, provide 'good prospects of success at relatively little cost' to the Communists.[20]

A communist cell on a night-time patrol – note the handheld gas lantern and simple camouflage. (Communist Archive/Albert Grandolini Collection)

Helping President Diem

There was also an appreciation, again in contrast to some of the historical writing, that the political aspect of the conflict – and the role of President Diem – was vital. For example, a 1962 report noted that 'it is a truism to say that this war is as much political as military' and that this would manifest itself in a struggle for control of the villages in South Vietnam.[21] It was acknowledged that 'the struggle for South Vietnam, in sum, is essentially a battle for control of the villages' and this had to take place through so-called 'rice

A youthful looking President Diem watches a military parade. Notice the Westerners in the background and the overt status of the Catholic Church: all would be used to undermine his regime in the future. (Albert Grandolini Collection)

A briefing given by senior ARVN officers before a raid on a Viet Cong stronghold. (Albert Grandolini Collection)

President Diem greets supporters from the various provinces of South Vietnam. (Albert Grandolini Collection)

The American military advisor, Colonel Edward Lansdale, in an early meeting with President Diem. Lansdale was one of the many 'Quiet Americans' advising Diem and was also one who recognised the need to limit his (and the American) national profile. (Albert Grandolini Collection)

roots' democracy whereby peasants would be encouraged to help implement political change.[22]

Also, whilst many advisors in South Vietnam believed that Diem was part of the problem, they also understood why he was so slow to embrace political change. For example, Maxwell Taylor stated in November 1961 that although Diem had a ruling style that sought to 'maintain all the strings of power in his own hands, while fragmenting power beneath him,' it was recognised that this was the administrative style 'of an old fashioned Asian ruler' and therefore culturally appropriate to South East Asia.[23]

Edward Lansdale is shown near retirement in 1963, as a major general. Lansdale had extensive counterinsurgency experience and was one of the few Americans that Diem trusted. (Albert Grandolini Collection)

1960 – troops on the streets of Saigon helping to support Diem's regime. The fixed bayonets would seem excessively threatening. (Albert Grandolini Collection)

Lansdale (in civilian attire, middle with briefcase) on yet another advisory mission – flying into Saigon to advise the president. (Albert Grandolini Collection)

Additionally, other cultural factors meant that the visible extent of American involvement had to be moderated in order to allow Diem 'to get credit for the defeat of the Communists' and therefore preserve 'Vietnamese prestige.'[24] Consequently, if American involvement was too overt or aggressive, this would discredit Diem and the 'progress toward the formation of a cohesive nation' would be slowed.[25] There was also a realisation that Diem was frightened of another coup attempt and that he was unsure of the nature and extent of American support. For example, Diem believed that there were Americans in Saigon who were 'very close to those who tried to kill him on November 11' 1960 and this limited his faith in many American advisors.[26]

Even a man who Diem trusted, Edward Lansdale, found it impossible to dissuade him that this was a fact.[27] As a result, it was established that the Americans needed to 'increase the confidence' of President Diem and assure him of American support at this

Military Assistance Advisory Group headquarters in South Vietnam. In the early years of the Kennedy Administration, MAAG officials worked closely with the South Vietnamese government. (Albert Grandolini Collection)

point in the conflict.[28] Unfortunately, this fear of another coup d'état also led to a fragmentation of resources under government control because Diem tried to avoid 'placing too much power in the hands of a single subordinate.'[29]

This created problems such as the 'inability to mobilise intelligence' and meant there were 'poor relations between the province chiefs and the military commanders.'[30] This reflected Diem's fear of creating a rival power base.[31] It also made it difficult for unified action to take place as palace intrigue and province rivalry all hindered effective communication and action.[32] Again though, as advisors noted, this fear may have been justified. For example, Taylor claimed that 'at the present moment, the most serious threat is posed by military officers, who might combine at any time with government officials to depose Diem': the president's caution was understandable.[33]

Infiltration into the South

There was also recognition of what needed to be done to help Diem. In particular, Lansdale (who seems to have understood the nature of the conflict better than many) explained that if the United States increased their efforts in 1961 they could frustrate the insurgents and allow the regime to go on the offensive in 1962.[34] In order to help persuade Diem to adjust his approach, it was stated that there were three essentials for progress at this time. Firstly, the Americans had to get close to their Vietnamese counterparts, raise morale and build up trust.[35]

Secondly, the Vietnamese had to start acting with greater vigour in their response to the insurgent threat and finally, President Diem

ARVN troops chase a Viet Cong suspect into the jungle. (Albert Grandolini Collection)

ARVN troops in training – note the rather basic camouflage adopted here: the more standard camouflage patterns had not been universally adopted in South Vietnam at this time. (Albert Grandolini Collection)

Another ARVN patrol introduced to try and deal with rising insurgent numbers. The man on point is armed with a shotgun while the rest of the squad has M-1 carbines. (Albert Grandolini Collection)

Viet Cong suspects captured and being prepared for interrogation. US advisors watch and guide ARVN in the correct procedures and techniques to use in such a situation. (Albert Grandolini Collection)

had to be persuaded to allow some form of political opposition to develop so as to reduce the chance of assassination.[36] This would also include removing his brother from power in order to help Diem establish control of the country.[37]

In addition to the political problems, another difficulty that the counterinsurgents recognised was the nature and extent of infiltration into South Vietnam. It was accepted that insurgent numbers were on the increase from around 4,000 in mid-1960 to over 12,000 by mid-1961.[38]

The 'Jorden Report' made clear that many of the Viet Cong groups were reinforced by soldiers returning from North Vietnam.

Map 1: The map depicts the personal travel history of one infiltrator into rural South Vietnam. It clearly shows that both land and sea routes were used for entering and exiting the country before and during the time period under study. (Map by George Anderson, based on TTU, 6-20-15A5-116-UA17-149_000001, A Threat to the Peace, Appendix N, p.78)

This meant that by the end of 1961, the Diem regime had to counter an insurgent body which was comprised of '70 percent locally recruited; 25 percent South Vietnamese trained in the north and re-infiltrated; 5 percent North Vietnamese regulars.'[42] The intelligence reports also noted that infiltration was by both 'land and sea from North Vietnam.'[43] Finally, in terms of infiltration, there was an acknowledgement that border patrols had to be increased and aerial surveillance 'over the entire frontier area' was needed to halt the flow of insurgents into South Vietnam.[44]

VC Control of South Vietnam?

The consequences of this infiltration were recognised in the 'Counterinsurgency Plan' of 1961. This noted the limited nature of government support and claimed that below province level in the 5th Military Region, 'no effective GVN control exists in many areas.'[45]

NSAM 52, which included the 'Gilpatric Report' also acknowledged that 'what amounts to a state of active guerrilla warfare now exists throughout the country' and it recognised (in agreement with other sources) that 'the number of Viet Cong hard-core Communists has increased from 4,400 in early 1960 to an estimated 12,000 today.'[46]

The report also stated that '58 percent of the country' was 'under some degree of Communist control, ranging from harassment and night raids to almost complete administrative jurisdiction in the Communist "secure areas".'[47]

It also recorded how many of these 'returnees' were former Viet Minh fighters who had been involved in the war against the French.[39] As a result of this infiltration one transit station alone accounted for over 400 infiltrators per month moving into South Vietnam.[40] Furthermore, there was a recognition that infiltration was 'accompanied by local recruitment' within rural South Vietnam itself.[41]

It is also interesting to note how Saigon itself was almost completely surrounded by insurgent held areas or zones of influence. Even at this stage of the conflict, the Americans were aware of the general location of many of the insurgents and knew that, in particular, they were heavily concentrated in the Mekong River Delta area.

There was also an understanding that within these areas the insurgents were setting up provincial level local government structures that were collecting taxes and harvests and conducting

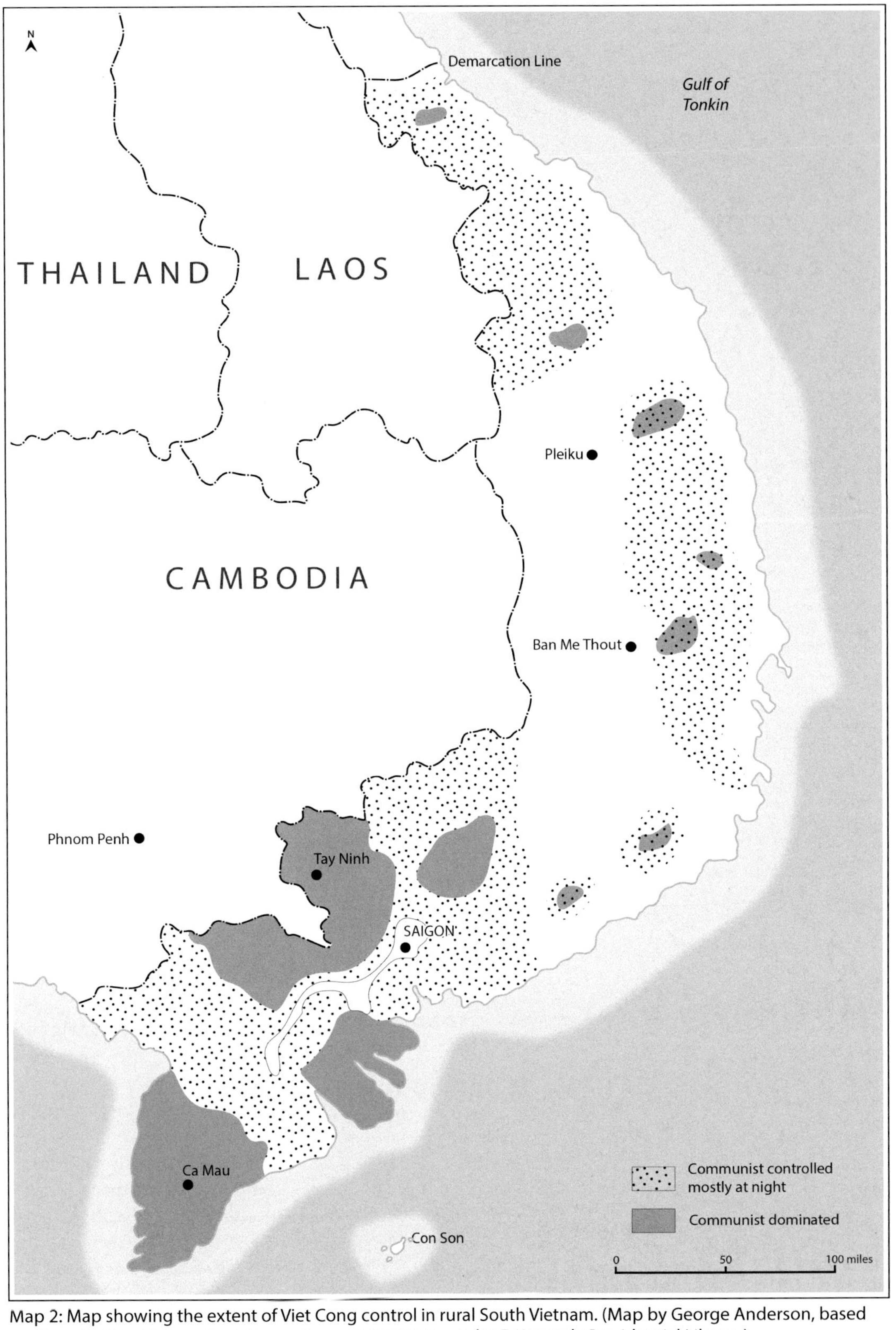

Map 2: Map showing the extent of Viet Cong control in rural South Vietnam. (Map by George Anderson, based on Report of the Vietnam Task Force, Annex 7, NSAM 52 – John F. Kennedy Presidential Library.)

indoctrination programmes.[48] The extent of Viet Cong influence was recognised in NSAM 52 which included a map (see Map 2) to show just how much of South Vietnam was under the jurisdiction of the Viet Cong at this time. The extent of Viet Cong control is shown clearly and even those areas that did not appear to be under insurgent influence during the day could be under VC rule at night.

By early 1962 – before the 'Counterinsurgency Plan' had really had a chance to take effect – it was estimated that control of this territory gave the Viet Cong 'access to at least 25 percent of the 2 million fit males between the ages of 15 and 49.'[49]

This meant that there were at 'least 25,000 Viet Cong organised into 22 battalions' with around '100,000 part-time, partially armed' support forces too.[50] In his 'Strategic Concept for South Vietnam' Hilsman went further and even managed to present figures estimating Viet Cong strength in various regions of the country. The map here (see Map 3) shows where these forces were concentrated, their number and the extent of American intelligence on the Viet Cong threat. As the conflict progressed, this gave the insurgents a significant amount of manpower to draw upon and together with consistent levels of infiltration, would allow the insurgents to pursue their revolution throughout this time period.

This understanding about insurgent location and strength built upon the initial assessment in the 'Counterinsurgency Plan' which commented that the Viet Cong were intending to 'eliminate any semblance of GVN control in rural areas, particularly the Mekong Delta, and establish so-called "liberated zones"' as a prelude to further action.[51]

Threatening the 'People'?

It is also important to note that American intelligence was aware of the methods used by the Viet Cong to recruit the South Vietnamese to support their cause. However, this support may not always have been given without intimidation being used against the population. For example, the 'Jorden Report' examined the extent to which coercion influenced the decision to join the Viet Cong. It noted that many joined the insurgency to protect their families and it quoted one 17-year-old saying he had joined because of threats made by the insurgents:

> They took my father away for 10 days and tried to force him to join their organisation. But my father refused. Then they took me and forced me to co-operate. They threatened to kill my father if I refused. That is why I joined them.[52]

ARVN casualties are readied for loading aboard a US Army H-21 helicopter. ARVN suffered a lot and in contrast to their initial reputation were – at least at the lower levels – a brave and tenacious fighting force. (Albert Grandolini Collection)

ARVN troops disembarking from a US Army H-21C on the way to ambushing a suspected Viet Cong cell. (Albert Grandolini Collection)

A Communist insurgent setting a trip wire across a jungle path. (Communist Archive/Albert Grandolini Collection)

Also, insurgent tactics for attacking the government and intimidating the population were understood. For example, government forces faced many different forms of violence that included 'armed attacks against agrovilles, land development centres, Civil Guard and Self-Defence Corps posts.'[53] As a result, the Acting Secretary of State for Defence, Nguyen V. Thuan, stated that between

Communist troops return to a friendly village in South Vietnam and celebrate a successful attack on an ARVN patrol. (Communist Archive/Albert Grandolini Collection)

Civilian Irregular Defense Group officers briefing ARVN before a patrol. Notice the variations in camouflage during this time period before standardised camouflage was adopted. (Albert Grandolini Collection)

'two and three hundred South Vietnamese troops were being killed each month.'[54] Insurgent activities at village level also included 'armed propaganda and leaflet distribution; taxing of the population for food, money, and medicines' and the 'kidnapping and murder of village and hamlet officials' as well as road and canal ambushes.[55] Estimates suggested that nearly 4,000 of Diem's officials had been assassinated or kidnapped between 1961 and 1962 alone.[56] All of these attacks helped to create fear and confusion within rural areas.

In addition, the insurgents often used subtle social pressure to influence villagers and use them as spies or to gain local support for their activities. Insurgents would cultivate friendships with family members, try and indoctrinate one or two individuals within a village group and then 'use them in our propaganda toward other people to take hold of the enemy situations.'[57]

Reports recognised that the real source of supplies and recruits was actually in 'the people and villages of South Vietnam' and that Hanoi had infiltrated these communities and recruited these people 'voluntarily or by force.'[58] Advisors were aware that the insurgents had an extensive spy or informant system because they appeared 'to have good intelligence on the plans and movements of government forces sent on anti-guerrilla missions.'[59] Even here though, advisors appreciated that there was a distinction to be made between having

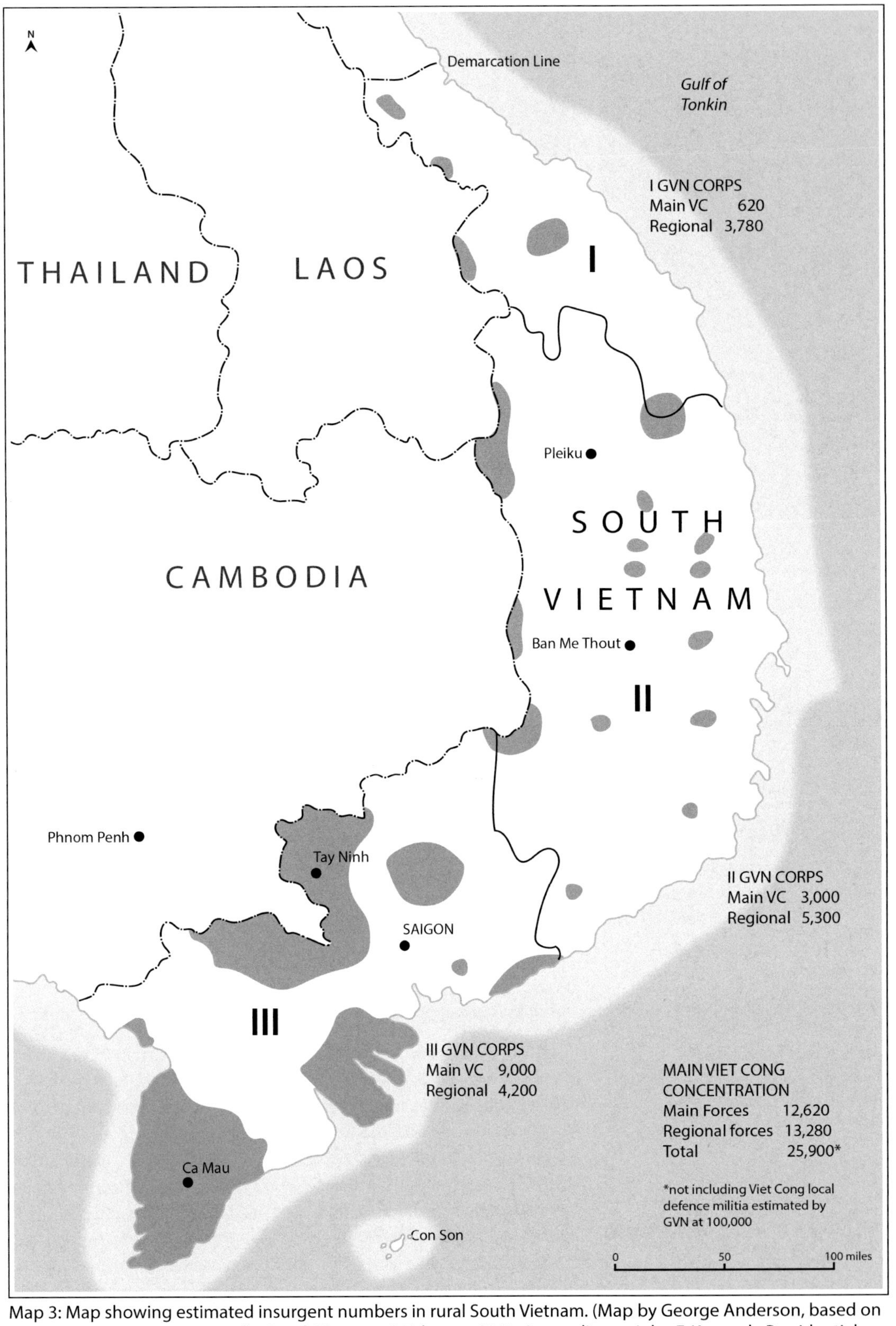

Map 3: Map showing estimated insurgent numbers in rural South Vietnam. (Map by George Anderson, based on Vietnam: A Strategic Concept for South Vietnam, 2 February 1962, Appendices – John F. Kennedy Presidential Library)

the support of the people and having access to the people: as long as insurgent contact with village communities continued they would be able to 'compel submission by terror and threat.'[60] The importance of the rural population was considered critical in the campaign as villagers were described as being 'local sources of strength' for the Viet Cong and it was maintained that the conflict could only be won by denying the Viet Cong access to the people.[61] This was developed further by Hilsman who recognised that simply sealing off the border with North Vietnam would not, in itself, end the conflict due to the role the rural villagers played in supporting the insurgents.[62] In essence, winning their political support was vital.[63] However, it is perhaps important to note here that Donnell and Hickey found that although only a small number of peasants 'perhaps no more than 4 percent' were definitely pro-Viet Cong, some '60 to 70 percent had divided political loyalties and were capable of occasional collaboration with the enemy' and therefore the struggle had to be focussed on shifting attitudes amongst the malleable.[64]

Finally, intelligence reports also commented on the structure of the rural insurgent cells and revealed that whilst the war was being directed from Hanoi, a basic cell would be established in a village which would receive its orders from district and provincial insurgent commands – which in turn were directed from North Vietnam.[65] It was understood that although most of the leaders and instructors came from North Vietnam, the majority of the personnel was 'recruited and trained locally' and were usually 'part-time guerrillas.'[66] It was claimed that this meant there were several thousand casual supporters who were 'innocent citizens' but who would join the insurgents to 'assist in intelligence, sabotage, propaganda, and terrorist operations.'[67]

Detailed Planning

The Counterinsurgency Plan and the Strategic Hamlet Programme

In response to the insurgent threat, detailed plans were developed to counter the insurgency. These included a comprehensive Counterinsurgency Plan and the introduction of the Strategic Hamlet Programme. In practical terms the counterinsurgency strategy involved increasing patrols on the ground, supporting the South Vietnamese economy, trying to get President Diem to begin political reform and building strategic hamlets to defend the rural population. The strategy recognised that a complex approach had to be taken that involved more than the simple killing of insurgents. Instead, as Thompson noted, the 'overall aim of any

Communist infiltrators transporting goods along one of the paths on the 'Ho Chi Minh' trail, in this case over makeshift but effective ladders crossing rough terrain. Many sympathisers had family connections to both North and South Vietnam. (Communist Archive/Albert Grandolini Collection)

Communist troops examine a captured weapons dump that include rifles, submachine guns and a mortar. Capturing ARVN supplies was a major source of weapons and ammunition for the Viet Cong (Communist Archive). (Albert Grandolini Collection)

counterinsurgency plan must be to win the people' and from this the 'killing of communist terrorists will follow automatically.'[68] It was also understood that the government would need to 'protect the villagers from being intimidated' by the insurgents and thereby cut off supplies being provided surreptitiously to the Viet Cong.[69] This meant using the 'oil-blot' method which revolved around establishing a secure village and then extending control 'slowly,

ARVN troops on patrol along a riverbank. The dense jungle to the right of the troops provided ample cover for snipers and the ambush/assault tactics used by the VC. (Albert Grandolini Collection)

ARVN troops being deployed in a rice paddy via US Army UH-1 helicopters as part of a pincer movement designed to trap Viet Cong soldiers. (Albert Grandolini Collection)

making sure no Viet Cong pockets are left behind, and using police units to winkle out the Viet Cong agents in each particular village.'[70]

After this, tactics labelled 'Spear and Net' would be used to locate, surround and then either capture or destroy the remaining insurgent forces.[71] Additionally, villages under attack had to be reinforced rapidly and even if conventional military operations were being used in a province, they should be 'secondary to the major task of extending security' in rural South Vietnam.[72]

Methods for 'extending' this security were varied in nature. They included, for example, excluding the population from 'prohibited areas' where they could be shot on sight if they entered, night-time curfews, the use of identity cards and even limited amounts of food control to try and starve insurgents into submission.[73] However, the main method of establishing security would be through the Strategic Hamlet Programme.

The strategic hamlets themselves were not a new concept. They were fortified villages that were based upon the British experience of counterinsurgency warfare during the Malayan Emergency, which in turn had probably been based around the French experience from their time in the Maghreb and Indochina.

A basic overview of a strategic hamlet. Notice the large entrance gate in the background and the way in which – even within a hamlet – groups could be isolated from each other by the clever positioning of fences. (Albert Grandolini Collection)

An aerial view of a strategic hamlet clearly showing the trenches and guard towers around the perimeter, the whole on high ground. (Albert Grandolini Collection)

In Malaya, the British had built fortified villages and settlements with the aim of separating the general population from the insurgents and thereby cutting off supplies of items such as food, ammunition and information. Transferring the concept to South Vietnam, these hamlets were designed to provide 'the peasants with an increasing degree of physical security from Communist intimidation' whilst enacting 'social, economic, and political reforms meaningful to the peasants in the context of their own traditions and expectations.'[74]

The aim was to improve the general environment of the rural population and as a result the same people would become more inclined to help the government and reduce their support for the insurgency. David Galula, a French counterinsurgency expert, said that the goal here was not just to destroy the insurgents' military forces but also to break up their political structures and bring about 'the permanent isolation of the insurgent from the population.'[75]

The Strategic Hamlet Programme was ultimately designed to reduce the National Liberation Front to 'hungry, marauding bands of outlaws devoting all of their energy to staying alive.'[76] The construction of hamlets also tied into the culture of South Vietnam because it was recognised that the erecting of fortified villages built upon the 'basic social unit of the country' and any strategy needed to start from the hamlet upwards.[77]

A CIA telegram in 1962 noted that basing counterinsurgency policy around the hamlet was a solid, sensible thing to do; it built upon the traditional structure of Vietnamese society, allowed the government to modernise aspects of Vietnamese culture and

David Galula – a French counterinsurgency expert. Some of his work was used to help inform American policy and it is even suggested that Diem's brother, Nhu, favoured using French counterinsurgency theory instead of taking American and British advice. (Albert Grandolini Collection)

South Vietnamese officials inspecting the perimeter defences of an unnamed strategic hamlet. The fence in the background would appear to be of little defensive use. (Albert Grandolini Collection)

therefore, through this modernisation, would help defeat the communist insurgency.[78]

Winning a 'War on Paper'?

Perhaps at this point is it also worth noting that a major problem with this strategy was the number of 'plans' put forward at this time. A discussion of the way in which the strategic hamlets were implemented across South Vietnam will provide some chronological context and also illustrate the competing nature of policies upon government strategy. Although 'Operation Sunrise' in March 1962 was often cited as being the beginning of the Strategic Hamlet Programme, there were different accounts given about the genesis of the strategy.[79]

For example, some of these accounts claimed that a programme 'of sorts' was already in place as early as 1960 when a Colonel Khanh fortified several villages in Ninh Thuan province.[80] As an alternative, it was suggested that Nhu himself stated that a Catholic priest in Truong Hoa district (in Darlac province) had requested 30 shotguns to defend a village and this was where the programme began.[81] In another explanation, Catton claimed that Vietnamese documents showed Diem had already started to devise a 'Counterinsurgency Plan' of his own before 1962.[82] This had been inspired by previous agroville attempts in the 1950s and sought to build upon success achieved in 1961 in Vinh Long Province by Major Le Van Phuoc in the village of Tan An.[83]

Despite these conflicting claims, the Vietnamese recognised the potential of the hamlet strategy and the first official 'strategic hamlet' was inaugurated in Tay Ninh province on 8 December 1961.[84] Once the location and building of the initial strategic hamlets had been established, the Vietnamese began constructing them in selected provinces. As part of the 'Delta Plan' agreed with Thompson, Diem began 'Operation Sunrise' in Binh Duong in March 1962. In addition, several other provinces began hamlet construction programmes. For example, 'Operation Sea Swallow' took place in

A guard post/protected official's office within a strategic hamlet. These varied in quality from fortified buildings to little more than wooden huts. Many provided only rudimentary protection for their occupants. (Albert Grandolini Collection)

This picture was often used to demonstrate the defences around a strategic hamlet. Notice the sharpened bamboo stakes and multiple lines of defensive spikes. It should be stressed that not every hamlet had this level of protection. (Albert Grandolini Collection)

Many strategic hamlets also trained their female occupants. Here a group of female militia patrol with an American advisor looking on in the background. (Albert Grandolini Collection)

A heavily defended fort/hamlet base. Notice the trenches, cleared fields of fire and extensive fortifications. American visitors were often taken to locations such as this to demonstrate the strength of the Strategic Hamlet Programme – however, most bases and defences came nowhere near this level of security. (Albert Grandolini Collection)

Another view of the defended hamlet/base seen in the previous photograph. In this instance, the base was defending a choke point in the river. Smoke can be seen from what appears to be an assault. It is unclear if this was a training exercise or an actual attack. As most VC attacks took place at night it is more likely to have been a simulation. (Albert Grandolini Collection)

Strategic Hamlet militia on patrol in the interior of such a hamlet. Again, the defences are stakes and high fences. Some of these perimeters were several kilometres in length and were almost impossible to defend. The bamboo spikes could be relatively easily pushed aside, though not quickly, and barbed wire took even more time. (Albert Grandolini Collection)

More perimeter patrols by the Strategic Hamlet militias. Although given rifles, many in these militias had no bullets or only enough ammunition to fire one or two shots at attacking insurgents. Despite this, the occupants of many hamlets fought incredibly bravely in the face of Viet Cong violence. (Albert Grandolini Collection)

Phu Yen province in May, whilst Operations 'Let's Go' in Binh Dinh and 'Red/Royal Phoenix' in Quang Ngai began in Autumn 1962. However, by May 1962, the original 'Delta Plan' had been quietly shelved and in August 1962, the Strategic Hamlet Programme was expanded to cover all of South Vietnam.[85] At the end of 1962, an estimated 3,225 hamlets had been built (with over 4.3 million people living in them), by June 1963 an estimated 7,205 had been built (containing 8.7 million population) and by September 1963 nearly 70 percent of the rural population lived in them.[86]

This expansion of the hamlet programme was further enhanced by USOM and specifically, the Office for Rural Affairs (and Counterinsurgency) headed by Rufus Phillips. Rural Affairs provided social and economic support for the strategic hamlets. It established pig breeding programmes, money for rural development and also set up provincial committees to allocate funds on a local basis to match local needs.[87]

In addition to the Vietnamese plans and the USOM aid effort, the Americans also devised their own strategies to support the campaign. Unfortunately, a lack of co-ordination meant that the plans did not always meet the envisioned reality: the American concepts of phased progression and hamlet construction did not always correspond to those of their Vietnamese counterparts. Whilst a basic 'Counterinsurgency Plan' was presented to President Kennedy at the start of 1961, this underwent several additions, amendments and modifications over the time period covered by this book.[88] Additions to the plan began in 1961 in the form of NSAM 52 which laid out counterinsurgency policy suggestions and included the 'Gilpatric Report' which outlined several key problems to be addressed.[89] The 'Staley Report' of July then laid out the financial recommendations for the strategy.[90] Further improvements were made with the 'Geographically Phased National Level Operation Plan for Counterinsurgency' which attempted to add a three phase sequence of actions – preparation, military and social reform – to the mix.[91] Modifications continued into 1962. Roger Hilsman put forward his 'Strategic Concept for South Vietnam' which laid out the counterinsurgency strategy in greater detail.[92] This drew upon his own discussions with Thompson and brought together many of the previous plans for implementation.[93] These plans eventually merged – either wholly or in part – and formed much of the initial counterinsurgency strategy for South Vietnam.[94] Then, to complicate matters even further, it was not until August of 1962 that an agreed South Vietnamese–American plan of action was completed.[95] This was followed in 1963, by a 'Comprehensive Plan for South Vietnam' which was discussed by the military and suggested that the war would be won by the end of 1965.[96]

All of these plans and reports fed into the wider counterinsurgency campaign but they also help illustrate why the strategy appears at times to be confused and haphazard. Finally, to add even greater complexity, this planning process was hindered by province and corps area boundary changes and the creation of new provinces in late 1963. In discussing these issues in 1962, Theodore Heavner wryly commented that it was 'easy to win a war on paper' and the assortment of planning documentation would indicate he had a point.[97]

Indeed, Hilsman recognised the confusion caused by this multitude of plans and in January 1963, outlined some of the common features of the various approaches and summarised them in a memorandum to President Kennedy. The overall strategy was described as having three main objectives:

> (1) to create the incentive for resistance in the basic population by providing for a flow upward of information on villagers' needs and a flow downward of government services, and by knitting them into the fabric of community decision-making; (2) to provide the basic population with the means and training for resistance; and (3) to cut the guerrillas' access to the villagers, their true line of communications, by essentially police-type measures for controlling the movement of goods and people.[98]

The Strategic Hamlet Programme would form a substantial part of this strategy and provide villagers with access to modernised facilities, improve democratic participation and enable the separation of the insurgents from the local population. The memorandum then went on to list three further, main military objectives for the overall strategy:

> (1) to protect installations vital to the economy and government; (2) to provide rapid reinforcement for villages under heavy attack; and (3) to keep the *regular* guerrilla units off balance and prevent them from concentrating by aggressive but highly discriminating and selective offensive military operations.[99]

Despite the haphazard implementation, the various plans were based on sound practice. The remainder of this section will demonstrate that the strategy underlying each plan (The Strategic Hamlet Programme) made military – if not administrative – sense.

The Strategic Hamlet Programme

The hamlets were designed, in theory, to follow a layout based around a common plan. This included:

> A fence of bamboo and barbed wire (which) is built around the entire hamlet, and a ditch or moat is dug around the fence; the ditch or moat, in turn, is encircled by an earthen mound. The area immediately around the village is cleared to permit fields of fire and to avoid giving guerrillas and terrorists hiding places close to the hamlet.[100]

These basic fortifications were designed to offer protection and security at night whilst giving the residents a chance to repel any attacks they might face. The actual physical nature of the hamlets (for example, size, layout or defences) varied from province to province and depended upon on the perceived threat that each rural community faced.

Whilst the actual criteria for completed hamlets stressed that 'fences, spikes, communication trenches' had to be built, these varied in quality.[101] In their survey of the Strategic Hamlet Programme undertaken in 1962, Donnell and Hickey claimed that they came across many successful strategic hamlets. Some were 'heavily fortified' strategic hamlets found 'in the "Operation Sunrise" area around Saigon' and these were 'largely or entirely surrounded by extensive earthworks' and many were 'studded with bamboo spears that project about 1½ feet.'[102]

However, they also came across hamlets where there was only a single military post surrounded by earthworks and limited defences such as 'thorn hedges, portable steel-spike boards, and a few hand grenades planted as land mines.'[103]

In addition to large, bamboo defences, it was also suggested that the hamlets included some form of command post in which leaders could station themselves in the event of an attack. A communication station was also deemed necessary in order to call in rapid response units to support the village in times of crisis.

The guard post at a strategic hamlet shown in mid-construction. The effectiveness of these materials in being able to withstand a full-scale VC assault was often questioned by advisors and ARVN officers 'on the ground' but was suitable for protection against small arms fire. (Albert Grandolini Collection)

The construction of a guard post at a strategic hamlet begins. The use of natural materials, readily at hand, eliminated need to transport sheet metal and concrete. (Albert Grandolini Collection)

Villagers constructing hamlet defences. This photograph was taken by a US advisory mission in Phu Yen. It is unclear if the labourers were local volunteers or compelled corvee labour. (Albert Grandolini Collection)

The hamlet Self-Defense Corps on patrol outside a village. (Albert Grandolini Collection)

The Self-Defense Corps stand guard outside a strategic hamlet. (Albert Grandolini Collection)

Any number of smaller villages would then be moved and relocated inside the hamlet for protection from the Viet Cong. Guard posts were to be established to counter attacks and allow for sniper fire to be aimed at insurgents, whilst punji stakes were introduced into trenches around each hamlet to provide additional security and protection. Donnell and Hickey noted that in many of the hamlets they came across, there was often a 'military post of concrete surrounded by another set of ditch, wall, and barbed-wire fortifications' to help repel insurgent assaults.[104] The hamlets were also designed to have observation towers, a defensive post to store weapons and a rudimentary alarm system such as a bell or bamboo drum was expected to be present.[105] Many hamlets were also furnished with radio sets that – in theory – allowed them to maintain direct communications with district security forces and request help when needed.[106]

Hilsman also envisaged a series of 'Strategic' and 'Defended' villages which would be built to protect the peasantry whilst trapping the insurgents in ever smaller areas of land. Strategic Villages were intended to protect populations considered to be under limited threat of attack and these would be in relatively secure areas whereas Defended Villages would be created along the 'periphery of Viet Cong concentration areas.'[107] Defended villages would be built in such a fashion as to form a belt along a population density line, enclosing the insurgents and preventing further expansion.[108] Hilsman put forward an 'ideal' layout for these villages in his report, 'A Strategic Concept for South Vietnam' (See Photo 1)

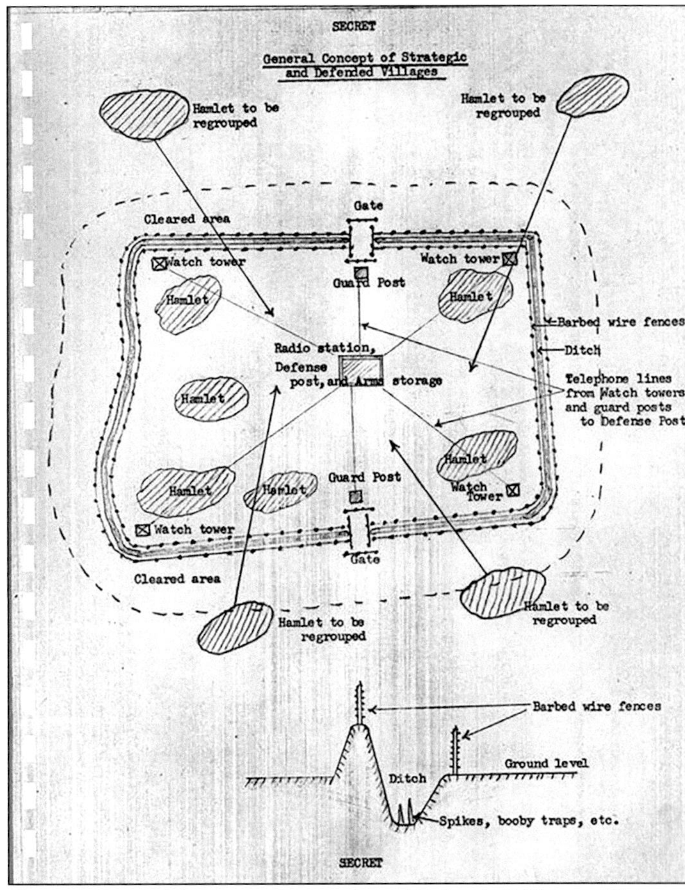

Photo 1: General Concept of Strategic and Defended Villages – Vietnam: A Strategic Concept for South Vietnam, 2 February 1962. A Strategic Concept for South Vietnam. (John F. Kennedy Presidential Library, with permission)

ARVN undergoing weapons training – notice the line of buildings within a strategic hamlet that can be seen on the horizon. The nearest soldier wields a .45-cal M3 'Grease gun' and the next man a .30-cal M1 Garand. (Albert Grandolini Collection)

Once these various villages or hamlets were constructed, the aim was to slowly isolate the insurgents from popular support and, through sweep operations, gradually track and eliminate the Viet Cong and drive them out of a province.

Hilsman believed that once the strategic and defended villages had been established, then effective counterinsurgency measures could be adopted.

Referring to Map 4, he explained how these tactics would work:

> Let us assume for purposes of illustration that the white area east of zones I and II is virtually free of Viet Cong, that zone I is moderately penetrated, and that zone II is virtually free but subject to incursions by Viet Cong irregulars from the south. In

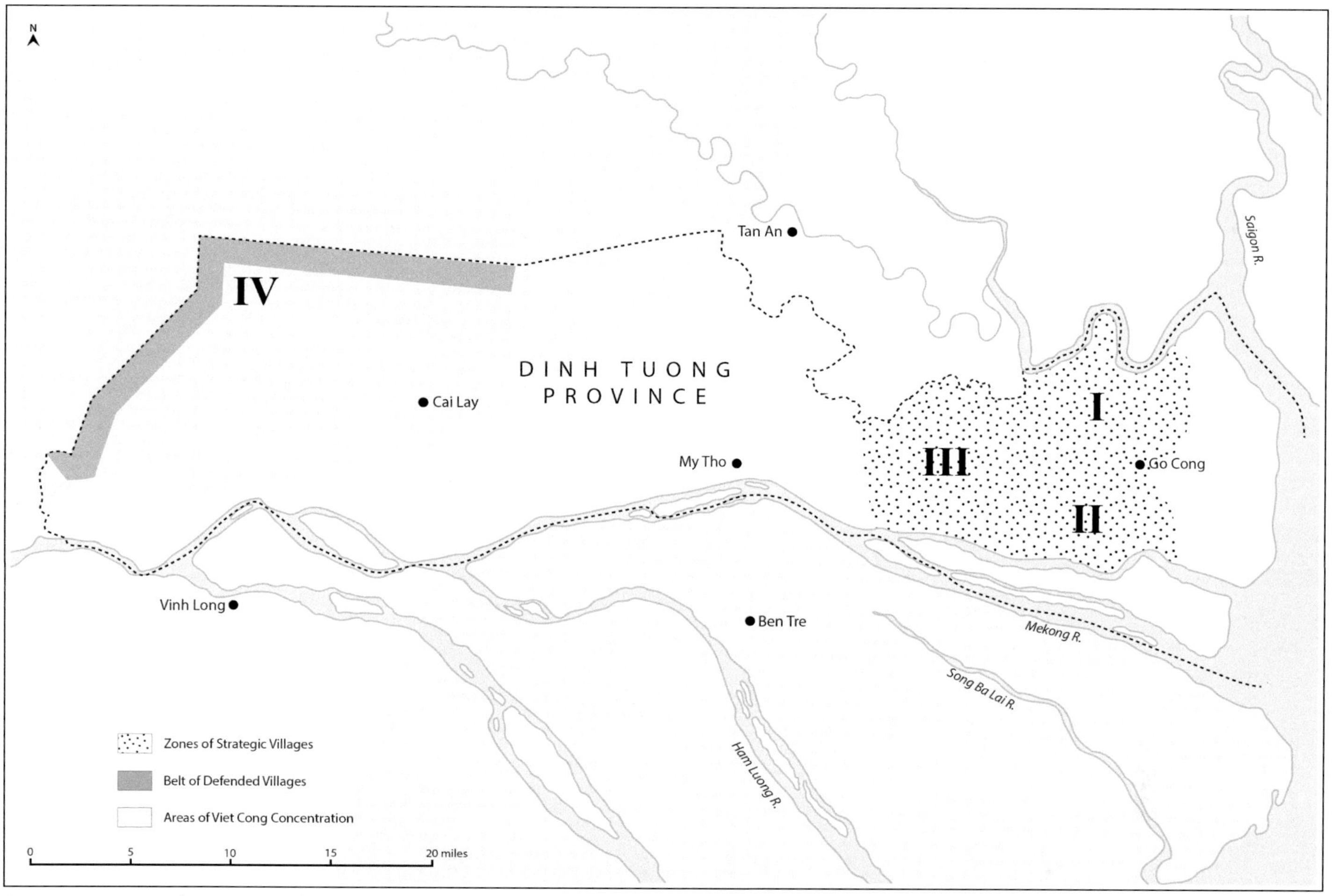

Map 4: Expansion of Strategic and Defended Villages into Viet Cong held territory (Map by George Anderson, based on original in Vietnam: A Strategic Concept for South Vietnam, 2 February 1962. John F. Kennedy Presidential Library)

ARVN forces deployed on yet another mission to hunt Viet Cong transported by USMC H-34 troopships. (Albert Grandolini Collection)

ARVN were relatively well-equipped for a South East Asian fighting force. Here an advisor demonstrates how an M2 flamethrower shooting napalm can be used in the field. (Albert Grandolini Collection)

the white area, strategic villages would not be necessary. Zone I would need strategic villages to protect its population from local Viet Cong, and zone II would need them to protect its population from incursions from the heavily penetrated area of the south. After zones I and II have been secured, the teams would move on to zone III.

At the same time as these zones of strategic villages are being constructed work would begin on a belt of *defended* villages in zone IV along the edge of the population density line to serve as a cordon sanitaire.

The regular forces of the South Vietnamese army would at the same time wage a sustained campaign of patrolling and appropriately conceived offensives against the regular Viet Cong forces with whatever troops it has available after discharging the essential tasks of defending vital installations and protecting the teams constructing strategic villages. Keeping the regular Viet Cong off balance is vital, since the Communists will make every effort to prevent the construction of strategic village zones.[109]

This strategy was designed to be gradually expanded and implemented in three phases. It was decided that the priority areas in Phase One would be where 'the vast majority of the people live, in the Mekong River delta and along the coasts,' and Phase Two would cover 'the other areas of heavy population density' and

Transport along the rivers and tributaries of the Mekong Delta was often by simple boat. This made travel a slow, laborious process and often meant that ARVN troops were vulnerable to ambush. Similar images suggest the boats and operators were local resources. (Albert Grandolini Collection)

A well-armoured river patrol boat. However, even these were vulnerable to sniper fire from the riverbank. The turret appears to be adapted from an M8 Greyhound armoured car. (Albert Grandolini Collection)

More American advisors in US Army vehicles leading an ARVN patrol into the jungle. It is unclear if this is a training activity or a genuine military situation. The gun installation and shield appear improvised. (Albert Grandolini Collection)

Again, advisors leading and training ARVN but this time in a river patrol. The boats, with armour and mounted weapons, are a substantial improvement over canoes. (Albert Grandolini Collection)

give increased attention to the Montagnard highland areas too.[110] Phase Three would see the borders closed.

It was felt that if the area had a population that was too dispersed for the strategic hamlets to be effective, items such as rice would be stored at 'protected sites' and 'then sold once a week at about half the price to the tribal peoples on a closely controlled ration basis to deny it to the Viet Cong.'[111] This would alienate the insurgents even further and lead to eventual victory. Phase One of the plan was intended to provide a foundation upon which successful counterinsurgency policy could be enacted. This would see public administration bodies set up in the villages to ensure a flow of information between Saigon and the provinces and President Diem himself set up a youth movement of over 300,000 members who would undertake labour and other tasks to improve local morale.[112] In addition, 2–3 police would be linked to each village to issue identity cards, control the movement and recording of supplies and people and attempt to 'filter out' hardcore Viet Cong.[113] Finally, the villages would receive help from agricultural credit teams, medical technicians and education specialists: all of these were designed to win over 'hearts and minds'.[114] Emphasis was also placed on developing organisations within the strategic hamlets. Political and social developments included the election of hamlet committees and the building of schools.[115] The introduction of the hamlets also led to roads being built and non-military construction such as 'small bridges, schools, administrative offices, assembly halls, youth movement quarters, and the like' increased markedly as the hamlets spread around the provinces.[116]

Other measures would also be undertaken in Phase Two, for example, a 'stepped-up programme of economic and social development' would take place which was designed to 'achieve maximum effect at the village level and to build up the progress made by the Civic Action teams during Phase I.'[117] Finally, Phase Three was designed to 'provide permanent protection at the borders' and to eliminate the 'remaining Viet Cong in the mountains and jungles of the less populated regions.'[118]

Hilsman felt that by this point in the process, 'suitably hardy, loyal and tough villagers will be resettled in permanently defended, strategic villages along the Cambodian and Laotian borders', blocking Viet Cong infiltration and allowing ARVN to pursue and destroy any insurgents still in hiding.[119]

Indications of Progress

Hunting the Viet Cong

There was compelling evidence of military success in South Vietnam as a result of the counterinsurgency strategy adopted. Reports noted the changing nature of insurgent attacks, Vietnamese peasants willing to fight against the Viet Cong and insurgent informers reflecting on the losses they had suffered.[120]

Although many reports were general in their nature, they illustrated how developing trends appeared to be optimistic. For example, USOM personnel indicated the positive impact that the strategy was having on South Vietnam. Phillips suggested as early as July 1962 that 'Vietnamese counterinsurgency efforts have become more effective in the last six months' and that extensive anti-hamlet propaganda and prisoner interviews indicated this was the case.[121]

This idea that the insurgents were being hurt was supported by William Colby, the CIA Station Chief in Saigon, who claimed that even communist sympathisers such as Wilfred Burchett had told him that the strategy 'had become so effective that in 1962 the year belonged to the government, and that was a communist appraisal of the fact.'[122] Although there was a feeling that no side clearly had 'the initiative,' there were signs of favourable trends developing.[123] For example, in a paper prepared for the Department of State by the Director of the Vietnam Working Group, it was noted that there were dramatic changes in rural morale, the people within the villages believed that the Diem regime would now win and that Viet Cong casualties were 'high, nearly 600 a week and going up.'[124]

Other general improvements were noted in a report by USOM in July 1962 which observed that it was possible to visit several previously heavily infiltrated insurgent provinces without the need for a military escort, whereas in the past, 'several civil guard companies would have been required.'[125] The same report also noted that in the Delta province of Vinh Binh, even by conservative estimates, a 'situation of almost complete insecurity' had been turned around in the space of a year.[126] It went on to say that '70 percent of the population and 59 percent of the area of the province were estimated to be under Government control by June' and that over 900 insurgents had been killed, over 250 had voluntarily surrendered and the hamlet militia were mainly responsible for this success.[127]

ARVN soldier with a machine gun awaiting the order to attack a VC jungle base. The soldiers' kit and dress show much more uniformity and combat readiness than images earlier in the book. (Albert Grandolini Collection)

These developing trends were reinforced in late December 1962 when a memo from Hilsman commented that the increasing attacks on the strategic hamlets were a clear sign that 'the hamlets have become a major Viet Cong target, suggesting that Viet Cong feel that their access to the people is being threatened.'[128] Furthermore, whilst some reports may not have claimed victory was imminent, they recognised that the situation on the ground was changing and improving because 'since the fall of last year, we have moved from a situation in which the VC were clearly winning to a stand-off' and that the Viet Cong were 'clearly further from their objective than they were in October 1961.'[129]

This theme was continued in reports issued in 1963. For instance, in a memorandum to President Kennedy in January, Hilsman noted that the 'Viet Cong, in sum, are being hurt – they have somewhat less freedom of movement than they had a year ago, they apparently suffer acutely from lack of medicines, and in some very isolated areas they seem to be having trouble getting food.'[130]

Further successes were noted in the assessment of the Hilsman-Forrestal trip which went on to say that 'our overall judgment, in sum, is that we are probably winning, but certainly more slowly than we had hoped.'[131] The report recognised progress made in the programme, acknowledged that improvements would take time but stated that the war was 'clearly going better than it was a year ago.'[132] This guarded optimism was reflected further in a report to the Joint Chiefs of Staff in January 1963, which noted that 'the situation in South Vietnam has been reoriented, in the space of a year and a half, from a circumstance of near desperation to a condition where victory is now a hopeful prospect.'[133] A Special National Intelligence

ARVN engaged on a deployment aimed at encircling and capturing the Viet Cong. In the early 1960s this type of activity put the VC onto the back foot and boosted morale within ARVN. Air transport, via a US Marine Corps H-34, was of tremendous advantage. (Albert Grandolini Collection)

Yet another deployment aimed at encircling and capturing the Viet Cong is facilitated by 'Huey' turbine-powered choppers. (Albert Grandolini Collection)

Estimate also claimed that 'Communist progress has been blunted and that the situation is improving' as a direct consequence of American involvement and a resulting increase in South Vietnamese capabilities.[134] Finally, reports recorded that the counterinsurgency strategy was winning over rural communities and that, in a reference to Phu Bon province, the people 'have freely chosen to align themselves' with the government of South Vietnam.[135] These positive comments all contributed to a common feeling that the counterinsurgency strategy was having an impact on the insurgents and had increased general safety and security.

In addition to the broad progress made under the 'Counterinsurgency Plan', the apparent success of the strategic hamlets and their effect on the insurgent operation was also discussed – with caveats regarding their rapid expansion – in several documents. For example, the 'Mansfield Report' noted that the strategic hamlets in certain areas were 'generally well organised and defended.'[136] Further praise for the hamlets came in a memo that boldly claimed that 'in the strategic hamlet concept, together with a quick military reaction, we have found the right formula' for further success.[137] This overall consensus continued even during the Buddhist Uprising of 1963. Phillips documented that 'the war was being won in Vietnam' and that 'extensive popular support was being won for the Government in the countryside by the Strategic Hamlet Programme.'[138] The positive effect of the Strategic Hamlet Programme was noted in further correspondence that claimed 'highly significant progress' had been made in the programme and it was 'an undertaking of major importance.'[139] Whilst the hamlets often varied in quality, this was acknowledged by the South Vietnamese themselves as an area in which improvement was needed.[140]

There was also a belief that as a result of the strategic hamlets, the Vietnamese government was increasing its control over rural areas. A memorandum of January 1963 noted that as of 1 December 1962, the Vietnamese government controlled just over half of the country. It claimed this amounted to:

> 951 villages containing about 51 percent of the rural population – a gain of 92 villages and 500,000 people in six months. The Viet Cong control 445 villages with 8 percent of the rural population – a loss of nine villages and 231,000 people in six months.[141]

This clearly illustrated the perceived extent of insurgent losses and was an indication of the apparent success of the initiative. Other indicators of the success of the hamlet strategy were noted in research memoranda which claimed that accomplishments were being spread over several provinces and villages. For example, in Ca Mao district (An Xuyen province) in the Delta, an area that was '95 percent controlled' by the Viet Cong saw 11,000 people resettled and the result was 'most appealing' to the people in the area.[142] Further successes were noted in Tam An (Bien Hoa province) where the Viet Cong were 'virtually eliminated' and defence posts were established and a village council was created.[143] As with the 'Counterinsurgency Plan', the general consensus at this time was that the Strategic

Low flying helicopter troop deployment (here via Marine H-34s) was a key advantage for ARVN in the early 1960s. Their rapid deployment initially caught the VC off guard. However, as the conflict progressed the insurgents adapted and melted away as the troops and helicopters approached. (Albert Grandolini Collection)

Helicopter deployment of ARVN forces clearly disrupted initial VC activity. Here, troops are being rapidly deployed in the field from H-21s – slowing down the insurgents' advance. (Albert Grandolini Collection)

ARVN troops securing a landing zone before rapidly moving out to engage with the enemy. Their materiel is largely American Second World War surplus to include the backpack radio. (Albert Grandolini Collection)

Hamlet Programme was giving every cause for optimism and was considered by the communists to be a 'threat of considerable magnitude.'[144]

Attacking their own Support

Attacks on the Strategic Hamlets

One indication of apparent success was the manner in which the insurgents were forced to step up their attacks on the strategic hamlets. This was caused by the separation of the villager (however brief) from the Viet Cong. This allowed the government to begin to establish a political base and, in some areas, build facilities that improved the lives of the rural communities. This in turn had the effect of starting to make the rural population anti-Viet Cong in both outlook and action. For example, whilst some hamlets were ineffective in defending their population, many provided a secure base from which to operate and were clearly frustrating the insurgents and making them increase their military activity. Reporting on a visit to the Delta and drawing on his Malayan experience, Thompson reported that escalating insurgent activity and increased attacks were actually a sign of success.[145]

Thompson warned that although the situation could be misinterpreted by the media based in Vietnam, the programme was seeing results.[146] Thompson claimed that the hamlets were forcing the Viet Cong to attack defended villages and this meant that they had 'admitted the hostility of the population and, therefore, their eventual defeat.'[147] He also said that the insurgents were losing the initiative because 'if they attack the hamlets, they are attacking the people whose support they must have to win the war.'[148]

This was also recognised in Washington. A White House memorandum said that increased terrorism by the Viet Cong would be an acknowledgement that they were losing and 'an admission of defeat'; although it also recognised that any such surge in activity would generate unfavourable reports in the press and would require 'steady nerves' to endure.[149] The hamlets, again in support of Thompson's analysis, were also described by Senator Mansfield as becoming a major Viet Cong target.[150] A further memorandum noted that the 'VC are reacting vigorously to the programme' including digging a 'three kilometre long tunnel in an attempt to get through the perimeter defences.'[151] The size of the forces involved in these attacks – 'six attacks against strategic hamlets exceeded platoon size' – also indicated just how threatened the insurgents felt by the programme.[152]

An ARVN special forces soldier in training. In this case he is being shown how to sneak up on and rapidly eliminate a VC guard. (Albert Grandolini Collection)

The Hoa Hao were one of several impressive militia groups that operated against the Viet Cong in South Vietnam – they were motivated by religious and anti-communist ideology. Here recruits are on parade. The Hoa Hao gained an impressive reputation amongst American advisors and at several points in the war it was suggested that they should be 'let loose' to track and kill VC around the country. (Albert Grandolini Collection)

This fear was also reflected in the violence meted out during raids on the hamlets. One Viet Cong interviewee commented that their hamlet had been attacked three times whilst another was attacked twice and, in the attacks, the 'communists killed about thirty to forty ARVN soldiers including the commanding lieutenant' and this contributed to insurgent unpopularity.[153] This would seem to support Thompson's view that more attacks indicated strategic success and people were turning against the insurgents.

Indeed, in a lecture in Santa Monica, James Farmer, who had recently returned from Vietnam, summed up the predicament that the insurgents faced: 'The Viet-Cong are faced with a dilemma. Their propaganda proclaims they are "fighting for the people." How can they be "fighting for the people" if they attack a strategic hamlet?'[154]

Strategic hamlet Self-Defense Corps in training. Not every region had access to the equipment on show here. (Albert Grandolini Collection)

Hoa Hao militia waiting to ambush a Viet Cong attack group. (Albert Grandolini Collection)

More ARVN troops and US advisors out in the field. The terrain of South Vietnam often made rapid deployment difficult and – helicopters aside – jungle patrols could be slow and ineffective. (Albert Grandolini Collection)

Farmer then went on to say that the Viet Cong 'have not yet found any really successful counter to the programme.'[155] Further support for this view was provided in a USOM report in June 1963 which suggested that where 'a large percentage of the population is grouped within good, viable, strategic hamlets the impact on the Vietcong has been considerable.'[156] The result was that the Viet Cong were being 'forced into violating their own doctrine by committing useless acts against the people.'[157] Therefore, attacks and activity around a hamlet were seen by Thompson as positive because the Viet Cong were 'being forced to react against them' and undermine their own claims to legitimacy.[158]

The aftermath of a VC attack on a transport train. Indiscriminate assaults on civilians often undermined the VC claims of fighting for 'the people' and made them increasingly unpopular. (Albert Grandolini Collection)

Thompson also argued that by 1963, the signs of Viet Cong activity in many places merely reflected the fact that they were seeking to 'improve their bargaining position' and launching co-ordinated attacks was a sign of this strategy.[159] Furthermore, Thompson went on to explain that by attacking seemingly inadequate defences or incomplete hamlets, they were deliberately targeting weaker, more vulnerable hamlets in pursuit of this aim and this was an indication of their own vulnerabilities.[160] He also suggested that these raids were a sign that the insurgents were being dispersed into the jungles and that there was now a real fear of being caught 'in the open by aircraft or helicopter borne forces' which was reflected in covert attacks at night and quick raids.[161]

However, Thompson advised that a lack of activity in other provinces was not always an indication of success. He warned that where there ought to be a lot of Vietcong activity but little was actually occurring, then this was a warning that 'the Vietcong have succeeded in maintaining their contacts inside such hamlets and are playing it quiet' to avoid drawing attention to themselves.[162] As will be seen later in this chapter, Thompson suggested that a better way to evaluate whether the Viet Cong had contacts remaining in an area was to judge the level and standard of recruitment. Lots of activity on this front would mean that the strategic hamlets were 'beginning to work well' because the Vietcong were 'being forced to react against them' and replace their losses.[163] Although the concept that if a government was being attacked more, that same government was winning the war does seem to be paradoxical, it was based on the extensive military and counterinsurgency experience of Thompson himself. However, these escalating attacks were not the only indications that the counterinsurgency strategy was working.

The South Vietnamese Fight Back

A further cause for optimism was reflected in the rural population becoming more aggressive in their response to the Viet Cong. Firstly, there was an increase in intelligence received that resulted in 'higher Viet Cong casualties including surrenders particularly at the village guerrilla level.'[164] In Quang Nai, USOM reported:

Despite ARVN having success with helicopter raids, the VC rapidly adapted. Here a recruit trains with a MAT-49 submachine gun and prepares to ambush troops as they are deployed to a drop zone. (Communist Archive/Albert Grandolini Collection)

> Following the failure of the VC attacks in April, the people in the countryside continued to show their allegiances to the Government, particularly by providing information on the VC. In one instance, two farmers reported a VC hiding place. This was especially significant because the informants stated that they had known of these VC for over a year but had not previously thought it advisable to report them.[165]

In addition to the increase in intelligence, there were indications that people were also joining the hamlet militia voluntarily, seeking to 'positively defend their hamlets' and many were embracing relocation to the hamlets themselves.[166] This empowering of the population was a major hamlet success and Phillips noted that not only were villagers now being aggressive in their own defence, they were also 'patrolling and staging ambushes outside their hamlets' and that if properly supported, he believed that the programme would work.[167]

As well as these generalised impressions, other measures were also highlighting favourable trends and progress. For example, there

ARVN troops being deployed in preparation for a major assault. Notice the soft terrain hindering the movement of the M-113 APCs in the background. (Albert Grandolini Collection)

were indications that the morale of the South Vietnamese forces had improved, this resulted in an 'increased aggressiveness' and had led to government forces capturing more weapons than they lost.[168] A memo to President Kennedy noted:

> For the first time since the war began in 1959, for example, the government forces began in September to capture more weapons than they lost. From January to August, government forces captured 2,728 weapons but lost 3,661. But in September and October, they captured 908 weapons and lost only 765.[169]

What is also interesting to note is that whilst statistical reports were often interpreted in a negative light, if Thompson's analysis of the situation was used, then positive trends could be extrapolated from most of the data gathered.

For example, a Department of State Research Memorandum offered a pessimistic appraisal of the situation in October 1963. It noted that there was 'an unfavourable shift in the military balance' and that the Vietnamese Government would be unable to maintain positive trends in the face of an 'accelerated Viet Cong effort.'[170] However, the same report showed that positive trends were developing in line with Thompson's analysis. For example, defections from the insurgents rose from 1,956 in 1962 to 2,485 by September 1963 which would support Thompson's claim that indicators in addition to simple military kills should be used to judge counterinsurgency success.[171] Additionally, the report stated that 'since July of this year, total incidents and armed attacks have increased appreciably.'[172] This was seen in a negative light, but again it ties in with Thompson's analysis that increased attacks were a sign of insurgent desperation.

ARVN rapidly deploying through paddy fields in South Vietnam. (Albert Grandolini Collection)

Hindering the Insurgency

Paralysing the Viet Cong

In addition to the military accomplishments, the 'Counterinsurgency Plan' and Strategic Hamlet Programme were affecting insurgent recruitment and their ability to travel freely around the country. Firstly, the hamlets were beginning to affect insurgent movement and mobility. The establishment of hamlets and GVN bases meant that 'mopping-up' operations would often take place and 'the VC were no longer able to operate openly any more': many insurgents were forced to take cover in forests and abandoned villages.[173]

This meant that insurgents were constantly on the move in some provinces and in their own words were becoming 'confused and frightened.'[174] The insurgents were also finding it harder to conduct their activities and noted in their own publications that every time they penetrated an enemy area they were 'all rounded up and pursued by the enemy. Our cadres and village self-defence members are

Self-Defense Corps on parade. The effectiveness of such units made the VC increase their attacks – often in desperation. (Albert Grandolini Collection)

More helicopters – again used to rapidly deploy ARVN forces. These UH-1s carry rocket pods and machine guns to assist in suppressing enemy fire in the landing zone. (Albert Grandolini Collection)

Another search and destroy patrol aided by vertical envelopment. Although the US advisors were officially non-combatants, they did have orders to shoot back and defend themselves should they be attacked. (Albert Grandolini Collection)

ARVN, militia and Self-Defense Corps in training. In late 1963 these forces inflicted heavy casualties on attacking VC units. (Albert Grandolini Collection)

US military advisors 'out in the field' and training ARVN in the use of American hardware; here M1 Garand rifles and Thompson submachine guns. (Albert Grandolini Collection)

attacked and driven away.'[175] This often marginalised the insurgent activity because they had to remain on the outskirts of a village and this made it difficult to get help from the rural community. One insurgent noted that from February 1962, the building of a strategic hamlet in Hoa Dinh meant that 'all the village party members as well as the guerillas had to flee from the village' and the insurgents' own organisations involving farmers, women and younger people had to be disbanded.[176] As well as affecting movement, the construction of the hamlets meant that many insurgents were beginning to find it hard to gain access to food and medicines.[177]

Intelligence reports suggested that government operations had 'destroyed Viet Cong food stores' and there were 'increasing reports of low morale as a result of hunger and the lack of medical facilities' which made the insurgents increasingly desperate in their search for food and medicine.[178] It was also reported that 'attacks on Vietnamese outposts' were 'frequently launched for the express purpose of acquiring medicines' and that this was having a negative impact on their support as the rural population was starting to feel 'an increased repugnance' towards the Viet Cong and their activities.[179]

In addition to affecting the Viet Cong's ability to acquire food and shelter, the hamlets were also altering the nature of village attacks and raids. Whilst some village raids were brutal, others focussed on attacking weaker or partially constructed defences and there appears to have been a change in the method and nature of insurgent activity.

Firstly, throughout 1962, there seems to have been a slight drop in the number of operations carried out from 1,900 incidents in March to 1,340 incidents by December of the same year.[180] However, the insurgent losses were actually growing from around 1,900 per month to over 2,750 per month by December of that year.[181] Initially, this might appear to contradict Thompson's claims but in fact these statistics confirm what he was saying: the higher casualty rate actually supported the notion that larger groups were raiding the hamlets and were concentrating on certain areas of less secure government control. This view was supported by intelligence reports which suggested that all of this activity indicated that the communists were 'engaged in a slow, though perceptible, increase in effort' to thwart the government and that the 'Communists will continue to wage a war of attrition, hoping for some break in the situation which will lead to victory.'[182]

Interestingly, the insurgents' own documents also support this view. For example, it was acknowledged that during the early stages of 1962 'the enemy has succeeded to complete the experimental phase of his plan' and the hamlets had 'caused us some temporary difficulties and has created some temporary favourable conditions for the enemy.'[183] Indeed, reports on the insurgent attacks on the strategic hamlets noted that even when an attack was launched, they had to withdraw the next day as a result of military forces within the hamlets themselves.[184] Finally, the insurgents also recognised that although their movement was on an 'upward surge,' they were not strong enough to take on the government which still had 'some strength': they needed to create 'favourable conditions for the fight to get the initiative' in the war.[185]

Recruitment and Retention

Secondly, the hamlets were affecting insurgent retention. Desertion rates increased and recruitment rates declined. As noted previously, there was evidence that desertions were increasing from around 75 per month in January 1962 to 215 a month by December of the same year.[186] This trend continued into mid-1963 with defections increasing 'from 200 per month in January to 450 in June' and around 2,000 battle casualties were being reported each month.[187]

Other factors, such as low morale, were also influencing the decision to abandon or defect from the Viet Cong. For example, 'hunger, sickness, and lack of munitions' were discussed in one report whilst another commented upon the 'physical fatigue, the fact that their families were living in poverty and neglect, and the idea that they (the insurgents) were rarely permitted to visit larger villages to find amusement and relaxation.'[188] Other reports noted the inability of the insurgents to regroup due to being vulnerable to artillery and air strikes.[189] The Chieu Hoi or 'Open Arms' programme was also praised for encouraging defections and diminishing the Viet Cong support base.[190] Finally, reforms in the strategic hamlets themselves were praised as being influential in swaying defectors. It was claimed that returnees from the North to the South were 'amazed at the economic and sociological progress that had been made' and this increased their propensity to defect.[191]

In addition to desertions and defections, insurgent recruitment was being adversely affected. There was a visible decline in the number of new recruits willing to join the insurgent movement. For example, one villager reported that 'forty to forty-five new recruits' would join every month from 1960 to 1962 but in 1963 'recruitment became even more difficult and only about twenty men per month could be obtained.'[192] Donnell noted that this lack of enthusiasm manifested itself in several other ways. Firstly, there was a shift away from 'relatively selective and voluntaristic' recruitment methods towards more forcible techniques.[193] These included 'abduction and forced indoctrination' and heavy recruitment quotas were imposed on villages to 'replace casualties and maintain the desired momentum toward an even larger main force' of insurgents.[194] Secondly, there was an easing up of recruitment standards from a 'stringent' examination in 1962 towards a criteria that was 'eased considerably' in 1963.[195] This again indicated how the insurgents were being hampered by the programme. Donnell went on to explain that his interviewees noted that whilst the 17 to 30 age bracket was generally retained as the target recruitment age, it began to be moved from age 'thirty to forty,' women were recruited and the health criteria for selection was simply 'adequate health and no contagious diseases.'[196] The effect of declining recruitment numbers also saw some Viet Cong cadres shift from voluntary to compulsory conscription: August 1963 was given as the time this changed.[197] Donnell's report also discussed how the insurgents were beginning 'to force all youths in the draft age to enlist' and techniques such as ambushes and kidnapping to

A US advisor training ARVN in 'mopping up' operations. (Albert Grandolini Collection)

obtain troops were widely used.[198] What is notable here is that this confirms Thompson's claim that eventually the insurgents would be forced to attack the very population whose support they relied upon. These recruitment problems also fed into the increased need for infiltration of units from outside of South Vietnam and this meant that troop numbers had to be reinforced from the North. This was commented upon in a report to the Joint Chiefs of Staff in 1963 that noted that despite losses, the insurgents were able 'to maintain their strength, or even increase it slightly' and that the 'infusion of cadres of leaders and technicians, from outside the country' continued at 'a significant rate.'[199] Some of this could be attributed to better intelligence gathering but it also reveals that the insurgents did not have an unlimited manpower pool to draw upon in South Vietnam and further demonstrates the success of the strategy.

A State of Mind

Psychological Barriers?

Finally, there was evidence that the counterinsurgency strategy, in addition to damaging insurgent operations and improving provincial security, was also having a positive psychological impact. President Diem considered the hamlet programme to be part of a 'state of mind' as much as a physical proposition and the mental aspect of establishing a defended base was almost as crucial as its physical construction.[200] This was because the hamlets represented a commitment from the rural population to support the government against the insurgent movement.[201] The construction of the hamlet was a symbolic occasion that sent out a signal to neighbouring areas about events taking place in that village or province. To quote the Province Chief of Phu Yen, the fence around the hamlet became a 'symbol of the common defence effort' and this gave greater momentum to internal organisation in the hamlet itself.[202] These fences also made the hamlet a visible, physical entity and acknowledged Vietnamese culture because many rural Vietnamese liked having 'hedges and fences' around their properties as they were a traditional symbol of security and family unity.[203] Additionally, an attack by the insurgents would then be seen as a symbolic violation of the new community which reinforced Thompson's view that the strategy would eventually force the insurgents to turn upon their own people.[204] Although sometimes seen as a negative, the control of the population also allowed for 'the physical separation of the people from the VC' and the hamlets were creating 'an enclave which they dare not approach to talk with, terrorise, or attack its

General Le Van Vien with a Cao Dai priest. The general was also leader of the criminal organisation Binh Xuyen and this shows how Diem's senior figures often had other, more criminal, connections. (Albert Grandolini Collection)

inhabitants': there was 'undeniable value in the physical separation' it offered.[205] Another way in which hamlet construction helped to support the rural population was that the very process of building a hamlet tended to 'bring loyalties into the open and force choice on the uncommitted' and helped combat Viet Cong influence.[206] Whilst it was true that some insurgent supporters could simply hide their sympathies, as Heavner noted, 'few peasants' were 'consummate actors' and as the hamlets were built, their loyalties would become apparent.[207] Finally, the very fact that a hamlet was even being planned for construction in an area provided a boost for the counterinsurgents. Donnell and Hickey noted that when a Rural Reconstruction Team moved into an area they would visit a village that was earmarked for relocation and 'try to learn about families with pro-Viet Cong sentiments.'[208] These families would then be 'regrouped near a military post for easier surveillance.'[209] A census would then be drawn up and this often prompted 'some pro-Communist individuals to flee the hamlet' to avoid identification and capture.[210]

A Changing Political Climate?

In addition to the psychological benefits of hamlet construction, there were also political advantages to be obtained from the programme. The simple fact that elections were taking place meant that the government control of the villages was now claimed by some as being legitimate. As such, an insurgent attack against village leaders was now no longer simply an attack on the government but 'an attack against them has become an attack on the people themselves.'[211] One of the reasons for this was that the hamlets introduced elections and hamlet chiefs were voted in by all the adult voters within a few weeks of the inauguration of the hamlet. A Council of Elders was also established and a Hamlet Management Board set up to oversee the running of the hamlet.[212] Advisors believed at the time that these measures allowed there to be greater response to the needs of the locals, they provided a link with Vietnamese tradition and also offered a degree of prestige to the individuals concerned.[213] The young – who were insurgent recruitment targets – were also involved in these programmes. The Rural Reconstruction Teams tried to organise a Republican Youth Movement in each hamlet which would receive political and military training.[214] Incidentally, it should be pointed out that the theoretical age range of 18 to 35 in the Republican Youth Movement was often extended up to 50 – which does make the name of the organisation a slight misnomer.[215] This youth group would also be drilled and trained with bamboo staffs and have a member elected to the village council.[216] This all created status within a village and it was noted that social status in the rural areas was often considered to be far more valuable than social status acquired in the West: the proliferation of groups across the age brackets created 'a vested interest in the success of the community' and the hamlet itself.[217] This was because the rural villagers had titles and official jobs which enhanced their standing in the local community.

The change in the political climate was also reflected in the increase in secret elections as people became more involved in running their own hamlets. Villagers were being given 'a stake in the local status quo' and consequently they were 'giving a good account of themselves' when combating the insurgents.[218] Furthermore, this separation of the people from the insurgents gave the government a chance to re-build its political base. It was recognised that the 'ultimate success of the programme is largely dependent upon the political spirit generated in the hamlets' and the hamlets helped facilitate this by bringing the population closer together.[219] This allowed the government to extend its control to the lower levels of society and use this control to present the counterinsurgent case.[220] This connection between the local population and the local officials also allowed the government to 'build a cohesive state in' which there was 'a political cause for fighting beyond, in this case, anti-communism.'[221] This was recognised by the insurgents who themselves appreciated that the most important form of control was to be able to manipulate the 'ideology of the masses.'[222] As a final point, the expansion of government influence had other, unforeseen benefits. One was the uncovering of corruption within village and province administrations. Several dishonest officials were identified, uncollected or misappropriated taxes were accounted

Militia seen dismounting from a truck, returning 'home' after a long day searching for VC. (Albert Grandolini Collection)

for and resource controlling monopolies were dissolved. Diem received praise for this and also for refusing to be bribed to change his mind.[223] One report acknowledged that a particular provincial official had unsuccessfully tried an 800,000 piasters bribe to retain his job but had been rejected.[224] All of this was notable because the Viet Cong would often target Government and village officials but instead of intimidating the local population, the attacks were now seen as an attack on the people.

Building a 'Better Life'?

A final, perhaps more tangible benefit, was that the strategic hamlets were building better amenities for people in rural areas and consequently winning their support. The British Advisory Mission noted that many programmes were reaching rural areas and introducing better facilities such as 'schools, dispensaries, wells, fertilisers, rat poison and even in some cases electric light.'[225] This was leading the peasant to reject communist approaches, made them more prepared to fight for themselves and increased recruitment to local village militias.[226]

The insurgents also recognised that the hamlets were allowing the government to 'recruit the young for their forces, organise more republican youth units, and their spies started again their activities' against the insurgent organisation.[227] One captured insurgent noted that in the strategic hamlet his operations were made more difficult because:

> The people were allowed to go out only after eight am and had to come back before six pm. Life there was very easy. The people were given cement to build pig pens and selected pigs for breeding.[228]

Indeed, this extension of government apparatus was so effective that by the end of 1962 an additional half a million people had been brought under government control.[229] The counterinsurgency strategy was clearly having positive effects; it was weakening the insurgent movement, hindering recruitment, starving insurgents and isolating them from the very population that they sought to control. It was also improving the lives of the rural peasant and encouraging him or her to fight back against the Viet Cong insurgency.

Faced with such a threat to their power, the Viet Cong had to retaliate.

2
THE INSURGENTS RESPOND

Viet Cong Strategy: The Anti-Strategic Hamlet Programme

When you look at a programme, you can see all the faults and you complain about them, but if you are on the enemy's side, it may be having quite an effect despite its faults.

—William E. Colby, CIA Station Chief in Saigon, commenting on the Strategic Hamlet Programme, Oral History Interview, 1 March 1982[1]

William Colby, in his role as CIA Station Chief in Saigon, was well placed to evaluate the impact of the Strategic Hamlet Programme on South Vietnam. He correctly pointed out that even with the problems and issues caused by the hamlets, the effect on the Viet Cong could not be underestimated. Having discussed the successes of the Strategic Hamlet Programme in the first chapter, this second chapter will consider Colby's statement and look at the insurgents' view of the programme and their response. It will show that Colby's assertion was correct and the insurgents were being hunted and hurt.

Whilst counterinsurgency strategies were being devised in Saigon and Washington and strategic hamlets were being built in the countryside, the insurgents were formulating their own schemes and techniques for subversion. They were drawing up plans to beat the counterinsurgency strategy. In particular, 1962 saw the distribution of the NLF 'Anti-Strategic Hamlet Programme' which – by its very creation – implied that the Viet Cong were worried about the Strategic Hamlet initiative, the 'Counterinsurgency Plan' and the direction of the war in general.[2]

In addition, the insurgents provided training leaflets, assessments of strategy and tactical documentation all intended to undermine the counterinsurgency plans. For example, this included documents such as 'Assessment of the Status of the Revolution in Vietnam' (which provided information on the problems caused by the strategic hamlets) and 'Experiences in the Anti-Strategic Hamlet Programme' (which outlined simple measures to undermine and destroy hamlet operations).[3]

Viet Cong suspects captured by an ARVN patrol. (Albert Grandolini Collection)

A Viet Cong prisoner is marched through a village after being caught in an ARVN sweep operation. (Albert Grandolini Collection)

Communists plan a raid on a strategic hamlet from the safety of a jungle base camp. (Albert Grandolini Collection)

The Viet Cong became increasingly worried as the Strategic Hamlet Programme rolled out across South Vietnam. One reason was that their supporters were being captured and interrogated – as shown in this photograph. (Albert Grandolini Collection)

Helicopters fire rockets onto jungle vegetation and possible VC bases – allowing the VC to suggest that the government were undertaking terrorist operations against the people. (Albert Grandolini Collection)

The Malayan 'Threat'

An Imperial 'Bastard'?

Advisors in South Vietnam often referred to British actions during the Malayan Emergency as a time when a Strategic Hamlet Programme had been successfully used to tackle a communist-backed insurgency.[4] They were not the only ones who believed the strategy was potentially successful: the insurgents were worried too. Documents reveal that the insurgents were worried about the hamlet programme, were losing popular support and were unprepared for the implementation of the strategic hamlets. They were also being forced to engage in combat on a regular basis as a result of increased American aid and involvement.

This insurgents' fear was justifiably based on the acknowledgement that the strategic hamlet strategy was built around the successful British policy used to counter communist insurgency in Malaya: they feared it being transplanted into South Vietnam.[5] Although the documentation that compares the Malayan and Vietnamese strategies clearly includes propaganda, it also demonstrates the anxiety that the insurgents were experiencing. For example, documents mention the 'repressing experiences of the British colonialists' being used to transform 'the rural areas and cities in South Vietnam into a system of jails.'[6] Whilst statements such as these were clearly emotive in nature, they illustrated the fear of subjugation and captivity that the hamlets represented to the insurgent mind-set. Similarly, archival sources also claimed that the Strategic Hamlet Programme was 'only a re-adaptation – but more wicked – of the plan to draw a line between two enemies' and that it was a 'mechanical, subjective repetition of the experience of the British imperialists in their repression of the revolutionary movement in Malaya.'[7] In addition, Osborne reported how Vietnamese national radio referred to Thompson as a 'terrorist commander of terrorist operations against the Malayan people' in a further attempt to link perceived Malayan oppression to Vietnamese rural resettlement.[8]

This theme continued in other radio broadcasts and there were efforts made to link the British, American and South Vietnamese forces into a coherent, oppressive, imperialist coalition who had:

> … approved the creation of a bastard, whose father is American and whose mother is British and which was put forward by the

> witch adviser Ngo-Dinh Nhu after months of scheming by Staley and Thompson – this is the state policy of strategic hamlets.[9]

This propaganda was clearly trying to undermine the hamlet strategy even as it spread across the nation. This fed into anti-American and anti-colonial narratives that also helped develop the insurgents' argument that South Vietnam was a victim of Western expansionism.

The Strategic Hamlet Programme Starts to Hurt the VC

This fear of the Malayan experience being successfully transplanted into South Vietnam was partly due to the effectiveness of the strategy being felt by mid-1962. A Communist evaluation for the period up to January 1963, split the insurgent response and the effects of the Strategic Hamlet Programme and the 'Counterinsurgency Plan' into two time periods.[10]

ARVN troops leave a village after destroying a Viet Cong base area and setting fire to the buildings. (Albert Grandolini Collection)

The first was from the end of 1961 to March 1962. Here the judgment was that the 'enemy was preparing his forces and preparing to attack the movement on a fiercer scale' whilst the insurgents continued their political activities.[11] The overall assessment of this time was that the 'general situation of the movement was unchanged, through these years.'[12] The second phase was considered to be from March 1962 to July or August 1962. Here the insurgents commented upon the increase in activities from the South Vietnamese Government, noted that they faced 'widespread attacks, particularly mop-up operations' and summarised that the 'combat situation became very violent and the movement encountered difficulties in a number of places.'[13]

These difficulties were also expressed in the 'Anti-Strategic Hamlet Programme' which commented that the hamlet policy at this time was to 'the enemy's temporary advantage' and the situation was becoming more challenging for the insurgents.[14] The 'Assessment of the Status of the Revolution in Vietnam' claimed it would also 'become more difficult for the revolution in the South, making this war more unrelenting and stubborn.'[15] There was also a tacit acknowledgement that by October 1962, 'the enemy successfully established 3,364 hamlets' which led, in the insurgents' own words, to a 'number of successes.'[16] This developing concern was articulated even further in documents from the start of 1963 such as the 'Communist Assessment of (the) South Vietnam Scene' where insurgents noted that in comparison to the previous agrovilles programme, the strategic hamlets were 'shrewder, bolder, and more widely spread.'[17] It went on to say that the hamlets were on a 'crueller and fiercer scale' and the insurgents were not yet able to 'clearly understand every new aspect of the enemy's parts and activities.'[18]

This fear of the potential success of the strategic hamlets forced the insurgents to acknowledge that the programme was dangerous and had to be sabotaged. Statements such as 'our most imperative mission now is to destroy this enemy scheme' and 'if the enemy can carry out his national policy of the strategic hamlets, then he will win' bear this out.[19] Finally, retrospective history by the insurgent movement, published in 1970, discussed the problems that the strategic hamlets were causing the insurgency. The NLF 'Study of War History' examined the programme in some detail. It noted how the 'enemy obtained a number of important results' in 1962.[20]

This report also acknowledged the 'many difficulties caused' that were driving the insurgents 'into confusion' and that they had sustained 'heavy losses' during this time period.[21] The document went on to claim that as ARVN expanded into insurgent held territory they were able to 'rapidly organise' armed units in villages to

ARVN parachute troops drop into Viet Cong held territory from US Air Force C-123s in preparation for search and destroy missions – severely damaging insurgent operations. (Albert Grandolini Collection)

ARVN and Self-Defense forces on patrol. (Albert Grandolini Collection)

Viet Cong prisoners awaiting interrogation show a mix of fear, defiance, interest and indifference on their faces. (Albert Grandolini Collection)

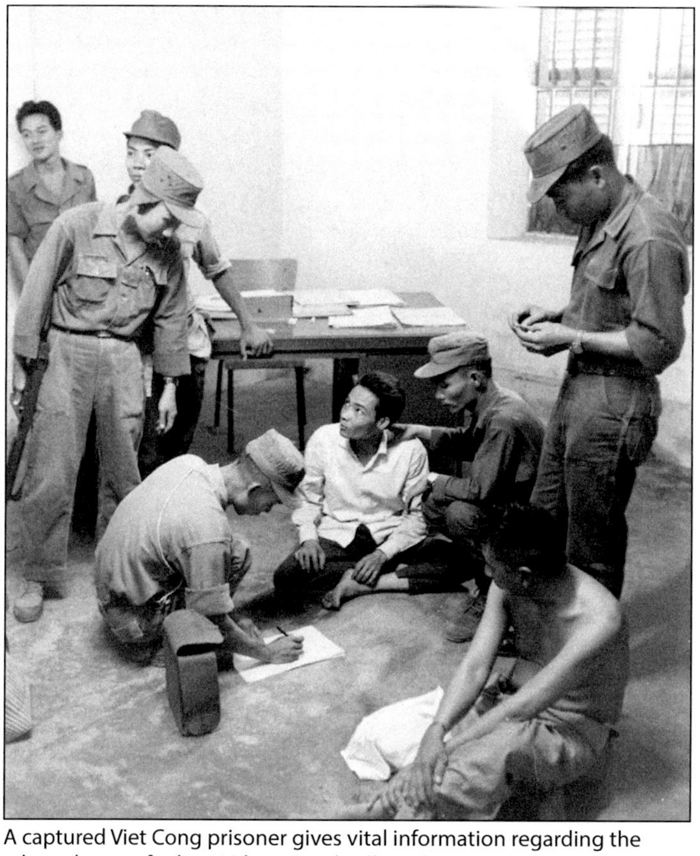

A captured Viet Cong prisoner gives vital information regarding the whereabouts of other VC bases and cells. (Albert Grandolini Collection)

combat the Viet Cong.[22] This in itself is an interesting admission because it demonstrates that the loyalty of the population may not have been as assured as previously imagined and that the rural Vietnamese were willing to switch sides in the conflict. This was supported further by comments in documents such as *Kinh nghiem chong pha ap chien luoc cua dong bao xa H (Khu II)* (*Experiences of Struggle with and Elimination of Strategic Hamlets of H Villagers*) in which the insurgents acknowledged that support for their campaign was declining 'very rapidly' and that the recruitment of young people and the expansion of the government spy network was making it very challenging for the Viet Cong to conduct their activities.[23]

It was also claimed that insurgents were often pursued by ARVN and were chased away by village self-defence forces which in turn was making it difficult for the insurgents to use their village networks for support.[24] What is noticeable here is that this would again seem to indicate that there was popular backing against the insurgent movement and the idea of automatic acquiescence to the insurgents was incorrect. These extracts may simply have been excuses used to justify insurgent failures but they also indicated that losses were being felt amongst the Viet Cong.

Taken by Surprise?

Insurgent documentation then went on to acknowledge just how the insurgency movement was unprepared for the scale and effectiveness of the programme. For example, the 'Communist Assessment of (the) South Vietnam Scene' commented that in the early stages 'there was a lack of alertness and the enemy plots and schemes were not carefully studied so that the leadership in the Party and the masses could formulate a tangible plan in time.'[25] This led to increased counterinsurgent success resulting in 'difficulties and disorder' amongst insurgent forces and 'confusion' in the face of enemy fighters.[26] There was a recognition that the hamlet programme had caught the Viet Cong at a time when they were not very strong and they needed to create better combat conditions to gain the initiative.[27]

Due to being taken by surprise, insurgent literature claimed that they had to be patient in the face of the hamlet programme and the time had not yet come for them to instigate a general insurrection.[28] Documentation also said that they needed 'more time to increase our strength in all aspects' because a 'tug of war' was taking place between both sides.[29] What is also interesting to note is the admission that the insurgency had perhaps over-reached itself at this time as the document goes on to claim that (original spellings retained):

Viet Cong cadres prepare for strikes on the strategic hamlets. (Communist Archives/Albert Grandolini Collection)

A VC supporter poses for a photo with clothing and weaponry similar to ARVN. (Communist Archives/Albert Grandolini Collection)

> Previously the movement had made rapid changes and the movement expanded quickly, but the areas were not consolidated greatly. When the enemy increased his forces and strongly counter attack, we did not possess and equip defence, did not have appropriate and effective methods to oppose enemy operations.[30]

This is an interesting point, particularly considering claims in the literature that the Diem regime expanded the hamlet programme too rapidly.[31]

It would seem that this rapid expansion caught the insurgents off guard and was effective in undermining their ability to strike back. This assertion was further supported by the recognition that the strategy had caused initial problems during the opening months of 1962.[32] This would support the contention that the hamlets were having an effect on the Viet Cong in 1962 in particular.

Finally, the insurgents remarked how American support was having a major impact on their activity. The fact that American intervention was 'making many new difficulties for us' was noted and reflected the problems that aid and advice had caused.[33] This American involvement had 'created a state of much fiercer combat' within South Vietnam and the insurgents were required to consolidate their power base whilst continuing their attacks against the regime.[34] Interestingly, American reports at this time also re-iterated the insurgent view, and in a letter to President Diem, dated 23 February 1963, General Harkins commented:

> What of the enemy? The VC know they have an adversary who, for the first time, is capable of defeating him. They have become the hunted instead of the hunter. Captured documents and personnel, plus other intelligence, reveal VC dismay and concern. However, he is a long way from defeat. He may have more military capability today than he did a year ago. But, he is being driven from the base of his support, the people.[35]

Although Harkins' views were optimistic, the rest of this chapter will show that his optimism was not misplaced.

Lightly armed VC recruits pose for the camera before an assault on the strategic hamlets. (Communist Archives/Albert Grandolini Collection)

Know your Enemy

Understanding Sun Tzu?

The Chinese strategist, Sun Tzu, had a maxim that in order to defeat an enemy, a commander must first get to know the strengths and weaknesses of a rival.[36] It would appear from the documentation that the insurgents agreed with him. For example, the 'Anti-Strategic Hamlet Programme' noted how the Viet Cong must 'understand clearly the complete scheme of the enemy' in order to be successful.[37] It is apparent that the insurgents, spurred on by setbacks, were determined to fully understand the nature of the threat that they faced. It is also interesting to note how they obtained a very detailed

VC recruits pose with their weapons after a training session. Their motley attire and mix of light weapons belied the threat they posed. (Communist Archives/Albert Grandolini Collection)

NVA soldiers help train VC recruits with a water-cooled M-1919 .30-cal machine gun. It is possible they are being shown how to shoot at aircraft. (Communist Archives/Albert Grandolini Collection)

Insurgents being trained in camouflage and jungle warfare while manning a recoilless rifle. (Communist Archives/Albert Grandolini Collection)

understanding of the day-to-day tactics that they encountered and just how thoroughly they understood the problems that confronted them. This was probably due in part to – as Higgins asserts – spies and infiltrators passing on detailed, secret information to the Viet Cong: the insurgents' inside knowledge was startling.[38] It also demonstrates that the insurgents would not have gone to all the trouble of finding out about the strategy or tried to understand the tactical repercussions if they did not feel it was a threat.

In very simple terms, the insurgents were conscious not only of the outline aims and strategies behind the plan but were also acutely aware of the various stages that would be undertaken as the plan was implemented. The insurgents recognised that the strategic hamlets scheme was aimed at separating people from the 'revolutionary forces' in order to undertake a step-by-step destruction of the revolution.[39] The insurgents went on to claim that the overall aim of the counterinsurgency strategy was one of isolation and elimination.

A Communist assessment in 1963 said the aims were:

> To isolate the South Vietnam revolution from North Vietnam and our faction; to regain the rural areas and the people; attack and separate the revolutionary forces from the masses so that these forces can be eliminated; quickly eliminate the revolutionary armed forces from the masses so that these forces while they are still weak; and surround, isolate, and destroy the revolutionary bases in order to crush and eliminate the revolutionary movement in all of South Vietnam.[40]

Captured documents such as 'VC Measures Against the Strategic Hamlet Programme' also noted that the general hamlet strategy aimed to eventually surround and isolate the insurgents.[41] This would create conditions for the government forces to 'annihilate our

Communist forces learning how to assault a target en-masse. (Communist Archives/Albert Grandolini Collection)

VC supporters boost morale after a rally and prepare to assault a strategic hamlet. (Communist Archives/Albert Grandolini Collection)

guerrillas' in conventional combat and 'establish a belt to surround, isolate, and constrict the liberated areas and our base areas in order to eliminate us.'[42] There was even knowledge of the terminology used by the counterinsurgents. The insurgents understood how white and yellow areas (where government forces were in control or partial control) would surround and isolate the red areas (containing insurgents) and 'exterminate the red areas.'[43]

The insurgents were also acutely aware of how the strategy was to be implemented on a zone by zone basis. This would be done by moving from relatively secure areas to insecure areas, establishing 'puppet administration machinery' and by using 'spies to oppress our people.'[44] The insurgents were also told that hamlets would be inhabited by a displaced population and a series of hamlets would then be combined into a combat zone or a strategic belt.[45]

People would then be 'used to oppose the revolution' and as a consequence 'our base areas and mountain areas which are thinly populated would then be surrounded by the white belts and thereby isolated.'[46] In addition, there was an understanding

US advisors in the field with ARVN. (Albert Grandolini Collection)

An ARVN soldier about to assault a suspected Viet Cong prisoner. (Albert Grandolini Collection)

ARVN soldiers removing Viet Cong propaganda from a village notice board. (Albert Grandolini Collection)

that a belt of demarcation lines would be established to allow the counterinsurgents to protect and consolidate their bases before attacking again.[47] The insurgents were also aware of the in-field tactical approaches that would be used against them with mop up operations being used in conjunction with the building of outposts and strategic hamlets.[48] This was a correct interpretation of the Diem–American strategy and shows how well informed the insurgents were in regards to the tactics being used at this time.

The insurgents also recognised specific policy goals and understood the multi-faceted nature of the government strategy. They were aware, for example, that a 'military, political, and economic' strategy was being devised.[49] The military aspects have already been discussed but in political terms, the insurgents knew that the aim was to 'completely isolate the people from our revolutionary armed forces.'[50] This would be done by simultaneously establishing 'enemy authority' in order to prevent 'our revolutionary propaganda.'[51]

Similarly, in economic terms, the insurgents realised that the result would be to 'destroy all sources of provisions' for them whilst accumulating vast stocks of American goods.[52] The social aspect of the programme was also acknowledged because the insurgents claimed it was designed to 'change the appearance of the rural area by a number of demagogic social reform activities' that consolidated the power of local landlords whilst introducing an education system that was 'servile and depraved.'[53] Whilst some of the language is very much based around propaganda, it is telling that some of the more successful hamlet schemes – such as building schools and land reform – were criticised in such terms and this again demonstrates how anxious the insurgents were about the programme and how they sought to dismiss government achievements. These measures were designed to win the 'hearts and minds' of the local population and were clearly having an effect on the insurgency. Finally, the insurgents were also mindful of the strengths and weaknesses of the Americans supporting the Diem regime. Whilst acknowledging that the strategic hamlets were 'good,' the insurgents also recognised that the scheme 'violated' the sentiments and interests of the rural population and that the 'enemy had many internal problems' to overcome.[54]

This correctly reflected inside knowledge of some of the disputes and arguments within the American establishment. At this point in the conflict, the insurgents were developing an understanding of the Strategic Hamlet Programme and recognised that it represented a threat to their campaign.

Self-evaluation

Initial Viet Cong Assessments

It is also apparent, when reading communist documentation, that the insurgents were constantly evaluating their own practice. The insurgents felt they were being threatened, they needed to understand the strategy they were facing but they also had to adapt their own approach to the Diem–American plans. As a result, the insurgents began an extensive self-evaluation in terms of their own strategy, their tactics and the methods they used amongst the people.

In November 1961, the USAF deployed its first combat unit – Detachment 2A of the 4400th Combat Crew Training Squadron – to South Vietnam as part of Operation Farm Gate. In addition to eight T-28Ds, and four SC-47s, this included four Douglas B-26/RB-26 Invaders. Left in bare metal overall, with engine nacelles in black, they wore the insignia of the Vietnam Air Force (VNAF) and, officially, flew 'combat training' in cooperation with them. They were used intensely, and most of the aircraft quickly showed heavy traces of cordite around the 12.7mm machine guns in their nose, and often around the cockpit all the way to the centre of the fuselage. This B-26, US-FY-serial 44-35530/35530, was shot down on 5 November 1962 while on a napalm strike mission in the Mekong Delta, killing the crew including two Americans and a VNAF observer. (Artwork by Tom Cooper)

The first US Army helicopter units deployed to Vietnam were the 8th and 57th Transportation Companies, which arrived at Qui Nhon and Can Tho in December 1961, respectively. Both were equipped with Piasecky CH-21B Shawnee helicopters, and saw extensive use in transporting troops and supplies. Due to the local conditions, their maximum load was reduced to nine fully-equipped troops – the type having been designed for cold weather operations. Early on, all CH-21Bs were painted in glossy olive drab (FS14087) overall. Through 1962, this was replaced by flat olive drab (FS34088). This example probably served with the 33rd Transportation Company, based at Tan Son Nhut starting in May 1962, and is known to have been shot down later the same year. CH-21Bs remained in service until 1964, when replaced by the well-known Bell UH-1 Huey. (Artwork by Luca Canossa)

The next USAF contribution to the early phase of the US involvement in Vietnam came in the form of the 346th Troop Carrier Squadron under Project Mule Train. Starting in January 1962, Fairchild C-123B Provider transports of this and six other squadrons were regularly forward deployed to Tan Son Nhut, and later to Da Nang and Don Muang air bases. As the force build-up increased it was consolidated as the Tactical Air Force Transport Squadron (Provisional) 2 (TAFTS(P)-2), in May 1962, and then the 315th Troop Carrier Group, in July 1963. As of the time, all the C-123Bs were painted in a single layer of clear lacquer mixed with 5 percent aluminium powder, and their highly polished finish mirrored the surroundings. The 'last five' of the US-FY-serial (54-0655 in this case) were always applied in black on the fin, and they wore VNAF markings as of 1961–1962. (Artwork by Tom Cooper)

The first helicopters of the US Marine Corps (USMC) to arrive in Vietnam were Sikorsky UH-34Ds of HMM-362, deployed to Soc Trang and Da Nang in April 1962, under Operation Shufly. All were painted in medium green (FS34102) overall – with either the matt or glossy finish, depending on the year of their production. Unlike USAF aircraft, they wore their full service title in white (applied in black in the case of other of USMC units that operated this type), together with unit insignia and the modex (YL 75 in this case). The modex was frequently repeated on the nose of the helicopter, and its 'last two' nearly always on the fin. National insignia was worn in four positions, including the top rear and the bottom of the cabin. (Artwork by Tom Cooper)

Within a year of arrival in South Vietnam, many of the Farm Gate aircraft began showing signs of wear. After two T-28s crashed due to catastrophic wing failures, they were replaced by Douglas AD6 Skyraiders, redesignated as the A-1E. Originally, Skyraiders were painted in gull gray (FS 26440) overall, but this rapidly deteriorated due to the elements, intensive use and heavy wear. Initially, only the 'last five' of their BuAer Number were applied on the fin (in this case, the complete number was 132665), but later on much bigger, single-digit designations were applied on the engine cowling. The aircraft of Operation Farm Gate remained officially a part of the VNAF until July 1963, when the detachment was re-organised into the 1st Air Commando Squadron, and, a few months later, into the 602nd Air Commando Squadron. (Artwork by Tom Cooper)

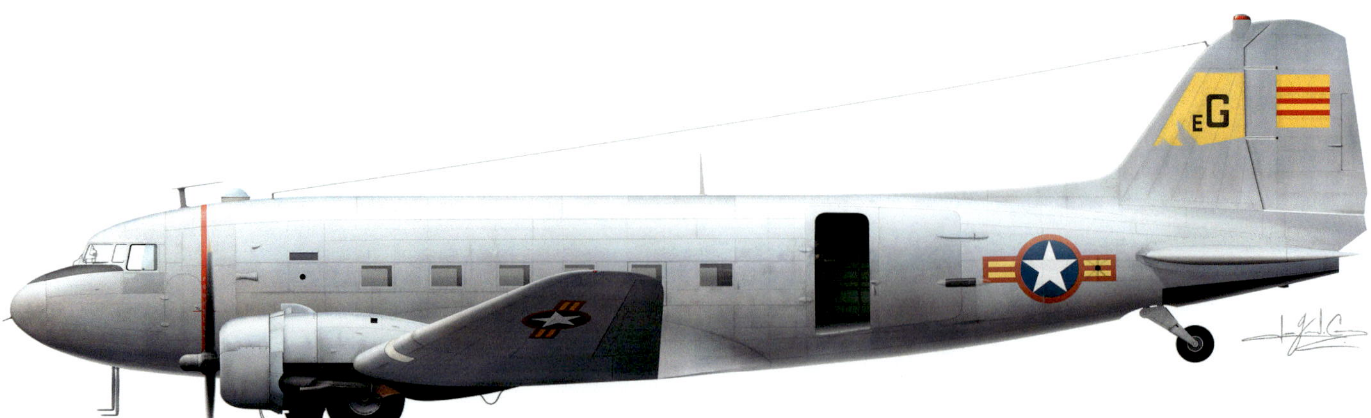

Officially established with French support in 1949, the VNAF was still a small, but already growing service as of 1955, when it received its first US-provided aircraft in the form of 32 Douglas C-47 Skytrain transports. On entry to service with the 1st and 2nd Transport Squadrons, and for several years after, these were left in aluminium overall, and wore a bare minimum of markings, including the aircraft code ('G') in this case, the unit code, and the national insignia applied in six positions. A few have retained the 'last five' of their US-FY-serial. Later on, the top fuselage sides and fin were painted in white. (Artwork by Luca Canossa)

US military aid resulted in the rapid growth of the VNAF – and especially a quick expansion of its Air Instruction Centre, at Nha Trang Air Base, which, in addition to the US instructors, included instructors from Canada, India, and Poland. In 1955, the Centre was re-equipped with Cessna L-19 Bird Dogs as basic trainers and North American T-6G Texans as advanced trainers. All the aircraft of the Air Instruction Centre were painted in yellow overall, and T-6s retained their black anti-glare panels on the forward fuselage. Thanks to their availability, the number of qualified pilots in the VNAF increased from 80 in 1955, to 163 only a year later, and then to 219 in 1957. (Artwork by Tom Cooper)

In addition to being used as basic trainers, Cessna L-19s and O-1A Bird Dogs were used by forward air controllers (FACs) to escort heliborne operations and truck convoys: whenever an ambush or enemy position was discovered, the FAC would quickly call for an air strike on the enemy position, or direct artillery fire. Operated by the 111th and 112th Observation Squadrons, most Bird Dogs used as FACs were painted in aircraft gray overall (FS16473), or in olive drab (FS34087). An exception were examples taken from the stocks of the US Marines – like this O-1A of the 112th Observation Squadron – which were painted in flat/medium green (FS34102) overall. Notably, the entire upper side of the wing was painted in white (FS35522), to be easier to spot by strike aircraft. Notice the double rocket launcher installed under the wing: this was used to launch rockets that marked targets. (Artwork by Tom Cooper)

The 1st Helicopter Squadron, VNAF, was established in April 1956, and equipped with a few Bell H-13s. In 1958, the unit received 10 Sikorsky H-19 Chickasaw helicopters, and in 1959–1960 its first Sikorsky UH-34D Choctaws. The insert shows one of the early Vietnamese UH-34s, which wore no markings other than the 'last five' of its BuAer Number (134486): the main illustration shows another example, which at least retained most of its maintenance and warning stencils, and had the 'Star and Bars' roundel re-painted into that of South Vietnam. Both were taken from ex-USMC stocks, and thus painted in flat/medium green (FS34102) overall. In early 1963, 1st Helicopter Squadron was re-designated the 211th Helicopter Squadron: together with 213th Helicopter Squadron, it continued operating H-34s well into the second half of the 1960s. (Artwork by Tom Cooper)

The constantly deteriorating military situation led the US to step up the provision of aid to South Vietnam: simultaneously with the introduction of Operation Farm Gate, the US began delivering North American T-28B/C/D and RT-28 Trojans to the VNAF. The first unit equipped with them became the 2nd Fighter Squadron, established at Nha Trang in December 1961. Co-located with the Air Training Centre, the unit was quickly worked up with help of US advisors, and starting in May 1962 maintained a permanent detachment at Da Nang. This T-28C was one of the Trojans known to have served at the latter base as of 1962–1963. It is shown in typical livery for this type, including gull gray (FS 36440) on upper surfaces and sides, and insignia white (FS17875) on undersurfaces. (Artwork by Tom Cooper)

This T-28C is known to have served with the 2nd Fighter Squadron at Nha Trang as of 1962. It was notable for having the propeller head, the rear canopy frame, and its wing-tips painted in yellow. Initially, most would have had the blind flight hood along the top of the cockpit: together with parts of the airframe, this was supposed to denote their use for training purposes. Eventually, the hood was replaced by green transparency which was installed to decrease the effects of the sun. Trojans could be equipped with up to six hardpoints, but most often only two were used: inboards for the installation of two pods for 7.62mm machine guns each containing 500 rounds, and outboards to carry two pods for nine 68mm unguided rockets – or two 250lb bombs (125kg). (Artwork by Tom Cooper)

In January 1963, 2nd Fighter Squadron was redesignated the 516th Fighter Squadron. The unit was meanwhile subordinated to the 12th Tactical Air Wing in Nha Trang, but continued maintaining a detachment of T-28s at Da Nang subjected to the operational control of the 41st Tactical Air Wing. By this time, the unit had adopted the tradition of applying its squadron insignia – a Tiger – to the fin of its aircraft. This T-28D showed traces of its aircraft code being overpainted in white and changed to 'T'. Usually, this was applied as the second letter, right after the unit code. (Artwork by Tom Cooper)

In response to Saigon demanding deliveries of advanced combat aircraft, in 1960 the USA helped replace worn out Grumman F8F Bearcats of the 1st Fighter Squadron, VNAF with a batch of Douglas AD-4 Skyraiders. All arrived painted in light gull gray (FS36440) overall, with black anti-glare panels in front of the cockpit, and black walkways along the wing-roots. Initially, they wore relatively few markings, including the aircraft code ('A' in this case), and the 'last five' of their BuAerNo (134497 in this case). The Skyraider proved a highly dependable, survivable, and versatile platform, capable of carrying immense payloads. The example here is illustrated as loaded with two 500lbs bombs (250kg), ten 250lbs bombs (125kg), and two pods for 5in (127mm) HVAR rockets (the latter installed on the outboard underwing pylon). (Artwork by Tom Cooper)

By 1961, the Bien Hoa-based 1st Fighter Squadron, VNAF included four – later six – flights, each of which applied a band in different colours and markings on the rear fuselage of its Skyraiders. This example was assigned to 'Satan's Flight'. As additional pilots completed their training, each of these flights served as nuclei for additional units. In 1962, the 1st Fighter Squadron was redesignated as the 514th Fighter Squadron, which was subordinated to the 23rd Tactical Air Wing – the insignia of which was applied on the engine cowling. This Skyraider is shown as armed with two 500lb bombs, eight 250lb bombs, and two M1A2/CBU-26 cluster bombs (the latter installed on outboard underwing hardpoints). (Artwork by Tom Cooper)

Another, rarely photographed flight of the 1st/514th Squadron applied a red fuselage band with white arrows on its aircraft, atop of their usual gull gray overall livery. Thanks to US support, the VNAF quickly worked up enough crews to establish additional units equipped with A-1Hs, including the 516th Fighter Squadron at Da Nang in December 1961, the 518th at Bien Hoa in October 1963, and the 520th and 522nd at Tan Son Hut in June 1964. This aircraft is shown as equipped with large BLU-26 napalm tanks installed on the inboard underwing hardpoint, and a total of twelve 250lb bombs (six under each wing). (Artwork by Tom Cooper)

The Willys MB jeep (left) was the primary utility vehicle of the ARVN and large numbers were deployed in nearly all of its units by the early 1960s. Some were modified to carry stretchers, for casualty evacuation, but the examples most present in the public conscience were those used by the Military Police in Saigon. Contrary to the highly standardised jeep, the Dodge WC series (right) was a heavier 4WD vehicle, manufactured in a range of purpose-designed variants. One of these was the WC-55, illustrated here as mounting a Browning M1919 7.62mm machine gun with a protective shield on its cargo deck. Trucks armed in this fashion were frequently deployed to escort convoys of supply trucks underway to strategic villages. As of the early 1960s, all were kept in olive green overall, and wore no markings except for their number plates. (Artworks by David Bocquelet)

The largest post-Second World War user of the US-made M8 Greyhound scout car – and its M20 variant with an open-topped armoured superstructure with a single M2 heavy machine gun – was France, which deployed dozens during the Indochina War of 1946–1954. Most were subsequently donated to the ARVN. The Vietnamese deployed them intensively, both for assault purposes and for truck convoy escorting tasks, but losses were heavy. Correspondingly, in 1962, the US supplied additional examples, which reinforced ARVN mechanised cavalry units, but were primarily deployed for rural patrols and road reconnaissance. Armed with a single 37mm M6 gun and one 12.7mm Browning M2HB machine gun, all the Vietnamese M8s and M20s of the early 1960s were left in olive green overall, and wore no markings other than their number plates. (Artwork by David Bocquelet)

The M24 Chaffee was a light tank equipped with the 75mm M6, a 7.62mm Browning M1919 machine gun installed coaxially, and 12.7mm M2HB machine gun mounted on a pedestal near the commander's cupola. France deployed its M24s in Indochina with success and then passed down about 50 survivors to the ARVN in the mid-1950s. The South Vietnamese deployed them – often in cooperation with M3 White and M8 Greyhound scout cars – in two 24-tank squadrons of their mechanised cavalry. For most of the late 1950s and early 1960s, they were deployed in small detachments, as 'motorised bunkers', and rarely far away from their bases. Two exceptions were their involvement in the 1955 operation against the Bao Dai criminal syndicate and the attack on the Gia Long Palace during the 1963 coup. (Artwork by David Bocquelet)

Many strategic hamlets had watchtowers and guard towers to help alert them to Viet Cong attack. These varied in quality but the one shown here is from Quang Ngai and is unusual in that it has more than one level. The towers also had a large drum on the top deck – these would be pounded to alert the village to potential attack. (Artwork by Anderson Subtil)

The Viet Cong improvised many traps aimed at maiming or killing ARVN soldiers. The punji stake trap shown here would often have the stakes covered in faeces – designed to cause further disease and injury to the unwary. These traps would be signposted to friendly units with the use of broken twigs, sticks laid out in parallel lines or even messages hung from branches containing phrases such as 'Kill Zone' or 'Please don't go'. (Artwork by Anderson Subtil)

In the early 1960s, South Vietnamese soldiers continued to use items inherited from the French, but they were already starting to receive an increasing amount of old American equipment from the Second World War. The soldier illustrated here wears a French model uniform, M1 steel helmet and characteristic South Vietnamese bat boots, very appropriate for the climatic conditions of Southeast Asia. The combat kit is from the North American model M1943, while the rucksack is a French model from the previous decade. The main weapon is a classic .45ACP caliber Thompson M1A1 submachine gun and the soldier also carries an Mk2 fragmentation grenade and two grenades to be fired from the M1 Garand rifle. (Artwork by Anderson Subtil)

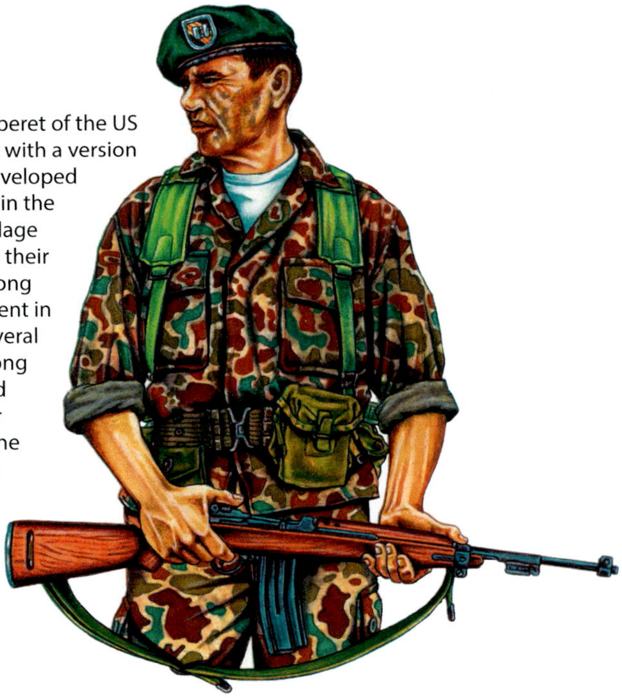

Easily recognisable by the signature green beret of the US Special Forces, this advisor wears a uniform with a version of the 'Duck Hunter' camouflage pattern developed during the Second World War. At this stage in the war, ARVN adopted many different camouflage patterns and some ARVN soldiers even had their own patterns made and shipped in from Hong Kong. At the beginning of the US involvement in Vietnam, this pattern was distributed to several of the elite US forces operating in the Mekong Delta. In the field, Americans often used old .30-cal M2 semi-automatic carbines in order to ensure ammunition compatibility with the troops they advised. (Artwork by Anderson Subtil)

This young girl – part of a regional guerrilla unit – wears the famous Viet Cong pyjamas, consisting of a black shirt with long sleeves and woollen trousers of the same colour, no different from the common clothing of many rural peasants in Southeast Asia. The footwear worn here are the 'Ho Chi Minh Sandals', an efficient item made from old truck tires and inner tubes. Note the protection over the shoulders – made of straw – used when carrying heavier equipment, such as the mortar bipod shown here. The cloth hat and canvas belt are of French origin, as is her weapon, a compact 9x19mm Parabellum MAT-49 sub machine gun, a weapon much appreciated for its simplicity, robustness and firepower. (Artwork by Anderson Subtil)

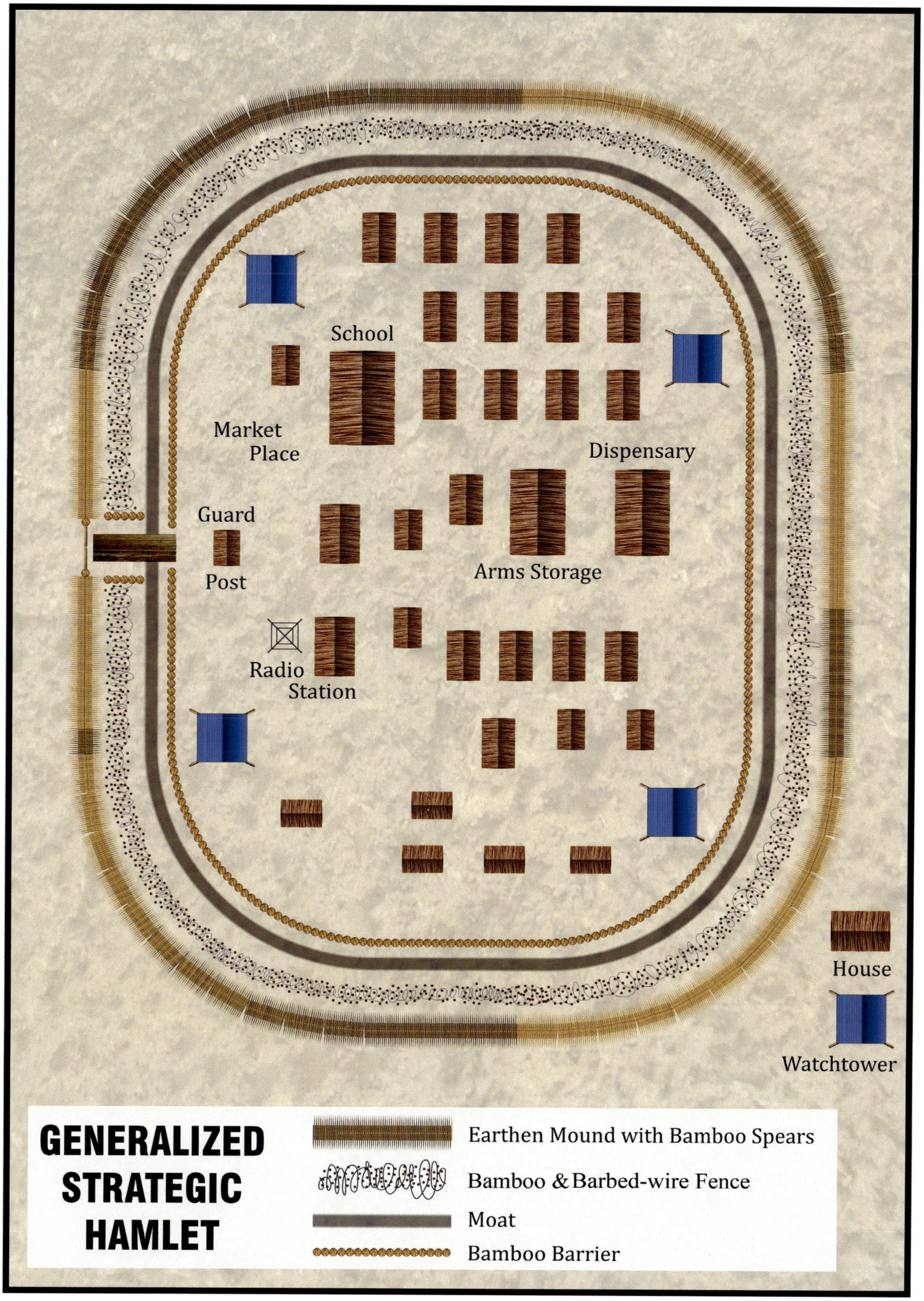

The centrepiece of the anti-Viet Cong strategy was the Strategic Hamlet Programme. In theory, these were heavily fortified villages in which Vietnamese peasants would be protected from VC attack. In reality, the quality of these hamlets varied enormously – the example drawn here shows the layout of an 'ideal' hamlet or defended village. Note the facilities aimed at winning 'Hearts and Minds': a dispensary, school and protected marketplace. (Artwork by Anderson Subtil)

Map of South Vietnam circa. 1960–1962. Notably, several provinces underwent boundary changes during the war and some – such as Phu Bon – were created in September 1962 and do not always appear on maps of this time period. The composite map here is designed for reference and to allow the reader to find provinces with ease. It is also worth noting that several of the provinces might not appear on earlier or subsequent maps from this time due to being merged with their neighbours or being created later in the conflict. (Map by George Anderson)

North Vietnamese forces train insurgent volunteers in preparation for infiltration into the South. (Communist Archives/Albert Grandolini Collection)

NVA forces and Viet Cong shooting at targets in the jungle. (Communist Archives/Albert Grandolini Collection)

The first point to make is that the Viet Cong acknowledged that they had been slow to respond to the threat they faced.[55] As noted previously, the insurgents commented that due to the rapid implementation, movement of government forces and strong ARVN attacks, the insurgents had been caught off guard and this meant that they 'did not have appropriate and effective methods to oppose enemy operations.'[56] The insurgents' self-analysis also noted that initially they had been slow to recognise the threat that they faced, were not clearly focussed on the government's plans nor did they have a deep understanding of the strategy overall.[57]

An insurgent poses with his equipment after training in North Vietnam. The barefoot soldier appears to have pineapple grenades on his belt. (Communist Archives/Albert Grandolini Collection)

VC recruits pose for photographs after basic training. (Communist Archives/Albert Grandolini Collection)

ARVN soldiers patrol a burnt-out base camp. Notice the wire used to tie up captured suspects. (Albert Grandolini Collection)

ARVN soldiers wade across a river whilst on patrol. (Albert Grandolini Collection)

One report, 'The Destruction of the Enemy's Strategic Hamlet Programme' went so far as to claim that the insurgents had 'underestimated the enemy work, thinking that the enemies could hardly succeed, and reacted negligently, inadequately and not in time' to the hamlet programme.[58] The acknowledgement that they had been 'slow in recognising the problems and in seeing clearly the enemy plots' actually gives support to the contention that the hamlets strategy had been successful because it shows that the insurgents were caught unawares and were being hurt as a result.[59]

Reports also commented on a negligence in some aspects of the insurgent response because they had 'reacted too slowly, underestimating the importance of the enemy plots.'[60] Many had also become complacent because when the hamlets were built some insurgent forces were able to overcome village resistance and so 'did not even bother to report to the higher echelon' their success.[61] This reveals a contradiction in the Viet Cong assessment of the hamlet programme. In some of the literature, the evaluation of the situation varies between claiming that they underestimated the counterinsurgency strategy and then stating that they simultaneously overestimated it too. For example, the 'Anti-Strategic Hamlet Programme' suggested that because of a variation in the approaches used to tackling the problem, the insurgents 'underestimated the enemy's scheme' whilst at the same time it claimed that they 'overestimated the enemy's strength and we became frightened; we were unable to have new initiatives, and found everything difficult.'[62]

This contradiction in assessment would indicate confusion within the insurgency movement but also highlights the attitudes and fears of the insurgents at this time. It may also help to explain why the hamlets were implemented with apparently varying degrees of success around the country.

Failures in Leadership?

One of the reasons suggested by the insurgents for this slow response was a failure in leadership. Some of this failure in leadership was based around the insurgents' belief that they were so strong and had so many 'good people' in their ranks that the enemy was 'unable to carry out their work.'[63] Initially, at least, many insurgent leaders did not see the hamlets as a threat and as a result they did not oppose the hamlet construction. One reason for this was that the insurgents felt that their senior leadership had not been direct enough in pointing out the dangers of the hamlet programme and did not concentrate 'well enough on the enemy's most dangerous schemes.'[64] As a consequence, the insurgents were not attacking the hamlets as repeatedly as they should have done.[65] A result of this breakdown in leadership was that the insurgency 'had not yet correctly specified the objectives of the guerrilla movement' and direction was sometimes vague and imprecise.[66] It is interesting to note that this assessment came from documents drawn up between January 1962 and June 1963 – the exact date is unspecified – and this could indicate just how long the insurgents took to respond to the initiative. This slow response was reflected in further statements which went on to claim that from 1962 onwards, the insurgents gradually gained 'tangible experience' of the counterinsurgency strategy and were able to correct deficiencies in their leadership and approach and 'stabilise the thoughts of the cadres and masses.'[67]

Again, what is noticeable here is what the document did not say but hinted at; for example, the mention of the need to stabilise the masses would indicate some form of instability in the ranks and the correcting of deficiencies would again indicate that there was a problem within the insurgent organisation. The insurgents went on to acknowledge that as a result of leadership failings 'military operations were not yet co-ordinated closely with the mass struggle' and as a result (and very tellingly when evaluating the hamlet's success), 'disorder emerged when faced with the new tactics of the enemy.'[68] Also suggested was unrest amongst rural supporters because 'the people, extremely confused, blamed the leadership' for not responding quickly enough to the hamlet programme and that only by providing 'timely and determined leadership' could the insurgency hope to prevail.[69]

There was also an understanding that the insurgency needed to consolidate and re-assess before going back on the offensive. The insurgents argued that although the revolutionary movement was becoming stronger, they were not powerful enough in 1962 to tackle

In the Delta region, small boats were often the most practical method of transport. Here ARVN soldiers cross a river whilst on patrol in the delta, the boat and operator apparently recruited locally. (Albert Grandolini Collection)

ARVN soldiers pose for the camera whilst on a break from their patrol duties. The standing soldier nearest to the camera is equipped with rifle grenades. (Albert Grandolini Collection)

the government forces.[70] This uneven development of insurgent military power had to be overcome in order to create advantageous conditions for a response.[71] The insurgents acknowledged that their movement had 'many shortcomings' because they were still very weak and did not have a uniform strategy.[72]

In recognition of the hamlet programme's effectiveness, they also noted that they were losing control of some areas 'because of the influences of the enemy movement, the grip on a number of our bases was deficient.'[73] Furthermore, the insurgents knew that they needed more time to 'increase our strength in all aspects, and especially in the military aspect' if they were to succeed.[74] Perhaps tellingly, the insurgents knew that time was a factor and the 'struggle to oppose and destroy the strategic hamlets will be a very long one, a very complicated one.'[75] This meant that resistance would see a 'pattern of seesaw movement, we may have to destroy (the same strategic hamlets) many times before the balance of forces changes.'[76] In fact, prolonging the struggle may actually have been a tactic of the insurgents. When assessing the situation in 1962, the Western Nambo committee stated that if the war was extended 'the enemy may get bogged down; they are unable to win and, the longer the war, the more handicapped they will be.'[77] Documents captured later in the war also revealed that the insurgents were aware of how they were being separated from the people and that they had to increase the level of their revolutionary activity and become, in their words, 'more decisive.'[78] This seemed to be taking effect by early 1963 as further documentation goes on to claim that the insurgents were getting stronger and that they were beginning to develop a response at a faster rate.[79]

Perhaps most revealing though, is the recognition that even with a struggle against the government going on in rural areas, the Viet Cong were not ready to commit to full scale open warfare. This was because they felt, even in 1963, that it 'was not possible' to launch the armed struggle too soon, before the situation had 'ripened.'[80] This would indicate that – even at this point in the war – the insurgents were still being damaged, were relatively weak and were unprepared for an escalation of the conflict.

Developing Strategies

Long and Short-term Approaches

The result of all of this self-analysis and knowledge was that the insurgents knew they had to respond to the threat they faced in a multi-faceted, methodical and co-ordinated way.

The insurgents were sensible enough to know that by opposing the counterinsurgency strategy they were embarking upon a 'long range mission' but they also knew that they had to adapt and change too.[81] The insurgents drew up specific tactics for dealing with the strategic hamlets and split these into several distinct steps; an overall strategy to increase insurgent effectiveness followed by a series of measures to be used before a hamlet was built, after it had been constructed and after it had been destroyed.[82] The stress here was on tactics that allowed the insurgents to 'cling to the masses' during the conflict.[83] The ultimate aim of the struggles would be to 'win over the people' and there would be both a political and a military campaign.[84] These struggles would run in parallel to each other and whilst the political aspect would be paramount, the party was to use the most appropriate means at any given time in order to achieve their goals.[85] Although the political struggle was seen as being the most important – with the military playing a supporting role – there were variations in the strategy.[86] In areas where the government was strong, a joint military and political struggle would be enacted, in areas where the enemy was weak, then military attacks would be the main tactic.[87] For example, if the strategic hamlets were being built in areas where the insurgent forces were strong, the strategy was to step up guerrilla activities and infiltrate the hamlets to a degree where it was hoped it would be possible for insurgents to take them over and build their own combat villages.[88] The decision to place an emphasis on a particular aspect of the struggle would depend

A woman and injured child are evacuated via river by ARVN soldiers. No record is given of their fate. (Albert Grandolini Collection)

Yet another successful patrol captures a Viet Cong suspect involved in the 'armed struggle' against the South Vietnamese government. (Albert Grandolini Collection)

on 'the current situation and level of balance between friendly and enemy forces' and here the insurgents were already displaying an adaptability and awareness that would go on to serve them so well in the rest of the conflict.[89] It was also recognised that the enemy forces had to be broken up, piece by piece, before any military offensive was launched.[90] The goal was to eventually isolate the Government of South Vietnam and ARVN from each other, from support within Vietnam and from the wider world community.[91]

Despite these variations in strategy, each particular facet of the 'anti-strategic hamlet plan' had distinctive features. For example, the political struggle was seen as being successful against Diem's regime because the insurgents believed that Diem's weak political base meant he had to use force to tackle the insurgency.[92] In turn, this made ARVN very aggressive and this was to the insurgents' advantage.[93] The political struggle would combat this aggression in several ways. Firstly, it would advance the 'patriotic movement' latent in South Vietnam and increase national unity.[94] Secondly, developing from this, the internal opposition to the American 'imperialist aggressor' would increase and the struggle against the strategic hamlets would intensify and thirdly, the insurgents would be able to successfully develop their local forces to pursue their overall aims.[95] Additionally, the insurgents hoped that their approach would stretch the resources of the South Vietnamese Government to breaking point and that Diem would have to 'spread out his troops everywhere' to combat the threat.[96] It was hoped that the struggle against the hamlets would eventually be made by

A company or more of ARVN soldiers, well supported by motor transport, return to base after an assault on VC positions. Smoke can be seen rising in the background. (Albert Grandolini Collection)

the people inside the hamlets themselves – with outside support being of secondary importance.[97]

However, despite these generalised political goals, it was also recognised that a 'simple political struggle' was not enough and an additional military or 'armed struggle' was necessary.[98] The military struggle was not simply about killing the enemy; it was also about combining approaches and tactics so that every military success would be followed by 'propaganda directed at the population and enemy troops to fully exploit our victories.'[99] This co-ordination between military success and psychological operations was to be further reinforced with activities that would 'indoctrinate' the people and allow the insurgents to win them over.[100] For example, one rural peasant commented that the Viet Cong propaganda, issued after a successful raid, told how they had come to 'liberate the people from these concentration camps so that they could go to their fields and freely farm their crops.'[101] This allusion to Nazi Germany was just one method used to undermine the government forces and it illustrated the crucial link between the psychological and military spheres.[102]

Three-stage Attack

Having devised a general strategy based upon a political-military offensive, the insurgents also devised a series of tactics or transitional steps to be used at each stage of the construction of a strategic hamlet. This involved measures to be implemented before the hamlets were built, tactics and offensive approaches to be used when attacking established hamlets and what to do once a hamlet was liberated.[103] The insurgents believed that this would be a protracted campaign. For example, Communist assessments noted that the struggle would be 'hard and long. The enemy activates, we destroy, he reactivates, we will destroy again.'[104] These assessments also suggested that the insurgents had to persevere and recognised that they had to make 'transitional steps in our way towards complete victory.'[105] As a result, the insurgents identified several key points at which to undermine and attack the hamlets and devised several strategies to be used at each transitional stage in the implementation of the Strategic Hamlet Programme.

Stage One

The first transitional step involved the tactics to be employed before the hamlets were built. Undermining the process from the start, 'right in the early stages,' was seen as being crucial to the overall effort to counter the hamlets.[106] The insurgents characterised this first phase as being when ARVN and Rural Reconstruction Teams would enter an area, perform propaganda activities that revolved around the purpose and usefulness of the strategic hamlets and also tell the people what they had to do if they wanted to oppose the communists.[107] The government forces would also perform sweep operations and assign materials, equipment and jobs to each family in a village.[108] Insurgent literature acknowledged that during this time period government 'propaganda is intensified, spies are sent everywhere to gather information …military operations are conducted in order to terrorise the people.'[109] The insurgents recognised that all of this was a sign that the hamlets were about to be constructed and they devised several responses.

The initial response was to ensure that the people were not separated from the insurgents and as such the guerrillas did not become disenchanted or lose their support base.[110] One way to do this was to infiltrate the village communities that were being reorganised. The 'Anti-Strategic Hamlet Programme' advised insurgents to be organised into cells beforehand and 'stay behind

NVA trainees pose for a photograph after a jungle exercise. (Communist Archive/Albert Grandolini Collection)

Communists prepare for a raid in the Mekong Delta. (Communist Archive/Albert Grandolini Collection)

and fight the enemy in a seesaw manner, in combination with the guerrilla forces.'[111] At the same time food was to be hidden in secret locations for collection at a later date, secret bases were established and the logistics of moving insurgents to these bases taken into consideration through forward planning.[112] Whilst this was going on, the insurgents were also told to gather together sympathisers in a hamlet and organise them into additional cells.[113]

These could operate from within the hamlet and 'lead the people who will stay inside the strategic hamlets' against the government forces.[114] Any villagers who had been identified previously as Viet Minh supporters were to be moved to other areas or to secret bases to avoid capture and interrogation even if they were not members of the Viet Cong.[115] A stress was placed in the literature upon keeping the support of the people at this stage and in addition to organising the military struggle, the District Committee had to assign members to study the local enemy plans, motivate local villagers and prepare for a counter-attack.[116] As well as motivating villagers to resist, the insurgents were also advised to 'approach good people and families' and then 'use them in our propaganda towards other people to take hold of the enemy situations' and undermine the hamlets from within.[117] Insurgent leaders were reminded that they should 'believe in the people's capability' and guide and council them at this stage of the conflict.[118]

Once the villagers had been organised, a meeting was to be held to tell people about the hamlets scheme, to inform them that their standard of living would worsen and to assign people tasks that would undermine the hamlet programme and destroy fences and spike pits.[119] It was stressed that villagers should be used as the main force in the conflict and they should eventually become 'secret armed forces' within the hamlets and engage in covert sabotage.[120]

There was an undercurrent of threat apparent here as the insurgents also mentioned punishing policemen and spies who helped enforce the government plans.[121] Finally, in order to encourage villagers to resist, sources gave concrete examples of places where villagers had been able to oppose government plans and overcome the hamlets.[122] This often took the form of a description of government atrocities followed by an account of successful counter-practices in other villages.[123] Whilst this often bordered on propaganda, it did occasionally detail ideas to use to counter the strategic hamlet strategy.

Viet Cong cadres entertain and inform a group of young children. Exercises such as this were crucial to VC propaganda and allowed them to claim they were winning the support of the 'people' (Communist Archive/Albert Grandolini Collection)

For example, in a document entitled *The People Should Support the Resistance Struggle against the Enemy's Strategic Hamlet and Army* the insurgents described how the villagers in the Khon Thon area had been forced to construct strategic hamlets, seen the 'blood-thirsty' ARVN kill and rape women and had 500,000 dollars stolen from them.[124] Taking into account the probable exaggerated claims of damage inflicted and money stolen, the document went on to say how villagers in other areas had responded to similar threats by refusing to go on work teams and how they united to protect themselves.[125] This united struggle, the encouraging of infiltration within the villages and the advice to keep cells secret would serve the insurgents well as they moved onto the second transitional stage of their assault on the hamlet programme.

Stages Two and Three

The insurgents knew that the second stage of resistance had arrived when villages began to be enclosed with fortifications, hamlet councils had begun their selection process and counterinsurgency measures such as the issuing of ID cards, taking family registers, implementing curfews and travel restrictions were imposed upon the people.[126]

Following on and linked in to the second stage was a third stage that saw social reform, medical care, school construction and insecticide spraying around the village take place.[127] Documentation noted that at this stage the insurgents could expect the enemy to 'assemble the people, they started to compel them to fell tress [sic], destroy the harvest, erect fences round the village.'[128] In addition, the insurgents had already encountered in this stage (in locations named only as Villages T and H) villages that were enclosed in fences and contained 'bunkers, spike fields, guard posts' and that were 'grouped together into an area encircled with barbed wire.'[129] As an aside, what is interesting to note here is that even the insurgents themselves recognised the effectiveness of some of the defensive counter-measures being used in the hamlet programme. This does seem to challenge some claims by historians about the relative weakness of the hamlet defences.

When tackling stages two and three, the importance of building bases was stressed. The insurgents' first step was to establish a chain of posts outside of the villages which would become 'fortified and long range stepping stone areas' which would vary in size and facilitate

South Vietnamese volunteers help the VC dismantle a bridge across a water channel in the Mekong Delta. (Communist Archive/Albert Grandolini Collection)

A Viet Cong cell wait to ambush an ARVN patrol. (Communist Archive/Albert Grandolini Collection)

NVA volunteers display their equipment – machine guns and recoilless rifles – in preparation for a possible move south. (Communist Archive/Albert Grandolini Collection)

NVA soldiers and Viet Cong volunteers examine the crashed wreckage of an ARVN helicopter. (Communist Archive/Albert Grandolini Collection)

'the constant movement of troops, as well as the transmission of direction to the people's movement.'[130]

This allowed for a shadow network to be established that would enable the various actors in the insurgency to meet, hide or simply recuperate from enemy attack. Again, it is interesting to note how the documentation claims that this establishment of bases was 'essential' because American aid, mopping up operations, air strikes and spies were acknowledged to be causing the 'oppression' of the revolution – which would again seem to indicate that the insurgents were being hurt.[131] The building of bases also tied into insurgent tactics at this stage because they allowed them to hide and keep secret their true numbers and their armament levels which they could then introduce into the conflict as a 'surprise move' to unsettle and undermine the government effort.[132] Additionally, the bases were to be used as centres where the insurgents could undertake what they termed a 'line casting position' or 'Tu the vot can cau'.[133] This was compared to a 'fisherman who tries to capture a fish by staying in one place and casting line out to catch fish in another place.'[134] It meant that the insurgents could influence villages from afar with propaganda conducted in the fields where people worked before returning to their safe haven at night.[135] This tactic of secrecy, whilst eminently sensible in an insurgent war, was extended to the hamlets themselves and any insurgents remaining in a village after it had been 'pacified' were told to maintain their cells and keep secret their links to the insurgency in anticipation of future conflict.[136]

Throughout each phase of resistance it was apparent that one of the major goals was to use the people to undermine the hamlet strategy. Captured documents, such as 'VC Measures against the Strategic Hamlet Programme' also mentioned how the main theme of the revolution at this stage was to 'motivate their hatred, indoctrinate them' to become involved in the insurgency and use the people to 'destroy the strategic hamlets.'[137] This notion of using the people to attack the hamlet initiative involved more than just fermenting insurrection inside the hamlet itself. One RAND interviewee noted:

> In 1962, when the national policy of strategic hamlets was carried out, my family moved to a strategic hamlet. I did not move with my family because I was influenced by VC propaganda. The VC said that the young men who lived in the strategic hamlets would be drafted or forced to labour very hard and might be killed by war. I was afraid that I would be killed; therefore, I remained in the village and was forced to work for the VC.[138]

This enabled the insurgents to stop young people moving to the local strategic hamlet. It denied the hamlet the young men who could enrol in combat training and enhanced their ability to communicate with people inside the hamlets themselves. It also

VC on a North Vietnamese firing range. (Communist Archive/Albert Grandolini Collection)

The Viet Cong were more than happy to include women in their fighting forces. Here, a young woman practices ambush tactics. (Communist Archive/Albert Grandolini Collection)

allowed for family members to be kept as part of the insurgent network, made communication between separate parts of a family easier to maintain and therefore kept the insurgents in contact with hamlet activities. Maintaining communication was vital as the insurgents wanted insurrection to come from within the hamlet and this could take several forms. For example, asking for freedom of movement in large groups would burden the hamlet militia and allow infiltrators to meet with people as they left the hamlet.[139] It would also 'maintain a line of communication for buying and selling goods with other areas' and keep open lines of contact.[140]

Military activities were also increased during the final two stages of the insurgency. Villagers were encouraged to dig pits with stakes inside to protect their property and advised to begin to form their own guerrilla groups.[141] In addition, the insurgents were told to use 'lightning concentration' and speed when attacking hamlets from the outside and surprise attacks on waterways and airfields were encouraged to undermine the government's mobility and night attacks were to be considered.[142] Increases in the size of Viet Cong forces involved in military operations at this stage were also observed. In Cochran's field study of insurgent morale, he noted that whilst propaganda incidents tended to be conducted by just one Viet Cong squad, in over two-thirds of cases attacks on the hamlets involved platoon or company-sized forces.[143] Indeed, the insurgents acknowledged how they had to 'concentrate' their troops in order to be successful.[144]

The VC transport a large aerial bomb through the jungle – possibly for future use in a hamlet attack. Large explosives were often used to breach perimeter fences or create diversions from the main assault (Communist Archive/Albert Grandolini Collection)

These attacks often took the form of a wall being blasted by recoilless weapons and this allowed the insurgents to breach the hamlet defences and enter the perimeter and overcome the hamlet militia.[145] Once a successful attack had taken place, the inhabitants were gathered together and there then followed a period of indoctrination where villagers underwent a 'lecture and recruitment session.'[146] Insurgent sympathisers were then 'planted in the crowd to whip up enthusiasm and even to set the pace by being the first to volunteer' for further activity.[147] This combining of the political and military struggle saw propaganda introduced whereby 'the people's interest should be brought up at all times,' effective resistance methods were explained to hamlet occupants and attempts were even made to 'gain the co-operation of enemy local government and army personnel.'[148] A flavour of this propaganda can be seen in a document from July 1962, entitled 'Let Us Develop the Fighting Spirit to Destroy the Americano–Diem Strategic Alliance' because it compared the hamlets to a jail.[149] It also mentioned Diem's cruelty and talked of the oppression that the people faced:

> As everybody knows, the so called "strategic hamlet" is used as a jail with all the necessary characteristics not only with barbed wire fences, guard towers but also with an oppression machine inside it. That is the highest and the most inhuman cruelty, of the Americans and Diem.[150]

The document then went on to praise the efforts of the people inside the hamlet, noted how they had revolted against oppression and even talked of how the soldiers inside the hamlet offered no resistance to the insurgent activity:

> The people have dissolved and paralysed the inside oppression machine. The people say courageously: "Dissolving the puppy government of the hamlet or the village, punishing the spies and policemen, the evil persons in the strategic hamlets to prevent the repairing of the oppression machine by the enemies, is similar to the killing of a snake by striking at his head." The strategic hamlet of Tan-Thanh in Chau Thanh district (Ben Tre province) has been destroyed a few hours after its construction, in the daytime. The enemies could not do anything because the interior oppression machine had been dissolved since the very beginning. The soldiers in the hamlet, moreover, have supported the people and have not fired a single shot.[151]

Communist soldiers pose after downing a US Army H-21 helicopter. (Communist Archive/(Albert Grandolini Collection)

It is interesting that this sort of propaganda not only commented on how successful the insurgents had been but it stressed the role that the people played in the destruction of the hamlets. It also offered an olive branch or concession to military forces in the hamlets as it noted how they did not resist the attack on Tan-Thanh and were, in effect, colluding with the local inhabitants. As such they are not mentioned as one of the group of people being 'punished' after the hamlet had been attacked.[152]

The effectiveness of this propaganda and the Viet Cong presence can be seen in the remarks made by a medical cadre, who commented that in their village, by 1963, the villagers 'saw the VC everywhere and we believed in their propaganda and their final victory. Therefore, we thought that joining the revolution was the best way to choose.'[153] This illustrates how the insurgents were skilfully combining the political-military struggle at this stage in the conflict but also using their political presence to intimidate the rural population.[154]

Post-Hamlet Activity

The set of tactics for the final stage of the struggle revolved around what to do once the hamlets had been destroyed. Interestingly, the insurgents did not want to reveal their full capacity after an attack and wanted cadres to remain hidden in case action needed to be taken in the future.[155] The 'Anti-Strategic Hamlet Programme' reminded the insurgents that they faced a 'long-duration' struggle and as such they had to maintain the secrecy of some of their cells, continue to infiltrate villages and other hamlets and be prepared to lead the villagers in future struggles.[156] The document went on to say that as well as the propaganda activities discussed previously, punishment and persuasion should be intensified in order to win over the people. Persuasion was to be focused around enemy troops; the aim was that if they could not be convinced to agree with the insurgents' goals, then they should at least be 'passive, in order to widen the scope of the front to isolate the wicked devils' and allow the insurgents to access the rural population.[157] In contrast, 'all possible means' were to be found to punish the 'wicked devils' who were hindering the revolution.[158] This was to be done by the use of terrorism to kill government officials and cause the 'common people and the troops to remain passive, neutral.'[159] This again indicates the fear that often lay behind Viet Cong tactics and hints at more sinister methods of control than the insurgents would openly admit.[160] This also illustrates that they could not always rely on voluntary rural support for their cause.

It can be seen that in response to the Strategic Hamlet Programme and the wider 'Counterinsurgency Plan', the insurgents developed a graduated, step-by-step strategy to help them win the conflict. This gave them a firm tactical basis from which to operate and ensured that, eventually, the insurgency would have a co-ordinated, unified answer to the government strategy. However, the insurgents did possess one other over-arching strategy that was to underpin the political and military struggles and that was to 'cling to the masses.'[161]

Cling to the Masses

Win 'Popular Support'

Perhaps the most crucial tactic that underpinned all of the other strategies was a central belief that winning the support of the people was the most important aspect of the conflict. Whilst it is notable that this was also the goal of the counterinsurgents, the captured documentation reveals the extent to which the insurgents would go to in order to win the assistance of the rural population. The insurgency recognised that 'the basic scheme of the enemy' was to isolate the population from the insurgents in order to deny them any leadership so they could then be 'exploited without reserve' by the Diem regime.[162] The insurgents acknowledged that this could potentially open up weaknesses in their campaign as 'they could not subsist and develop' if denied this access.[163] As a consequence of this, the insurgency stressed just how vital it was, at all stages of the conflict, to remain in contact with the people. The 'Anti-Strategic Hamlet Programme' emphasised that 'we must find all possible means to cling to the masses, under any circumstances' as that was the only way to maintain the struggle and develop the insurgency.[164] The so-called 'CRIMP Document' of 1963, went even further and underlined the importance of the people in a counterinsurgency conflict:

ARVN on patrol in the Delta. In places, the terrain made rapid movement on the ground almost impossible. (Albert Grandolini Collection)

Communists examining and unloading captured supplies. (Communist Archive/Albert Grandolini Collection)

> The armed forces must progress from small to large from weak to strong and three types of armies must exist; the revolutionary army must genuinely be the Army of the people, developed from the people, serve the people, be in close liaison with the people and have the support and participation of the people.[165]

This stress on the general population would serve as the ultimate asset of the insurgency itself. This strength was also reflected in the insurgents' use of the masses to attack the strategic hamlets from the 'inside and outside.'[166] Thus, by being close to the population 'many favourable conditions' occurred from which dissent could emerge.[167]

The insurgents used several methods to try and obtain this support. As previously touched upon, family ties were considered vital. Members of families could persuade their own relatives to either join the insurgency outside the hamlet or work from within to destabilise the project.[168] Families of troops not involved in the fighting were also targeted with propaganda that encouraged them to mobilise and combat the government attacks.[169] Education was also used to get 'first and foremost the workers, peasants and intellectuals' to understand the revolutionary movement and promote the 'highest degree of revolutionary fighting spirit' in the South Vietnamese.[170] Additionally, whilst the Strategic Hamlet Programme was a mainly rural-based strategy, the insurgents also acknowledged that the battle in the cities needed to be maintained and the role of the people accelerated here too. The cities were considered to be places that were ripe for insurrection as they were 'continually under the grip of the enemy' and were 'composed of masses who have a relatively high degree of awareness, realise who the enemy and the friends are, and continually have their hearts with the revolution.'[171] Finally, the 'Needs of the Revolution' noted that cities should not be left 'quiet' at this time and that the enemy 'must be kept worrying about dealing with friendly forces every day and every hour.'[172] This unrest was to be achieved through what was called a 'Public-Opinion Movement' whereby students, workers and those deemed to be intellectuals were encouraged to condemn Diem and try and 'ruin' the hamlet programme.[173]

In conclusion, the insurgents not only knew about the strategy that they faced but that it was causing them grave concern. They were suffering setbacks on the military front and they were also worried about the increasing American support for the Diem regime. The insurgents re-evaluated their tactics, stepped up their infiltration of the hamlets and began to re-draw their political-military strategy. One way to do this was by winning over the people.

3
THE X-FACTOR

Winning the 'People'

Lansdale said, "There's something missing" and McNamara said, "What?"
and Lansdale said, "The X-Factor,"
"What's the X-factor?"
"Well, the X-factor is what do the people think?"
"There's no way we can calculate this in any way numerically".
—Rufus Phillips recalls a conversation between General Edward Lansdale and Secretary of Defense, Robert McNamara.[1]

One of the major problems that the Diem regime faced was finding a way to prevent the insurgents from gaining access to the local population whilst simultaneously attempting to win popular support for government reforms. However, as Phillips observed, this presented a difficulty for the Diem–American alliance because they did not have sufficient systems in place to adequately measure the attitudes and outlook of the rural Vietnamese.[2]

As a result, they faced a struggle to win over the people, isolate the Viet Cong from the rural population and prevent insurgent infiltration. This would deny the Viet Cong access to recruits, supplies and information and limit their ability to hide from

South Vietnamese peasants being 'escorted' to a new strategic hamlet. (Albert Grandolini Collection)

government forces.[3] Indeed, both sides in the conflict were mindful that the aid of the Vietnamese populace was crucial for success in the wider war. The insurgents themselves were fully aware of the importance of popular backing and of the need to influence the rural communities whom they sought to govern. The 'Anti-Strategic Hamlet Programme' recognised the importance of winning popular support when it noted that 'the reason is very simple, the Party and the People are one, the guerrillas are the people, and the people themselves have carried out the guerrilla war; this is what the imperialists would have never known.'[4]

Similarly, the Diem regime, through its Strategic Hamlet Programme, was also seeking to win over the co-operation of the rural population and they too acknowledged that 'the war being waged in Vietnam is primarily a series of small political as well as military wars being fought in the hamlets for the loyalty and support of the hamlet people.'[5] Who would win this battle?

Establishing a Narrative

Americans and France: Two Sides of the Same Coin?

American involvement in the conflict allowed the insurgents to cultivate propaganda to counter the information being issued by the Diem regime. The insurgents did this by developing several narrative themes to support their insurgency. They were able to paint the Americans as imperialists who – much like the French before them – were seeking to use the counterinsurgency strategy to establish a new colony in South East Asia.

Although officially there was no formal commitment of American troops to South Vietnam at this time, numerous 'advisors' such as Rufus Phillips, John Donnell and generals such as Edward Lansdale were involved in the battle for South Vietnam. They were either in the country helping out with economic initiatives and

The effects of an ARVN patrol are clear: this woman is distraught and the photograph reveals how counterinsurgency practice can lead to a loss of popular support. (Albert Grandolini Collection)

Entrance to a VC information point in a village – providing assistance to the rural Vietnamese – being set ablaze by ARVN personnel. (Albert Grandolini Collection)

An ARVN patrol – unfortunately, these patrols allowed the VC to establish an anti-colonial narrative and undermined government efforts to support the local population. (Albert Grandolini Collection)

The tragedy of war: Civilian Irregular Defense Group officers honour a fallen comrade. (Albert Grandolini Collection)

US helicopter pilots involved in close air observation in South Vietnam. Although they had no 'official', formal combat role, they were involved in ground support and troop transport during this time period. (Albert Grandolini Collection)

US advisors lead ARVN officers on a training exercise in the Mekong Delta. (Albert Grandolini Collection)

military training or were suggesting political reform and providing advice in Washington.[6]

As *The Times* reported in 1963, many of these advisors were military personnel and it was an 'academic question' whether or not they were 'military effectives.'[7] It went on to say that the vast majority of the Americans were 'attached to field units, where they have orders to shoot if they are shot at' and to counter the violence and propaganda coming their way.[8] By April 1963, the number of American personnel in Vietnam was over 13,000 (10,000 of which were troops) and they had many different tasks.[9] For example, Civil Guard training was undertaken by MAAG in 1961 and regular search and destroy missions were being undertaken to help ARVN combat insurgent activity at this point in the conflict.[10]

One of the consequences of this increased American involvement was that it allowed the insurgents to suggest an anti-colonial and anti-imperial struggle was motivation for their actions. For example, the insurgents commented in 'Assessment of the Status of the Revolution in Vietnam' that the 'US imperialists will make the struggle longer and more difficult.'[11] Translated documents discussed how the struggle against Diem was a 'continuation and completion of the whole country's struggle against imperialism and feudalism' and stated how South Vietnam was being 'transformed into a new

US supplied helicopters fulfilled a variety of roles in South Vietnam. Here supplies are airlifted as a sling load by an H-21 to ARVN units in the field. (Albert Grandolini Collection)

Despite being from an earlier time period (1955), this photograph – with troops patrolling the streets – illustrates how chaotic South Vietnam was, even before formal US intervention in the early 1960s. The recoilless rifle carried by one soldier suggests the kind of combat anticipated. (Albert Grandolini Collection)

In another photograph from 1955, a torched jeep gives an indication of the potential for violence and chaos within the nation – and the idea that the war was a continuation of the conflict that began against the French. (Albert Grandolini Collection)

An ARVN M-113 APC advances along a river with the crew at full alert. The .50-cal machine gun would make quick work of any enemy watercraft. (Albert Grandolini Collection)

An ARVN patrol sets fire to flags of the National Revolutionary Movement from a VC supporting outpost. (Albert Grandolini Collection)

colony and a military base of the Americans; South Vietnam society is half colonial and half feudal.'[12]

Insurgent documentation went on to claim that the American support for the Strategic Hamlet Programme was 'clear evidence of their desire to control South Vietnam' and was a continuation of previous policies of 'terrorism and oppression' pursued by the Diem regime.[13] This attack on American involvement was developed further as the insurgents declared how American troops had moved illegally into South Vietnam and that the Strategic Hamlets were a 'dark plot' to 'transform the country into a US colony' where the security offered by the hamlets was actually a ruse for 'the oppression of the people.'[14] This attack on the Americans not only allowed the Viet Cong to undermine support for the hamlet programme, it also skilfully allowed the insurgents to further destabilise Diem and portray him as a 'lackey' of US imperialists.[15] This line of attack could be effective because it allowed the Viet Cong to depict the Diem government as traitors to the people of South Vietnam.[16]

There was also a clear policy to not only link the Americans to previous attempts by Diem to control South Vietnam but also to connect them with earlier French colonial practices. Farmer, when returning to the United States from South Vietnam, commented that the increasing Americanisation of the country meant that there was 'little difference between the French colonials and the American advisors' in the eyes of many South Vietnamese.[17] This was apparent as early as 1956, as one village security member noted that the Americans 'were supposed to be advisers for the GVN but I realised that they came here only to replace the French and swallow the country.'[18]

ARVN and Self-Defense Corps dismantle a VC information post. (Albert Grandolini Collection)

Soldiers rest by a defended post after a long patrol. (Albert Grandolini Collection)

A benefit of US involvement was increased military capacity. Here ARVN soldiers hunt the VC from atop an M-113 armoured personnel carrier armed with a .50-cal heavy machine gun. (Albert Grandolini Collection)

Here we see the M-113 being used to confront the VC in open combat. The Vietnam countryside was not always conducive to movement of armoured vehicles, limiting their value. (Albert Grandolini Collection)

Here we see ARVN troops disembarking from US Army helicopters. (Albert Grandolini Collection)

Others commented that 'the people were being led to believe that the original revolution which started against the French had never really been completed and had only lay dormant for several years after the Geneva Agreements,' whilst yet another claimed that the people 'think that this is the continuation of the former revolution.'[19]

This narrative helped develop, in the words of Theodore H. White, 'the gross fact of race-hatred, hatred of the white man in general, originally of the French, now converted by clever Communist tactics into a hatred of Americans' within South Vietnam.[20] White went on to remark that the insurgents had developed, in his words, a derogatory name for Diem that suggested Diem was an American puppet, claiming that 'the Commie tag for Diem is "Mei-Diem," meaning "America's Diem"' and this was enabling them to damage Diem even further.[21]

An American Paradox?

However, it should be noted that these anti-colonial themes relied on the rural population being politically literate in order to be effective and this was not always the case. For example, although it is interesting to note that anti-American materials constituted a large part of insurgent propaganda, other RAND interviewees commented that some rural communities simply did not grasp the wider geo-political picture and simply disliked Diem as opposed to linking him to American benefactors. For example, one commented that 'at that time, I did not fully understand this question of Americans being imperialists, but I could understand very well that Ngo Dinh Diem was maintaining a dictatorial family rule in South Vietnam' and this may have been a greater factor in causing rural unrest.[22]

It is also interesting to note that whilst the insurgents were clearly using American involvement to portray their struggle as being anti-colonial, they also recognised that there was an inherent paradox in this involvement: the American connection may have been helping the insurgents. The insurgents acknowledged that greater American participation could actually be beneficial to their cause because the people would become more united in their struggle.

Suspected Viet Cong are shackled together and await interrogation. The blanket raids and heavy-handed nature of much of the ARVN activity alienated many South Vietnamese. (Albert Grandolini Collection)

Militia and Self-Defense Corps pose before embarking on a patrol. (Albert Grandolini Collection)

The 'Anti-Strategic Hamlet Programme' noted that 'the more the US intervene, the more contradictions there will be' because 'the people will be more united in the fight of national liberation.'[23]

It also recognised that world public opinion would move their way as 'the more the US intervene, the more support we will have from the people of the world, especially the people of the socialist countries, and of Asia.'[24] The insurgents pointed out that as Diem was so closely linked to the American administration, they would both become 'more isolated' on the world stage as the conflict progressed.[25] This linking of American imperialism with Diem's own failings was successful in the minds of many rural South Vietnamese to the extent that one RAND interviewee noted that, 'I also realised that the dictatorial regime of Mr. Diem did not differ from the French regime' and this helped undermine the democratic legitimacy of much of the administration.[26]

Nationalism and Class Warfare

Linking with this anti-colonial account was a second narrative that was distinctly nationalist in its approach and focus. The 'Needs of the Revolution' noted that this 'imperialist' aggression would actually be used as a unifying force to enable South Vietnamese society to 'obtain the union' of the many to fight the Diem government.[27] Propaganda went on to claim that the people now had a common enemy in the US–Diem administration and the people were ready to undertake a 'sacrifice of the parts to save the whole' because they faced 'a fight to keep themselves their land, their homes, their own lives and the lives of their families.'[28] This point was developed further by RAND interviewees. One commented that he joined because 'I had heard the propaganda: "liberate the South, struggle against Diem and the Americans".'[29] A former Viet Minh fighter supported this view and recalled how he had returned to South Vietnam because 'being a South Vietnamese by birth, I felt it was my duty to return to South Vietnam and help the South Vietnamese people fight the Americans and liberate our fatherland.'[30]

Other, more subtle narratives were also developed within this Nationalist theme. For example, class war and land redistribution were also apparent in insurgent documentation. Class war featured in the 'Manifesto of the South Vietnam National Front for Liberation' and it claimed:

> My-Diem (US-Diemists) represent a collection of capitalists, businessmen and landowners, and the ruling class which is feudalistic, reactionary and depredatory to the people of SVN. At the present time workers, belonging to the oppressed class, are being subjected to cruel depredations (especially farmers). If you want to be liberated, it is evident that you cannot sit back and expect them (My-Diem) to willingly hand back your rights to you on a plate. They would rather lull you to sleep, urge you to feel happy with your condition and look forward to a better condition in your afterlife.[31]

This use of class warfare was not a new tactic and Donnell noted that Marxist-Leninism had been gradually diffused through Vietnamese society in the 1950s and 1960s which provided a further incentive to the insurgent movement.[32] Other RAND interviewees noted that they had been seduced by the Viet Cong's land redistribution too. One village deputy leader said that upon entering a village the insurgents 'gave land to the poor people who did not have a piece of land to work upon for a living. The land they gave belonged to those landowners who were not present at the time.'[33] Similarly, a village party member recalled how in 1961,

One consequence of the strategic hamlets was forced population resettlement. Here a village is forcibly moved from their ancestral home to the 'safety' of a strategic hamlet. (Albert Grandolini Collection)

'I was a poor peasant in my village. The VC took over and ordered me to join the Front and gave me land in exchange for my work with the Front.'[34] One of Donnell's interviewees described the land redistribution process that took place in his area in 1963:

> All the villagers including the landowners were convened in a meeting. The cadres openly asked those who owned many rice fields to give one part of their property to the poor countrymen. None of them dared refuse. Some bargained but at last all had to accept the share suggested by the cadres. [to obtain land] one had only to be landless or who own less than five cong… the share varied from two to five cong, according to the economic status of each one. I obtained five cong for myself.[35]

A cong was 1,000 square meters or one-tenth of an acre and so was a considerable amount of land to 'give' to peasants who may have had very little. It also helped win support for the Viet Cong and allowed them to portray themselves as benevolent benefactors of the rural poor.[36] In addition, some farmers who did own their own property were recruited by promises of secure land ownership after the revolution. One noted:

> I lived in the countryside. I had my own house and my own land. In 1961, the Viet Cong rose up in the area. I was frequently propagandised by them. They told me that they led the revolution in order to enable the farmers to protect their land. I realised that the VC were doing right because I, myself, was a farmer as well. Therefore, I joined the Front.[37]

Yet more population resettlement. Notice the none too subtle use of a gun to ensure compliance. (Albert Grandolini Collection)

Madame Nhu poses with female militia members and a handgun. Madame Nhu was often cited as a reason for Diem's unpopularity but accusations of corruption and influence over the president may have been overstated. (Albert Grandolini Collection)

The Diem regime was considered to be extravagant and out of touch by many South Vietnamese. Here we see a US major general and South Vietnamese officials engaging in the sort of indulgent banquet that fermented such views. (Albert Grandolini Collection)

Unsurprisingly, the poor who received this land became insurgent supporters and the wealthy, who lost the land, resented it. A hamlet guerrilla noted how the farmers became 'angry because of the losses they had to sustain' and this set the 'rich and middle farmers against the poor peasants.'[38] It also led to some farmers beginning to 'distrust the Front itself.'[39] This in turn meant that 'the dissatisfied villagers started to take revenge on the cadres and they began bringing out information to the GVN authorities' which undermined some Viet Cong attempts to win popular support.[40]

A portlier Diem inspects an ARVN parade. Notice the US observers watching in the background. (Albert Grandolini Collection)

Other Nationalist strands involved religion and attacks on President Diem. Diem's Catholicism was a source of resentment for some rural Vietnamese and although religion as such was rarely discussed in the anti-hamlet propaganda, it did provide a focus for fermenting limited rural unrest. One peasant farmer noted that in Diem's regime 'during the first three years, it had had good administration. But after that, it became a nepotistic government divided into factions, and it only took the Catholics into its service' and the insurgents exploited this by controlling religious activity in the villages they occupied.[41]

This allowed the insurgents to influence not only the flow of information through churches and other religious groups but it meant many Catholics fled their posts and left a vacuum of power for the insurgents to control. One cadre rather chillingly noted that 'when the VC took over, the Catholics were no longer seen' which may have been the intention of the insurgents all along.[42]

The final part of the Nationalist narrative strand was aimed at undermining Diem himself. American advisors were aware of the attempts to weaken Diem's government and in a paper prepared by the Country Team Staff Committee, dated Saigon, 4 January 1961, they noted that there was an 'active and partly successful campaign of the Viet Cong to discredit President Diem' and this was having a negative impact on his presidency.[43] Much of this propaganda referred (as discussed previously) to Diem as a 'lackey' of the Americans and claimed that Diem was using a 'false label' of Personalism to inflict injustices onto the rural Vietnamese.[44]

Personalism was essentially Diem and Nhu's attempt to transpose a social and political ideology borrowed from French philosophy and make it suitable for developing nations. Personalism mixed individual freedom with community responsibility and appeared to complement Asian Confucian values. Unfortunately, it was often used to justify forced labour and oppression.[45]

Strategic Hamlets or Concentration Camps?

The last narrative thread that the insurgents established was based around the Strategic Hamlet Programme itself. The insurgents claimed that the hamlets were an attempt by the regime to control the people and once the hamlets were built they would allow Diem to 'apply terrorism, menace and oppression measures upon the villagers' of South Vietnam.[46]

The propaganda – in a rather gruesome way – listed the many alleged crimes being committed by the Diem regime as they sought to implement the hamlet policy. For example, one such extract compared the Diem–American alliance to Hitler:

> In the course of these military operations conducted by the American officers, some people have been beheaded, disembowelled, women have been raped, 12 years old girls as well as 60 years old women… The US–Diem's crimes have no parallel even during the Dark Ages, or during the fascist domination of Hitler. Hate, resentment, sorrow, poverty, overfilled Vietnam up to the skies, from the countryside to the cities.[47]

A bus crosses a rotting bridge. The decaying infrastructure of many parts of South Vietnam caused a problem for the counterinsurgency forces. Although investment improved the road network, in many places the weather determined the pace of travel. (Albert Grandolini Collection)

US supplied equipment allowed for rapid deployment in the appropriate terrain. Here ARVN cross a ford built with US aid dollars. (Albert Grandolini Collection)

Another example of US supplied equipment supporting the work of ARVN. Here an M-114 APC equipped with multiple machine guns patrols a village housing suspected Viet Cong. (Albert Grandolini Collection)

The propaganda went on to mention forced labour, compulsory monetary contributions and extended so far as to claim that even the Americans themselves 'could not tolerate the crimes committed by US–Diem.'[48] The document also drew out the negative impact of the Strategic Hamlet Programme on the rural economy. This may have been aimed at countering some of the more successful government initiatives such as pig breeding and school building but it helped to portray the forced relocation of the peasantry into the new hamlets in a negative light.

The propaganda described in detail the demolition of villages, homes and civic and religious buildings. It also described the destruction of economic bases that the rural economy relied upon such as the damage to paddy fields and the looting of homes and rural farms. One extended extract illustrates some of the language used and demonstrates how government corruption was also cleverly inserted into the literature:

> Hundreds of military operations were conducted, with the participation of all branches of the services, thousands of homes have been burned, dozens of temples, pagodas, churches, have been destroyed, thousands of hectares of orchards, gardens, have been destroyed, fruit trees cut down, rubber trees cut down, paddies looted or burned, buffaloes, oxen, pigs, plundered or killed, millions of ducks and hens conveniently disposed of in the bags of soldiers and officers…[49]

Considering the nature of propaganda and the exaggerated accounts it often contained, these were claims that resonated with the rural population. For example, one villager recounted that the Viet Cong had told him how the people would be unable to plant crops and would 'die of hunger' as a result of Diem's policies.[50] This approach to stirring up fear about the consequences of the Strategic Hamlet Programme showed how the insurgents were developing a clear narrative to complement the anti-imperialist and Nationalist agendas that they were also pursuing. However, these agendas would only be relevant and useful if the insurgents were able to gain access to, and control of, the rural population and the next section will examine how this was achieved.

Infiltrating the Villages

A 'Shadow' Government?

Whilst the insurgents' narratives may have been persuasive, they had to gain access to the general population in order to garner support for their revolution. It is important to note here that there was a real distinction to be made between having the co-operation of a community and having access to that community. In an address in Detroit in 1962, George W. Ball argued that this contact with the people was key to winning them over.[51] He said that whilst the insurgents did not have the complete support of the people, 'so long as they have access to the people, they can undermine confidence, disrupt local government, and compel submission by terror and threat.'[52] It was this ability to contact and interact with the rural peasantry that was more crucial than simply persuading people of the value of the insurgents' cause. Phillips concurred with this and said that often policy makers made grand plans and lost sight of the

Here we see volunteers helping rebuild roads damaged in an ARVN attack. (Communist Archives/Albert Grandolini Collection)

An entrance to a secret Viet Cong base. The entrance is well-hidden and defended much like a strategic hamlet. The VC had lots of these outposts scattered around the countryside. (Communist Archives/Albert Grandolini Collection)

fact that it was 'events on the ground that drives things' and here the Viet Cong held a crucial advantage.[53]

National Intelligence estimates suggested that Viet Cong numbers were 'probably small in most villages' but this actually missed the point as extensive infiltration leading up to 1961 meant the insurgents already had the access to the population that Ball had discussed.[54] Much of this access was historical and came from areas of Viet Minh support and although it differed widely from province to province, it was, in the words of Special National Intelligence Estimate 14.3 / 53–6, 'the most important element of the Viet Cong paramilitary effort.'[55] Although Donnell and Hickey reported that some villages had been under insurgent control 'since 1945 or earlier,' most of the RAND interviewees gave from around 1959 to 1961 as the point when infiltration into villages really began.[56]

Specifically, the majority of RAND interviewees gave 1960 as the point in which infiltration increased but one even claimed that it had begun as early as 1955.[57] This allowed some villages to fall under the complete control of the insurgents. One commented that the infiltration was so extensive that the insurgents 'had cut off communication to the village, and so, the GVN was not able to come in' and could not influence the villagers and encourage them to counter the revolutionaries.[58] Additionally, this infiltration allowed the insurgents to develop safe havens which they could use for 'training, resupplying and resting their combat units.'[59] They could also build their own bases which in one case 'included a 200-man hospital, a basic training centre, an ordnance depot, and a battalion base camp.'[60]

Indeed, in War Zone D in the far south of the country, a Vietnamese ranger report noted that in the period 1962 to 1963 they had discovered a hidden base. It described the base network as follows:

> What best could be described as an inner fortress deep within the forested sanctuary. The rest areas and the training camps of the VC combat units were located within this inner fortress, while the security forces operated around the outer perimeter of Zone D. Spotted throughout the zone was an extensive network of way stations that were used as stop-over points for units and supplies infiltrating from North Vietnam. The way stations were about 15 to 20 kilometres apart and served very much the same purposes as our stage coach stops of the old west. They were whimsically referred to as the VC's Howard Johnsons.[61]

Although it could be argued that an infiltration network was already in operation before the Strategic Hamlet Programme came into effect, it permitted the Viet Cong to interact with the local populace, allowed them to move freely around certain parts of the country and meant that they were able to establish a shadow government in these areas.

This shadow government was described by Hilsman in 'A Strategic Concept for South Vietnam' and he acknowledged that infiltration allowed the insurgents to set up 'permanent, full-time government operations.'[62] This enabled a 'kind of shadow administration, functioning at night while the Government of Vietnam functions by day' to take effect.[63] This claim was supported by a guerrilla identified only as a Member of (the) Hamlet Propaganda, Culture and Indoctrination Section, who said that insurgent control was absolute in his area:

> From the beginning of the uprising (the VC uprising movement) in 1960 until 1963, the VC completely controlled the area surrounding hamlet and village. During that period, they set up a government which operated openly in the village. This VC government had all the related services attached to it: Security; Military Proselyting: Propaganda, Culture, and Indoctrination: Armed Forces; and so on.[64]

The shadow government had several key features and many advantages for the Viet Cong. It meant that a chain of command and

A US H-21 helicopter arrives to resupply an isolated base or hamlet. Many of these bases were built by corvee labour – both the VC and the Diem regime used unpaid labour to construct their bases of operations. (Albert Grandolini Collection)

Construction begins on an isolated outpost. Note the only access to the area was via helicopter. (Albert Grandolini Collection)

communication was established and according to a CIA report of February 1962 this extended 'from the regional committee down to the interprovincial, provincial, district, township, village and hamlet echelons.'[65] This allowed for orders to be quickly sent around the country and enabled the insurgents to organise rapidly in response to government activity.[66] It also meant that by destroying the hamlet democracy, the Viet Cong could then 'set up revolutionary organisations' to pursue their goals.[67] For example, a Village Front Committee would be appointed. This was described (again in the words of a RAND subject) as having the following structure:

When the Village Front Committee was first organised (1960 to 1962) it had a fairly good composition. It was composed of:

- A Chairman
- A Vice Chairman (an outstanding villager or a representative of a religious group)
- Representatives of other people's associations (chiefs of Executive Sections of the Farmer's, Youth and Women's Association)
- Heads of various services
- Representatives of religious groups
- Representatives of outstanding citizens (rich farmer, business firm owner, etc.)[68]

Some villagers claimed these appointments were made via a democratic process, whilst others claimed undue outside interference and suggested that 'in short, the Front Committee had the name, but the Party had the power. All important posts were held by Party members.'[69]

In addition to forming local government networks, this administrative base also gave the Viet Cong a chance to tax the local population to help fund their war effort. A Department of State report alleged that much of this taxation was gained via threats of extortion made to the local population. In 'A Threat to the Peace: North Vietnam's Effort to Conquer South' it was claimed that this taxation came from a variety of sources:

"Taxes" are extorted from the local population. Landowners and plantation operators often must pay a tribute to the VC as the price for not having their lands devastated. Similarly, transportation companies have been forced to pay the VC or face the threat of having their buses or boats sabotaged. Officials and wealthy people have been kidnapped for ransom by the VC. The VC have often stopped buses, taken the money and valuables of all on board, given them a lecture on the "glories of communism," and turned them loose.[70]

Where the peasantry were too poor to provide money, they had to pay in kind. One villager noted that from 1961 onwards 'the VC forced the young men and the farmers from my hamlet to go into the mountains to thresh rice for them. All told, about 30 persons were forced to go, including myself' and this provided the insurgents with the food they needed to survive if money was not forthcoming.[71]

This 'taxation' also extended to robbery of government officials and the setting up of illegal export networks where 'in the areas south of Saigon, the Viet Cong add to their revenues through considerable export trade by junks with Singapore, principally in tobacco.'[72]

However, paying this taxation could also be a cause of resentment. A Deputy Village Head of Finance commented that the villagers were essentially split in their support for the insurgency because 'half the population in the village was inclined to respond favourably to the Front, and the other half did not like it because their personal interests were infringed upon, and because they had to contribute too much taxes.'[73] These taxes were collected in various ways. One captured insurgent noted:

A wounded ARVN soldier and several South Vietnamese villagers are evacuated via helicopter to safety. Many of these evacuees later revealed surprising levels of support for the VC. (Albert Grandolini Collection)

> The VC cadres had confiscated 1 hectare of rice field which belonged to us and left my wife only 0.7 hectare to work on. The taxes they forced my wife to pay for that much land were not reduced accordingly. In 1961, my wife complied with the Front requirements in crop collecting by remitting 5 gia of paddy. In 1962…my wife had to pay 15 gia of paddy for each year instead of 10. I do not know how much they will force her to pay this year.[74]

Whilst taxation – in money or in kind – was beneficial to the insurgent cause, perhaps the final reason why the insurgents were able to effectively infiltrate the rural areas was that they relied on family ties to help develop and cement relationships. Aspects of this have been briefly mentioned in previous chapters and Phillips, in his report into counterinsurgency in July 1962, noted that although in places such as Quang Ngai the insurgents tended to live in bases in the mountains, they relied upon the support of local families with Viet Cong connections.[75] These connections to rural families were vital within Vietnamese society because 'loyalty to the family being perhaps the most important duty of a Vietnamese' meant that the insurgents could rely upon this tradition and covert backing to supplement their activities.[76] Phillips estimated, for example, that around five thousand Viet Cong regulars in Quang Ngai were maintained by 'some twenty thousand families with Viet Cong relatives' and this allowed the insurgents to function effectively.[77]

These family connections formed 'the main source of their support within these areas and within the population at large.'[78] In addition to providing supplies for the insurgents these familial connections also provided the insurgents with a valuable information network. Again Phillips noted that many families with Viet Cong connections 'were being used as informers to keep the rest of the population under control' and this helped extend the covert and shadow network of the insurgency.[79] This almost subtle use of informers and fear played a major part in controlling the rural population.[80]

Indeed, the Viet Cong themselves acknowledged that families were vital to their cause and that it would be necessary 'to mobilise the families of the troops into the fight struggle in order to curtail the violent drive of the enemy's attack.'[81] It was also suggested that family ties could be used to support the insurgency when there was no viable insurgent network within an area.[82] This was referred to as being able to 'build the people in the inside' to enhance their revolutionary prowess.[83] This use of the family and breaking the influence of these families was, again as Phillips noted, 'the single most difficult problem the Government faced in combatting the Viet Cong.'[84]

Therefore, as a consequence of infiltration, the insurgents were able to mobilise support for their cause and have a base for their activities. The insurgents were able to organise themselves on a regional and village level too. However, this would not be enough to successfully combat a national government strategy without the insurgents' ability to direct operations and control guerrilla activities on the ground. The insurgents' had an excellent military organisation and an expansive and effective communication network which allowed them to guide operations across borders and nations.

Insurgent 'Cell' Organisation and Communication

Familiar Communist Organisation

The insurgents in South Vietnam were, according to American intelligence, organised along lines that followed a 'familiar Communist pattern' that allowed them to communicate, plan and organise their attacks and activities effectively.[85] The insurgents structured their active cells, as noted above, along traditional guerrilla lines and these were set up to be similar to the Administrative and Resistance Committees used by the Viet Minh in the war against the French.[86] In *A Threat to the Peace* this structure was described as follows:

A Viet Cong booby trap ready for deployment. The VC excelled in using jungle materials to maim and injure ARVN and the rural peasantry. (Communist Archive/Albert Grandolini Collection)

VC await an aerial assault/troop deployment armed with a .30-cal machine gun. (Communist Archive/Albert Grandolini Collection)

> The basic unit is the cell of a few persons in a village or neighbourhood. Village units are subordinate to the district headquarters and these in turn are controlled by the provincial party headquarters. Above the latter are the regional or zonal headquarters which take their directions from Hanoi.[87]

Within the various cells, the insurgents divided their forces into 'concentrated forces, guerrillas, and self-defence militia' and these had numerous features.[88] For example, the concentrated forces were the main fighting units and were regarded as the 'most effective striking force' whilst the guerrillas were 'less well equipped and trained.'[89] The guerrillas were, in the words of one RAND subject 'supported by the village, lived together and were on permanent duty' although their fighting effectiveness may have been called into question.[90] Finally, the self-defence militia or people's combat forces were 'poorly equipped and only partly trained' and were 'provided with simple arms, such as grenades in order to set traps, plant land mines and make spike traps.'[91]

This final group was often not involved in the fighting and they would regularly remain in villages to farm the land and were not organised into groups or teams.[92] In terms of the leadership of each section, at the hamlet level there would be a Hamlet Unit Leader and one Assistant and the specific details of military operations would be left up to the 'discretion of the local VC commanders.'[93] This provided flexibility and potentially allowed for innovation and adaptability in response to the local conditions. However, promotion to the leadership positions may have been based more upon the perceived loyalty of an individual rather than their military talent or tactical acumen. As one Village Party Committee Member noted, 'I was promoted to that position by the higher authorities because I never violated discipline and I was said to have good revolutionary values' as opposed to being an outstanding combatant.[94] Yet another found himself 'promoted to be a squad leader' just three months after signing up.[95]

Communication Networks

In order to co-ordinate these various cells and groups, the insurgents developed a wide-ranging communications network made up of broadcasting stations in and around South Vietnam.[96] These broadcast stations were known as Liberation News Agency (LNA) stations and a Special National Intelligence Estimate 10-62 of February 1962, noted that there were '48 stations and 65 communication links' in the region and that these served as 'organs for information' for the insurgents and their members.[97] Additional propaganda would be issued and cadres were allowed to send messages to their loved ones.

This organisational structure and communications network allowed the insurgents to keep open lines of information and it also enabled orders to be given out: commanders could rapidly mobilise or reinforce their own troops in a combat zone. *A Threat to the Peace* described how these networks were used to support the insurgents' efforts:

> The official government radio in Hanoi is used both overtly and covertly to support the Viet Cong effort in South Viet-Nam. It disseminates a heavy schedule of propaganda, of course, praising the regime in the North, hailing the real and imagined successes of other Communist states, and attacking the Government in the South and all who are friendly to that Government. Recorded messages from individuals directed to loved ones and family members in the South are broadcast regularly. Their clear purpose is to influence morale adversely and weaken the will to resist. Captured agents have testified that the broadcasts are used sometimes to send instructions in veiled code to Viet Cong representatives in the South.[98]

The networks extended into Laos, Thailand and Cambodia. This allowed Hanoi to distribute orders to units in the field and co-ordinate military strategy. It also enabled them to circumvent the Demilitarised Zone and appear to remain within the letter – if not the spirit – of the Geneva Accords.

Finally, the insurgent infiltration of villages and their wide-ranging information network was supported by extensive spying operations within many of the regions of the South. Some of these groups were responsible for orientating agents arriving from the North, some gave instructions and tasks for new arrivals to complete whilst others acted as couriers for equipment, weapons and supplies.[99] CIA reports commented that this network was an important factor in the insurgents' success and that because this system existed throughout the entire countryside, the Viet Cong were able to maintain intelligence gathering operations at 'virtually every level in the South Vietnamese military and civil establishment.'[100] This set of contacts allowed for intimidation of the local population too. In fact, this had been ongoing since 1959. One RAND interviewee noted that 'almost all of the youth of the village were clandestine VC already' and if he had not joined the organisation he 'would have been interrogated and investigated – and terrorised.'[101] In addition to monitoring the local population, these networks would also send political cadres into villages to 'subvert the village' and try and indoctrinate the locals with insurgent

Not everyone in South Vietnam appeared hostile to ARVN. Here the troops are welcomed into a rural village. (Albert Grandolini Collection)

Troops on a recon mission evaluate potential village targets. (Albert Grandolini Collection)

propaganda.[102] This was extended to include so-called sleeper cadres who would look for new recruits and monitor the villages for signs of decreasing levels of support. These sleeper cadres would infiltrate villages and watch the local population. One villager noted that in 1961, a *can bon am vung* (sleeper cadre) arrived in their village and he described their actions:

> They (the sleeper cadre) report to the Viet Cong right away when there is any trouble, or when the Viet Cong come they are the people who make the contact. They are the ones who report, not the people. There is a small number of Viet Cong who stay all over the village. They live there like common people. It could be that they put one man in this group of houses, one man at another group of 50 houses, or one person in a hamlet. Whenever something unusual occurs they report to the higher ranks.[103]

This not only provided a solid flow of information to the insurgents, it also helped to sow distrust amongst the villagers themselves. This reduced the effectiveness of co-ordinated government operations and meant that informers were harder to cultivate because they did not know who to trust in a village at any one time. For example, one villager recalled how the names of those opposed to the revolution would be sent to the Viet Cong and this added to the sense of being permanently 'watched' by the insurgents.[104]

The Michigan State University Vietnam Advisory Group Collection noted in their study entitled *My Thuan: A Mekong Delta Village in South Vietnam* that suspicion was rife, even before hamlet construction occurred:

> The Viet Cong tactic of sowing distrust among the villagers has apparently been successful in the My Thuan area. One informant stated, for example, that the civil guards are ineffective because they do not trust each other. There is constant suspicion that one's friends, neighbours, or comrades-in-arms may be Viet Cong cadres. Since there are indications of justification for this fear, one of the government's most important means of combatting the Viet Cong, the use of informers, has been temporarily crippled. Unless confidence is restored in the government's ability to thwart the Viet Cong, it can be expected that security conditions will continue to deteriorate.[105]

This fear of infiltrators was justified. Donnell's study of why people joined the insurgent network revealed that a particular tactic of the Viet Cong was to attack a strategic hamlet at night, summon the inhabitants and after having collected 'contributions' to the insurgent cause, identify potential new recruits.[106] This was done by using spies and informers who would then seek to persuade prospective soldiers to join up:

> The VC often plants agents in these crowds to pick out onlookers responding enthusiastically to the message and reporting them to cadres who follow up these leads with personal visits. Such face-to-face appeals usually involve careful advance collection of information on the target individual with particular attention to personal problems that might make him particularly susceptible to certain appeals.[107]

This method of infiltration, indoctrination and coercion was not only successful, it was also expanded to include other areas of Vietnamese society. For example, the Special Group for Counterinsurgency noted that by April 1963, the Communists had penetrated not only rural areas but also had extensive links within the government, labour and student organisations that could provide information to support their cause.[108]

After a firefight, injured VC, dead ARVN and other casualties are prepped and ready for transfer back to base. (Albert Grandolini Collection)

Safety and Stomachs

Dividing the 'People'

Whilst the insurgents were clearly developing an effective information network, the sources also make clear that not every rural Vietnamese was an enthusiastic supporter of the 'Revolution'. Indeed, American advisors at the time were fully aware that it was difficult to ascertain the true feelings of the villagers in the South and that 'the only straws in the wind point in different directions' regarding loyalty to a particular side in the conflict.[109]

One reason for this was that when defending the strategic hamlets, some villagers had defended their homes bravely, whilst others had 'merely let the Viet Cong in or supplied what they wanted without reporting the incident to the authorities.'[110] Indeed, later in the conflict, one RAND subject said that when it came to loyalty to the cause, 'the people now only care about their safety and their stomachs. Whichever side can give them security and a chance to make a living, will receive their support' and this section will go on to demonstrate that he was, in part, correct.[111]

In his report on counterinsurgency in South Vietnam, Phillips noted that during the implementation of the Strategic Hamlet Programme – apart from the mountain areas of Tay Ninh province – there was no 'evidence of a shift toward voluntary support of the Viet Cong.'[112]

In many areas they had failed to establish new bases and were relying on villages that they used to hold in their fight against the French.[113] One reason given for this was that if the villagers supported the insurgents then this could make them targets for government attack. A hamlet cadre noted that 'since the Communists were in control of the village (1962), every day, the village was the site of heavy artillery shelling from the GVN position in nearby hills.'[114]

The constant shelling 'caused many dead and much damage.'[115] Donnell noted that this often meant the Vietnamese villagers 'who had lived in a state of insecurity for several years' took a short-term view of the future and were not particularly effusive in their support for either side in the conflict.[116] Indeed, it was quite possible for villagers within one community to support both the Viet Cong and the Diem regime. This mixed support for the insurgency or the government was reflected in a map drawn up by an insurgent who sketched a plan to illustrate how allegiance was split within his village of Hoa Quang in Phu Yen Province (see Map 5). This strategic hamlet was burnt down in 1962.

The same interviewee noted that after the village was attacked again (in 1963), ARVN soldiers fled and their supporters eventually changed allegiance.[117] This would appear to support the claim that the villagers tended to favour whoever was in control of their area.

ARVN troops await evacuation by a US Army H-21 helicopter after a successful patrol. (Albert Grandolini Collection)

One reason why support for the Viet Cong was not absolute was that many villagers were not always happy with the way that the insurgents treated them. A memo to President Kennedy in 1963, noted that there was real resentment against Viet Cong taxes and people were very suspicious about supporting the insurgency based on stories of violence and oppression that they were hearing from the North.[118] In addition, in a letter from Lansdale to Taylor in November 1961, it was noted that Viet Cong methods had 'alienated' the rural peasant but that they were often too scared to resist the influence of the insurgents.[119] As well as suspicion and alienation,

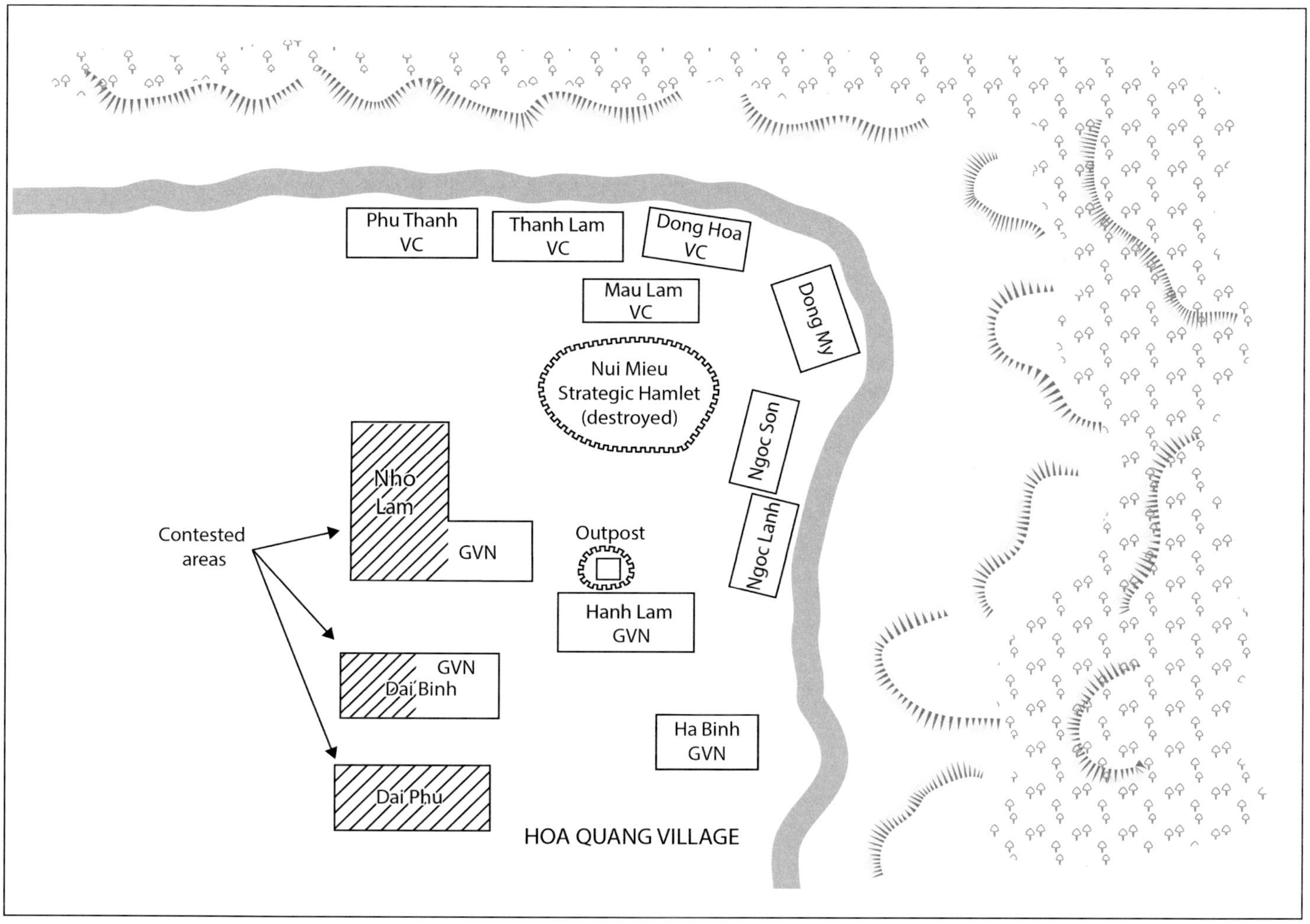

Map 5: Map showing support for either the Viet Cong or the Diem regime within the village of Hoa Quang. (Map by George Anderson, based on Studies of the National Liberation Front of South Vietnam Interviews 139.)

ARVN troops pensively await field deployment from a H-21 helicopter. In many isolated communities, air drops and air lifts were the only feasible way to attack the VC. (Albert Grandolini Collection)

another reason for not always supporting the insurgents was that the promises they made did not always match reality. A Deputy Village Head noted that 'all the Front's policies and plans sounded good only in principle. When it came to actual help, assistance, then the results were not anywhere to be seen.'[120] He went on to say that villagers would often put on a show of support for the insurgency 'but inwardly, they were all fed up.'[121] This was particularly true of the middle classes who he said were very unhappy because they had to 'dig roads, trenches, spike pits etc.' and engage in hard manual labour.[122]

Fear of the VC

However, even though many rural Vietnamese may have been ambivalent in their attitudes towards both sides in the conflict, many were not prepared to go against the wishes of the insurgent movement. One of the main reasons for this was fear. This manifested itself in several forms. Firstly, many rural Vietnamese did not feel physically protected and they would be 'prudently co-operative' in order to avoid 'individual acts of terror and retaliation' from the insurgents.[123] Phillips felt that this was a particularly important factor because the villagers he had spoken to said they lacked protection. They would, he argued, have stopped helping the Viet Cong if they did not feel that without government protection this would be 'tantamount to committing suicide.'[124] Secondly, the insurgents often used fear as a weapon. Lansdale noted, for example, that 'the Communists cut off heads' as a way to maintain control.[125] Kidnapping was also used as a 'stick' of terror and people were 'simply too frightened to talk about them' to outsiders.[126] Even in the early stages of the counterinsurgency programme in 1961, hamlet chiefs were threatened and intimidated if they tried to support the Diem regime.[127] Finally, subtle family influence was applied to add fear and cloud the minds of people who refused to join the insurgents or who wanted to sign up with ARVN. For example, social pressure was applied to young men who did not want to join the insurgency. One 16-year-old who joined in 1963 said 'if I had not joined the Front, I would have had to leave my village to go to work elsewhere, because the young women of the village would have ridiculed me and I would not have been able to stand their contempt.'[128] This social pressure could also be applied to those drafted into ARVN. One unnamed recruit talked of how potential ARVN soldiers were persuaded of the dangers of joining up to fight the insurgency. He claimed:

> I joined the Front in 1963. I got the draft order from the village authorities. One of my cousins advised me not to go into the ARVN. He said that to be a government soldier would be the end of my life but it would be good to be a combatant of the Front. Joining the Front might save my life.[129]

The way in which fear was used as a weapon of the insurgency is developed more in Volume 2 but these comments would seem to indicate that the support of the rural South Vietnamese was available to both sides. It was just that the Viet Cong seemed better able to influence rural communities to act in their (the insurgents') interests.

This final chapter has shown that as American involvement increased, the insurgents developed convincing anti-American narratives that in turn fed into a wider anti-Diem rhetoric and spurred on a Nationalist response. It has also shown that whilst the Strategic Hamlet Programme was attempting to re-establish government structures and democratic processes, the insurgents had already put in place their own systems of government to run alongside those of the Diem regime. Simply put, the gains made under the Counterinsurgency Plan and the Strategic Hamlet Programme were undermined by insurgent propaganda, infiltration of South Vietnamese villages and peasants under constant fear of their lives. Despite being 'hunted' the insurgents were able to re-organise and maintain their revolutionary movement in the face of government attack. In summary, the many gains made by the US-backed administration were undermined by an adaptable and shrewd insurgent organisation. Paul Harkins was correct when he claimed that the Viet Cong were being hunted, unfortunately the prey he was after was incredibly resilient, flexible and intelligent and was able to turn the tables on its pursuers.

The second volume in this series will examine why attempts by the counterinsurgents to reverse these trends and win 'hearts and minds' could not turn the tide against the insurgency and change the course of the war.

CONCLUSION

One reason for writing this book was that the sources encountered in the Kennedy Library and those produced by RAND and USOM did not match the widely held historical narrative about the Vietnam War. These documents revealed that a detailed, comprehensive strategy for South Vietnam was in place.

They also showed that there were many skilled and committed Americans involved in South Vietnam who understood the nation, cared deeply for its people and were desperate to defeat communist violence and expansion. The same was equally true of their South Vietnamese allies. Similarly, the documents written by the Viet Cong and the interviews with South Vietnamese civilians, ARVN and the VC themselves, revealed just how close the insurgents came to being defeated. The hope is that this book (together with the second volume) will help correct the historical record. American advisors and their South Vietnamese partners all courageously risked (and gave) their lives fighting a ruthless, violent insurgency.

It is regrettable that their sacrifice in the face of communist terror has largely been forgotten. The next volume in this series will show why things began to go so badly wrong.

ARVN troops lie in wait for a potential VC cell to pass their way. (Albert Grandolini Collection)

ARVN and the Self-Defense Corps pose for a picture whilst preparing to defend their homes. (Albert Grandolini Collection)

BIBLIOGRAPHY

ARCHIVES AND MANUSCRIPT SOURCES

JOHN F. KENNEDY ARCHIVES, BOSTON, MASSACHUSETTS

PRESIDENTIAL PAPERS – PRESIDENT'S OFFICE FILES

Country Files

Vietnam: General, 1960–1961
Vietnam, General, 1961
Vietnam, General, 1962
Vietnam, General, 1963
Vietnam, Security, 1961
Vietnam, Security, 1962
Vietnam, Security, 1963
Vietnam Subjects, Jorden Report
Vietnam Subjects, MAAG, Counterinsurgency, Part I–VII

Counter-insurgency

31 March 1959–13 January 1962
Departments and Agencies
Justice: Counterinsurgency (U.S. Army report), May 1961
Air Force: Counterinsurgency, 1962

Countries

Vietnam: General, 1963: 22 September–5 October: Defense cables
Vietnam: General, September 1963: 18–21: State cables

MEETINGS AND MEMORANDA (GENERAL)

Key national security problems: General, 1961: March–September

National Security Council meetings, 1963: No. 519, 2 October 1963
Special Group (CI): Subjects: Meetings, 8 June 1961–2 November 1962

Meetings and Memoranda (Staff)

Rostow, Walt, 1961
Taylor, Maxwell, 1961: September–December

National Security Action Memoranda

NSAM 52: re: Report of the Vietnam Task Force
NSAM 65: Joint Program of Action with the Government of Vietnam
NSAM 111: First Phase of Vietnam Program
NSAM 124: Establishment of the Special Group (Counter-insurgency)
NSAM 163: Training Objectives for Counterinsurgency
NSAM 182: Counterinsurgency Doctrine

National Security Files (General)

Vietnam, General, 1961: January–March
Vietnam, General, 1961: August
Vietnam, General, 1963: September

PRESIDENT'S OFFICE FILES (GENERAL)

Departments and Agencies

Air Force: Counterinsurgency, 1962
President's Office Files
General Correspondence 1962: HA

Regional Security Files

Southeast Asia, 1961

Gilpatric, Roswell L., Personal Papers

Hilsman, Roger, Personal Papers

Countries Files, 1961–1964. Vietnam: "A Strategic Concept for South Vietnam, 2 February 1962"
Countries Files, 1961–1964. Vietnam: Hilsman trip, December 1962–January 1963: Basic report and "Eyes Only" annex
Countries Files, 1961–1964. Vietnam, 27 August 1963

Komer Series, Counterinsurgency

Oral History Collection

Ball, George W.
Bell, David
Bundy, William P.
Burke, Arleigh A.
Cooper, Chester
Forrestal, Michael V.
Gilpatric, Roswell L.
Krulak, Victor (Harold)
Lansdale, Edward G.
Rostow, Walt W.
Wheeler, Earle

Liddell Hart Centre for Military Archives, London

The John F. Kennedy National Security Files, 1961–1963
US Armed Forces in Vietnam. 1954–1975
Vietnam Documents and Research Notes Series: Translation and Analysis of Significant Viet Cong / North Vietnamese Documents

Miami University Library: Oxford, Ohio

OCLC Number: 1658815. Rand Vietnam Interview Series V, Microfilm Collection V: Viet Cong Organizational Activities at Hamlet / Village level

THE VIETNAM CENTER AND VIRTUAL VIETNAM ARCHIVE, TEXAS TECH UNIVERSITY, LUBBOCK, TEXAS

Colby, William Collection

Donnell, John Collection

Questionnaire (I) For POW's and Ralliers
Studies of the National Liberation Front of South Vietnam Interviews
The CRIMP Documents
The Strategic Hamlet Program in Kien Hoa Province, South Vietnam: A Case Study of Counter-insurgency

Drachnik, Joseph Collection

Lehovich, Vladimir Collection

Michigan State University Vietnam Advisory Group Collection

Nulsen, Charles (Bob) Collection

Oral History Project

Phillips, Rufus Collection

Pike, Douglas Collection

Assessment and Strategy
Democratic Republic of Vietnam
Insurgency Warfare
Intra Ministry Committee for Strategic Hamlets
Military Operations
Monographs
National Liberation Front
Other Manuscripts
Statistical Data
The Early History of Vietnam

Shelton, William Collection

US Marine Corps History Division Vietnam War Documents Collection

Vietnam Archive Collection

Captured Documents
Background Information and Areas of Knowledgeability

ONLINE ARCHIVES

CIA ARCHIVES, WASHINGTON D.C. [ONLINE]

CIA History Staff – Center for the Study of Intelligence Memoranda and Miscellaneous

FOREIGN RELATIONS OF THE UNITED STATES [ONLINE]

Volume I: Vietnam, 1961
Volume II: Vietnam, 1962
Volume III: Vietnam, January–August 1963
Volume IV: Vietnam, August–December 1961
Volume VII: Vietnam, 1961–1963 National Security Policy

LYNDON B. JOHNSON PRESIDENTIAL LIBRARY [ONLINE]

Oral History Interviews

Ball, George
Bundy, William
Colby, William E.
Cooper, Chester
Davidson, Phillip
Durbrow, Elbridge
Forrestal, Michael F.
Gilpatric, Roswell
Harkins, Paul D.
Hilsman, Roger
Lansdale, Edward G.
McNamara, Robert S.
Phillips, Rufus
Pike, Douglas
Wheeler, Earle G.

NATIONAL ARCHIVES, WASHINGTON D.C. [ONLINE]

US–Vietnam Relations 1945–1967, Volume IV.A.4: Evolution of the War. U.S. Training of Vietnamese National Army, 1954–59
US–Vietnam Relations 1945–1967, Volume IV.A.5: Evolution of the War. Origins of the Insurgency
US–Vietnam Relations 1945–1967, Volume IV.B.1: Evolution of the War. Counterinsurgency: The Kennedy Commitments and Programs, 1961
US–Vietnam Relations 1945–1967, Volume IV.B.2: Evolution of the War.

Counterinsurgency: Strategic Hamlet Program, 1961–63
US–Vietnam Relations 1945–1967, Volume IV.B.3: Evolution of the War. Counterinsurgency: The Advisory Build-up, 1961–67
US–Vietnam Relations 1945–1967, Volume IV.B.4: Evolution of the War. Counterinsurgency: Phased Withdrawal of U.S. Forces in Vietnam, 1962–64
US–Vietnam Relations 1945–1967, Volume IV.B.5: Evolution of the War. Counterinsurgency: The Overthrow of Ngo Dinh Diem, May–Nov. 1963
US–Vietnam Relations 1945–1967, Volume IV.C.1: Evolution of the War. U.S. Programs in South Vietnam, November 1963–April 1965
US–Vietnam Relations 1945–1967, Volume V.A: Justification of the War. Public Statements. Volume I: C–The Kennedy Administration
US–Vietnam Relations 1945–1967, Volume V.B.4: Justification of the War. Internal Documents. The Kennedy Administration. Book I
US–Vietnam Relations 1945–1967, Volume V.B.4: Justification of the War. Internal Documents. The Kennedy Administration. Book II

RAND, SANTA MONICA, CALIFORNIA [ONLINE]

RAND Research Reports, Vietnam, 1962–1973
RAND Interview Series, Vietnam, 1965–1972

GOVERNMENT PUBLICATIONS

Military Reports and Handbooks

Armed Forces Information and Education Department of Defense, *Handbook for U.S. Forces in Vietnam* (Washington: US Government Printing Office, 1966)
MACV, *Counterinsurgency: Lessons Learned Number 61: Salient Lessons Learned* (San Francisco: United Stated Military Assistance Command, Vietnam, 1967)
MACV, *Counterinsurgency: Lessons Learned Number 63: Search and Rescue Operations* (San Francisco: United Stated Military Assistance Command, Vietnam, 1967)
MACV, *Counterinsurgency: Lessons Learned Number 68: Viet Cong Base Camps and Supply Caches* (San Francisco: United Stated Military Assistance Command, Vietnam, 1968)
Petraeus, General D.H., Amos, J.F., & Nagl, J.A., *US Army Marine Corps Counterinsurgency Manual* (Chicago: University of Chicago, 2007)
United States Army Special Warfare School, *Program of Instruction for Military Assistance Training Advisor* (MATA) (North Carolina: Fort Bragg, 1962)
United States Marine Corps, *FMFM–21: Operations against Guerrilla Units* (Washington DC: Department of the Navy, 1962)

RAND Research Reports

Anderson, M., Arnsten, M., & Averch, H., *RM–5239–1–ISA/ARPA – Insurgent Organization and Operations: A Case Study of the Viet Cong in the Delta, 1964–1966* (Santa Monica: RAND Corporation, 1967)
Carrier, J.M., & Thomson C.A.H., *RM–4830–2–ISA/ARPA– Viet Cong Motivation and Morale: The Special Case of Chieu Hoi* (Santa Monica: RAND Corporation, 1966)
Cochran, S.W., *16157–ISA/ARPA – Motivation and Morale: Some Questions – Some Answers* (Santa Monica: RAND Corporation, 1967)
Davison, W.P., *R–1024–ARPA – User's Guide to the Rand Interviews in Vietnam* (Santa Monica: RAND Corporation, 1972)
Davison, W.P., & Zasloff, J.J., *RM–4983–1–ISA/ARPA – A Profile of Viet Cong Cadres* (Santa Monica: RAND Corporation, 1966)
Donnell, J.C., & Hickey, G.C., *RM–3208–ARPA – The Vietnamese 'Strategic Hamlets': A Preliminary Report* (Santa Monica: RAND Corporation, 1962)
Donnell, J.C., *14436–IBA/ARPA – Viet Cong Recruitment: Why and How Men Join* (Santa Monica: RAND Corporation, 1966)
Goure, L., & Thomson, C.A.H., *RM–4699–1–ISA/ARPA – Some Impressions of Viet Cong Vulnerabilities: An Interim Report* (Santa Monica: RAND Corporation, 1965)
Goure, L., *RM–4517–1–ISA – Some Impressions of the Effects of Military Operations on Viet Cong Behavior* (Santa Monica: RAND Corporation, 1965)
Goure, L., *RM–5522–1–ISA/ARPA – Inducements and Deterrents to Defection: An Analysis of the Motives of 125 Defectors* (Santa Monica: RAND Corporation, 1968)
Kecskemeti, P., *'Insurgency as a Strategic Problem'* (Santa Monica: RAND Corporation, 1967)
Kellen, K., *RM–5013–1–ISA/ARPA – A Profile of the PAVN Soldier in South Vietnam* (Santa Monica: RAND Corporation, 1966)
Kellen, K., *RM–6131–1–ISA–ARPA– Conversations with Enemy Soldiers in Late 1968/Early 1969: A Study of Motivation and Morale* (Santa Monica: RAND Corporation, 1970)
Koch, J.A., *The Chieu Hoi Program in South Vietnam, 1963–1971* (Santa Monica: Rand Corporation, 1973)
Komer, R.W., *R–957–ARPA – The Malayan Emergency in Retrospect: Organization of a Successful Counterinsurgency Effort* (Santa Monica: Rand Corporation, 1972)
Pearce, R.M., *RM–552–1–ARPA – Evolution of a Vietnamese Village – Part I: The Present, After Eight Months of Pacification* (Santa Monica: Rand Corporation, 1965)
Pearce, R.M., *RM–4692–1–ARPA – Evolution of a Vietnamese Village – Part II: The Past, August 1945 to April 1965* (Santa Monica: Rand Corporation, 1966)
Sweetland, A., *17634–ARPA/AGTLE – The Analysis of the HES (Hamlet Evaluation System)* (Santa Monica: RAND Corporation, 1968)
Zasloff, J.J., *RM–4703/2–ISA/ARPA – Political Motivation of the Viet Cong: The Vietminh Regroupees* (Santa Monica: RAND Corporation, 1968)

Special National Intelligence Estimates 1960–1963

Special National Intelligence Estimate, *63.1–60, Short Term Trends in South Vietnam* (Washington DC: Director of Central Intelligence, No 344, 23 August 1960)
Special National Intelligence Estimate, *58–61 Probable Communist Reactions to Certain US Courses of Action with Respect to Laos* (Washington DC: Director of Central Intelligence, No 253, 21 February 1961)
Special National Intelligence Estimate, *50–61 Outlook in Mainland Southeast Asia* (Washington DC: Director of Central Intelligence, No 364, 28 March 1961)
Special National Intelligence Estimate, *50–61 Outlook in Mainland Southeast Asia* (Washington DC: Director of Central Intelligence, No 364, 03 April 1961)
Special National Intelligence Estimate, *10–2–61 Likelihood of Major Communist Military Intervention in Mainland Southeast Asia* (Washington DC: Director of Central Intelligence, No 320, 27 June 1961)
Special National Intelligence Estimate, *58–2–61 Probable Reactions to Certain Courses of Action Concerning Laos* (Washington DC: Director of Central Intelligence, No 69, 05 July 1961)
Special National Intelligence Estimate, *14.3 / 53–61 Prospects for North and South Vietnam* (Washington DC: Director of Central Intelligence, No 370, 15 August 1961)
Special National Intelligence Estimate, *TS 142405–c Probable Communist Reactions to Certain SEATO Undertakings in South Vietnam* (Washington DC: Director of Central Intelligence, 10 October 1961)
Special National Intelligence Estimate, *10–62 Communist Objectives, Capabilities, and Intentions in Southeast Asia* (Washington DC: Director of Central Intelligence, No 352, 21 February 1962)
Special National Intelligence Estimate, *10–62 Communist Objectives, Capabilities, and Intentions in Southeast Asia* (Washington DC: Director of Central Intelligence, No 86, 21 February 1962)
Special National Intelligence Estimate, *58–5–62 Probable Communist Reactions to Certain US Courses of Action with Respect to Laos* (Washington DC: Director of Central Intelligence, No 370, 31 May 1962)
Special National Intelligence Estimate, *68–5/1–62 Communist Reactions to Additional US Courses of Action in Laos and North Vietnam* (Washington DC: Director of Central Intelligence, No 371, 12 June 1962)
Special National Intelligence Estimate, *53–63 Prospects in South Vietnam* (Washington DC: Director of Central Intelligence, No 361, 17 April 1963)
Special National Intelligence Estimate, *14.3–63 The Impact of the Sino–Soviet Dispute on North Vietnam and its Policies* (Washington DC: Director of Central Intelligence, No 358, 26 June 1963)
Special National Intelligence Estimate, *53–2–63 The Situation in South Vietnam* (Washington DC: Director of Central Intelligence, No 354, 10 July 1963)

Memoranda and Miscellaneous

CIA Telegram, *Strategic Hamlets* (Washington DC: Director of Central Intelligence, 20 February 1962)
CIA Telegram, *Hamlet Programs* (Washington DC: Director of Central Intelligence, 03 July 1962)
CIA Telegram, *Strategic Hamlet Situation in Central Vietnam* (Washington DC: Director of Central Intelligence, 05 October 1962)
CIA Telegram, *Progress of Free Elections in Strategic Hamlets* (Washington DC: Director of Central Intelligence, 26 November 1962)
CIA Report, *Vietnam 1961–1968 Review of Judgements in INR Reports* (Washington DC: Director of Central Intelligence, Declassified 1985)
Memorandum for the Director, *South Vietnam's Leaders* (Washington DC: Director of Central Intelligence, 02 September 1963)
Memorandum for the Director, *Probable North Vietnamese Reaction to Certain Clandestine Operations* (Washington DC: Director of Central Intelligence, 20 December 1963)
CIA Documents, *Counter Insurgency Critical List* (Washington DC: Director of Central Intelligence, 25 July 1962)
CIA Documents, *Minutes of the Meeting of the Special Group (Counterinsurgency)* (Washington DC: Director of Central Intelligence, 21 August 1962)
CIA Documents, *Minutes of the Meeting of the Special Group (Counterinsurgency)* (Washington DC: Director of Central Intelligence 23 May 1963)
CIA Documents, *Minutes of the Meeting of the Special Group (Counterinsurgency)* (Washington DC: Director of Central Intelligence, 12 December 1963)

General

Commonwealth of Australia, *Parliamentary Debates: Melbourne and the Strategic Hamlets,* The Vietnam Center and Archive, Texas Tech University, 1963. [Online]. Available: http://www.virtualarchive.vietnam.ttu.edu/starweb/virtual/vva/servlet.starweb#

NEWSPAPERS, MEDIA AND PERIODICALS

The Times, London

Unknown Correspondent, 'American Guerrilla Experts for Vietnam', *The Times,* 15 May 1961

Unknown Diplomatic Correspondent, 'British Mission to South Vietnam', *The Times,* 18 September 1961.

Unknown Special Correspondent, Saigon, 'Vietnam Village Defence Pledge. 3M. Peasants Affected.' *The Times,* 21 April 1962

Unknown Correspondent, Saigon, 'Lessons of the War in South Vietnam', *The Times,* 21 January 1963

Unknown Correspondent, Saigon, 'Vietnam Dilutes its Democracy', *The Times,* 1 July 1963

Unknown Defence Correspondent, 'The American Strategic Revolution 3 – fierce Dedication of Fort Bragg.', *The Times,* 31 July 1963

Unknown Special Correspondent, Saigon, 'New Vigour in South Vietnam War on Communist. Popular Support for Regime leads to Aggressive Spirit', *The Times,* 12 November 1963

Unknown Special Correspondent, Saigon, 'Strategy in Vietnam', *The Times,* 31 March 1964

Unknown Correspondent, 'Vietnam as Seen from Peking', *The Times,* 29 March 1965

Unknown Defence Correspondent, 'Vietnam, The War No One Can Win', *The Times,* 16 July 1965

Unknown Correspondent, 'Strategy in Vietnam', *The Times,* 14 July 1967

MEMOIRS

Giap, Gen. V.N., & Dung, Gen. V.T., *How We Won the War* (Ypsilanti, Michigan: RECON Publications, 1976)

Herrington, S.A., *Silence was a Weapon. The Vietnam War in the Villages: A Personal Perspective* (Novato, CA: Presidio Press, 1982)

Luce, D. & Sommer, J., *Vietnam – The Unheard Voices* (Ithaca and London: Cornell University Press, 1969)

McNamara, R.S., *In Retrospect: The Tragedy and Lessons of Vietnam* (New York: Random House, 1995)

Neese, H. & O'Donnell, J. (eds), *Prelude to Tragedy: Vietnam 1960–1965* (Annapolis: Naval Institute Press, 2001)

Phillips, R., *Why Vietnam Matters: An Eyewitness Account of Lessons not Learned* (Annapolis: Naval Institute Press, 2008)

Sharp, Admiral U.S.G., *Strategy for Defeat: Vietnam in Retrospect* (Novato, California: Presidio Press, 1978)

Tang, T.N., *A Vietcong Memoir* (San Diego: Harcourt Brace Jovanovich, 1985)

Templer, R., *The Conduct of Anti-terrorist Operations in Malaya* (Third Edition), (Malaya: Director of Operations, 1958)

Thompson, R., *Defeating Communist Insurgency: Experiences from Malaya and Vietnam* (London: Chatto and Windus, 1966)

Thompson, R., *Make for the Hills: Memories of Far Eastern Wars* (London: Leo Cooper, 1989)

Thompson, R., *No Exit from Vietnam* (London: Chatto and Windus, 1969)

Truong, N.Q., *Territorial Forces* (US Army Center for Military History: Washington DC, 1981)

Zumwalt, J.G., *Bare Feet, Iron Will: Stories from the Other Side of Vietnam's Battlefields* (Jacksonville: Fortis Publishers, 2010)

PUBLISHED SECONDARY SOURCES

Books

Addington, L.H., *America's War in Vietnam – A Short Narrative History* (Bloomington: Indiana University Press, 2000)

Ahern, T.L., *CIA and Rural Pacification in South Vietnam* (Washington, DC: CIA History Staff – Center for the Study of Intelligence, Declassified, 2009)

Ahern, T.L., *CIA and the Generals. Covert Support to Military Government in South Vietnam* (Washington, DC: CIA History Staff – Center for the Study of Intelligence, Declassified, 2009)

Ahern, T.L., *CIA and the House of Ngo. Covert Action in South Vietnam, 1954–63* (Washington, DC: CIA History Staff – Center for the Study of Intelligence, Declassified, 2009)

Ahern, T.L., *Good Questions, Wrong Answers. CIA Estimates of Arms Traffic through Sihanoukville, Cambodia, During the Vietnam War* (Washington, DC: CIA History Staff – Center for the Study of Intelligence, Declassified, 2004)

Ahern, T.L., *The Way We Do Things: Black Entry Operations into North Vietnam, 1961–1964* (Washington, DC: CIA History Staff – Center for the Study of Intelligence, Declassified, 2005)

Ahern, T.L., *Undercover Armies. CIA and Surrogate Warfare in Laos 1961–1973* (Washington, DC: CIA History Staff – Center for the Study of Intelligence, Declassified, 2009)

Aldred, J., *British Imperial and Foreign Policy, 1846–1980* (Oxford: Heinemann, 2004)

Allen, C., *Plain Tales from the British Empire* (London: Abacus, 2008)

Anderson, D., *Shadow on the White House: Presidents and the Vietnam War, 1945–1975* (Lawrence: University Press of Kansas, 1993)

Anderson, D.L., & Ernst, J., *The War that Never Ends: New Perspectives on the Vietnam War* (Lexington: The University Press of Kentucky, 2007)

Arnold, J.R., *Jungle of Snakes – A Century of Counterinsurgency Warfare from the Philippines to Iraq* (New York: Bloomsbury Press, 2010)

Arreguin-Toft, I., *How the Weak Win Wars: A Theory of Asymmetric Conflict* (Cambridge: Cambridge University Press, 2005)

Asprey, R.B., *War in the Shadows: Classic History of Guerrilla Warfare from Ancient Persia to the Present* (St Ives: Little, Brown and Company, 1994)

Baker, M., *Nam: The Vietnam War in the Words of the Men and Women who Fought There* (London: Abacus, 1982)

Ballard, J.R., & Cordesman, A. H., *Iraqi Security Forces, A Strategy for Success, Terrorism and Political Violence* (Washington: The National War College, 2007)

Ball, S.J., *The Cold War: An International History, 1947–1991* (London: Hodder-Arnold, 1998)

Barber, N., *The War of the Running Dogs: How Malaya Defeated the Communist Guerrillas, 1948–1960* (London: Cassell, 1971)

Bayly, C., & Harper, T., *Forgotten Wars: The End of Britain's Asian Empire* (London: Penguin Books, 2007)

Beckett, I.F.W., & Pimlott, J., *Counter-insurgency: Lessons from History* (Barnsley: Pen and Sword Military, 2011)

Beckett, I.F., *Insurgency in Iraq: A Historical Perspective* (Carlisle, PA: Studies Institute, U.S. Army War College, 2005)

Beckett, I.F., *Modern Insurgencies and Counter – Insurgencies: Guerrillas and their Opponents since 1750* (London: Routledge, 2001)

Beckett, I.F. (ed.), *The Roots of Counterinsurgency: Armies and Guerilla Warfare, 1900–1945* (London: Blandford Press, 1988)

Berman, L., *Lyndon Johnson's War: The Road to Stalemate in Vietnam* (New York: W.W. Norton and Company, 1989)

Bew, J., Frampton, M., & Gurruchaga, I., *Talking to Terrorists: Making Peace in Northern Ireland and the Basque Country* (London: G Hurst & Co, 2009)

Birtle, A.J., *U.S Army Counterinsurgency and Contingency Operations Doctrine 1942–1976* (Washington, D.C.: Center of Military History, United States Army, 2006)

Boot, M., *Invisible Armies: An Epic History of Guerrilla Warfare from Ancient Times to the Present* (New York: Liveright, 2013)

Bourke, J., *An Intimate History of Killing: Face-to-Face Killing in the Twentieth Century* (London: Granta Books, 1999)

Bradley, M.P., & Young, M.B. (eds), *Making Sense of the Vietnam Wars: Local, National and Traditional Perspectives* (Oxford: Oxford University Press, 2008)

Bragg, C., *Vietnam, Korea and US Foreign Policy 1945–75* (Oxford: Heinemann, 2005)

Brigham, R.K., *Is Iraq another Vietnam?* (New York: Public Affairs, 2006)

Brown, A., Elder, S., Gilbert, A., & Williams, R. (eds), *War in Peace: Conventional and Guerilla Warfare since 1945* (London: Orbis Publishing, 1981)

Brown, T., *JFK: History of an Image* (London: I.B. Tauris & Co Ltd, 1988)

Browning, P., *The Changing Nature of Warfare* (Cambridge: Cambridge University Press, 2006)

Burleigh, M., *Blood and Rage: A Cultural History of Terrorism* (London: Harper Perennial, 2008)

Burleigh, M., *Small Wars, Far Away Places. The Genesis of the Modern World: 1945–65* (London: Pan Macmillan, 2013)

Callwell, C.E., *Small Wars: Their Principles and Practice,* 3rd edition (Lincoln: University of Nebraska Press, 1996)

Caputo, P., *A Rumour of War* (New York: Henry Holt and Company, 1996)

Carlton, E., *War and Ideology* (London: Routledge, 1990)

Carruthers, S.L., *Winning Hearts and Minds: British Governments, the Media and Colonial Counter-Insurgency 1944–1960* (London: Leicester University Press, 1995)

Carter, J.M., *Inventing Vietnam. The United States and State Building, 1954–1968* (Cambridge: Cambridge University Press, 2008)

Catton, P.E., *Diem's Final Failure: Prelude to America's War in Vietnam* (Lawrence: University of Kansas, 2002)

Cassidy, R.M., *Counterinsurgency and the Global War on Terror: Military Culture and Irregular War* (Stanford, California: Stanford University Press, 2008)

Cawthorne, N., *Vietnam: A War Lost and Won* (London: Arcturus Publishing, 2003)

Clodfelter, M., *The Limits of Airpower: The American Bombing of North Vietnam* (New York: The Free Press, 1989)

Clutterbuck, R., *The Long, Long War: Counterinsurgency in Malaya and Vietnam* (Westport: Praeger, 1966)

Conboy, K., & Andrade, D., *Spies and Commandos. How America Lost the Secret War in North Vietnam* (Lawrence: University Press of Kansas, 2000)

Cooley, J., *Unholy Wars. Afghanistan, America and International Terrorism* (London: Pluto Press, 1999)

Connable, B., *Embracing the Fog of War: Assessment and Metrics in Counterinsurgency* (Santa Monica: RAND, 2012)

Cordesman, A.H., *Rethinking the Challenge of Counterinsurgency Warfare: Working Notes* (Washington: The Center for Strategic and International Studies, 2005)

Cordesman, A.H., *The Long War: The United States as a Self-Inflicted Wound,* (Washington: The Center for Strategic and International Studies, 2007)

Corum, J.S., *Bad Strategies – How Major Powers Fail in Counterinsurgency* (Minneapolis: Zenith Press, 2008)

Cosmas, G.A., *MACV The Joint Command in Years of Escalation, 1962–1967* (Washington, D.C.: Center of Military History, 2006)

Cox D.G., & Bruscino, T., *Population-Centric Counterinsurgency: A False Idol?* (Fort Leavenworth, Kansas: Combat Studies Institute Press – US Army Combined Arms Center, 2011)

Crockatt, R., *The Fifty Years War: The United States and the Soviet Union, 1941–1991* (Abingdon: Routledge, 1995)

Croke, K., *Rethinking the War on Terrorism: The Lessons of Counterinsurgency Doctrine* (Washington: Progressive Policy Institute, 2006)

Dallek, R., *John F Kennedy: An Unfinished Life, 1917–1963* (London: Penguin, 2004)

Damms, D.V., *The Eisenhower Presidency, 1953–1961* (London: Pearson Education Limited, 2002)

Daugherty, L., *The Vietnam War – Day by Day* (Birkenhead: Snap Productions Ltd, 2002)

Davis, R.G. (ed.), *The U.S. Army and Irregular Warfare 1775–2007* (Washington, D.C.: Center of Military History, United States Army, 2008)

Deery, P., *Malaya, 1948: Britain's 'Asian Cold War'?* (New York: International Center for Advanced Studies New York University, 2002)

Dinh Tho, T., *Pacification* (Washington D.C.: US Army Center of Military History, 1980)

Dixon, N., *On the Psychology of Military Incompetence* (London: Pimlico, 1976)

Dorland, G., *Legacy of Discord. Voices of the Vietnam War Era* (Washington, DC: Brassey's, 2001)

Duiker, W.J., *The Communist Road to Power in Vietnam* (Colorado: Westview Press, 1996)

Dumbrell, J., *Rethinking the Vietnam War* (Basingstoke: Palgrave Macmillan, 2012)

Dumbrell, J., & Ryan, D. (eds), *Vietnam in Iraq: Tactics, Lessons, Legacies and Ghosts* (London: Routledge, 2007)

Edwards, O., *The USA and the Cold War, 1945–63* (Abingdon: Hodder Murrray, 2002)

Ellsberg, D., *Secrets: A Memoir of Vietnam and the Pentagon Papers* (New York: Penguin Books, 2002)

Elliott, D.W.P., *The Vietnamese War: Revolution and Social Change in the Mekong Delta, 1930–1975* (New York: East Gate Books, 2003)

Feaver, P.D., & Kohn, R.H. (eds), *Soldiers and Civilians: The Civil–Military Gap and American National Security* (Cambridge, MA: MIT Press, 2001)

Freedman, L., *Kennedy's Wars: Berlin, Cuba, Laos, and Vietnam* (New York: Oxford University Press, 2000)

French, D., *The British Way in Counter-insurgency, 1945–1967* (Oxford: Oxford University Press, 2011)

Fitzgerald, F., *Fire in the Lake* (London: MacMillan, 1972)

Fitzgerald, D., *Learning to Forget: US Army Counterinsurgency Doctrine and Practice from Vietnam to Iraq* (Stanford: Stanford University Press, 2013)

Gaddis, J.L., *Strategies of Containment: A Critical Appraisal of Post-war American National Security Policy* (Oxford: Oxford University Press, 1982)

Gaddis, J.L., *The Cold War* (London: Penguin Books, 2005)

Gaddis, J.L., *The Long Peace: Inquiries into the History of the Cold War* (Oxford: Oxford University Press, 1987)

Gaddis, J.L., *We Now Know: Rethinking Cold War History* (Oxford: Oxford University Press, 1997)

Galula, D., *Counterinsurgency Warfare: Theory and Practice,* 2nd edition (London: Praeger Security International, 2006)

Gardner, L.C., & Young, M.B. (eds), *Iraq and the Lessons of Vietnam* (New York: The New Press, 2007)

Gat, A., *A History of Military Thought from the Enlightenment to the Cold War* (Oxford: Oxford University Press, 2001)

Gelb, L., & Bett, R., *The Irony of Vietnam: The System Worked* (Washington DC: Brookings Institution Press, 1979)

Giglio, J.N., *The Presidency of John F. Kennedy* (Lawrence, Kansas: The University of Kansas, 1991)

Gilbert, M.J. (ed.), *Why the North Won the Vietnam War* (New York: Palgrave, 2002)

Gill, D.C., *How We are Changed by War: A Study of Letters and Diaries from Colonial Conflicts to Operation Iraqi Freedom* (New York: Routledge, 2010)

Goodwin, J., *No Other Way Out: States and Revolutionary Movements, 1945–1991* (Cambridge: Cambridge University Press, 2001)

Gompert, D.C., *Heads We Win: The Cognitive Side of Counterinsurgency (COIN)* (Santa Monica: Rand Corporation, 2006)

Gompert, D.C., & Gordan, J., *War by Other Means. Building Complete and Balanced Capabilities for Counterinsurgency* (Santa Monica: Rand Corporation, 2007)

Graebner, N.A., *The Cold War: Ideological Conflict or Power Struggle?* (Boston: D.C. Heath and Company, 1963)

Graessner, S., Gurris, N., & Pross, C., *At the Side of Torture Survivors: Treating a Terrible Assault on Human Dignity* (Baltimore: John Hopkins University, 2001)

Grob-Fitzgibbon, B., *Imperial Endgame: Britain's Dirty Wars and the End of Empire* (Basingstoke: Palgrave Macmillan, 2011)

Guan, A.C., *The Vietnam War, 1962–64: The Vietnamese Communist Perspective* (New York: McGraw Hill, 2000)

Gurman, H. (ed.), *Hearts and Minds: A People's History of Counterinsurgency* (New York: The New Press, 2013)

Gwynn, C., *Imperial Policing* (London: Macmillan, 1936)

Halberstam, D., *The Best and the Brightest* (New York: Ballantine Books, 1969).

Halberstam, D., *The Making of a Quagmire: America and Vietnam during the Kennedy Era, Revised Edition* (Lanham, Maryland: Rowman & Littlefield Publishers, 2008)

Hall, M., *The Vietnam War* (Harlow: Pearson Education Limited, 2000)

Hammes, T.X., *The Sling and the Stone: On War in the 21st Century* (St.Paul: Zenith Press, 2006)

Hammond, W., *Reporting Vietnam: Media and Military at War* (Lawrence: University Press of Kansas, 2000)

Hanson, V.D., *An Autumn of War: What America Learned from September 11 and the War on Terrorism* (New York: Anchor Books, 2002)

Hanson, V.D., *Why the West has Won* (London: Faber and Faber, 2001)

Head, W., & Grinter, L., *Looking Back on the Vietnam War: A 1990 Perspective on the Decisions, Combat and Legacies* (London: Praeger, 1993)

Hearden, P.J., *The Tragedy of Vietnam* (Abingdon: Pearson Education, 2016)

Hernon, I., *Britain's Forgotten Wars: Colonial Campaigns of the 19th Century* (Stroud: Sutton Publishing, 2002)

Herring, G.C., *America's Longest War: The United States and Vietnam* (New York: McGraw Hill, 2002)

Hess, G.R., *Vietnam and the United States* (Boston: Twayne Publishers, 1990)

Hess, M., *Then the Americans Came: Voices from Vietnam* (New York: Four Walls Eight Windows, 1993)

Heuser, B., & Shamir, E. (eds), *Insurgencies and Counterinsurgencies: National Styles and Strategic Cultures* (Cambridge: Cambridge University Press, 2016)

Hickey, G.C., *Village in Vietnam* (New Haven and London: Yale University Press, 1964)

Hilsman, R., *To Move a Nation. The Politics of Foreign Policy in the Administration of John F. Kennedy* (New York: Delta Publishing, 1967)

Hoffman, B., *Insurgency and Counterinsurgency in Iraq* (Arlington: RAND Corporation, 2004)

Holland, R.F., *European Decolonization, 1918–1981* (London: Macmillan Education, 1985)

Hosmer, S.T., & Crane, S.O., *Counterinsurgency: A Symposium, April 16–20, 1962* (Santa Monica: Rand Corporation, 2006)

Hunt, D., *Vietnam's Southern Revolution: From Peasant Insurrection to Total War* (Amherst: University of Massachusetts Press, 2008)

Hunt, M. (ed.), *A Vietnam War Reader: A Documentary History from American and Vietnamese Perspectives* (North Carolina: University of North Carolina Press, 2010)

Ives, C.K., *US Special Forces and Counterinsurgency in Vietnam: Military Innovation and Institutional Failure, 1961–1963* (London and New York: Routledge, 2007)

James Joes, A., *Resisting Rebellion: The History and Politics of Counterinsurgency* (Lexington: The University Press of Kentucky, 2006)

James, L., *The Rise and Fall of the British Empire* (London: Abacus, 1994)

Jennings, R.S., *The Road Ahead: Lessons in Nation Building from Japan, Germany, and Afghanistan for Postwar Iraq* (Washington: United States Institute of Peace, 2007)

Joes, A., *The War For South Vietnam* (Westport: Praeger, 2001)

Kahin, McT., *Intervention: How America became involved in Vietnam* (New York: Anchor Books, 1986)

Kaiser, D., *American Tragedy: Kennedy, Johnson and the Origins of the Vietnam War* (Cambridge: Belknap Press of Harvard University Press, 2000)

Karnow, S., *Vietnam: A History* (Harmondsworth: Penguin, 1987)

Kennedy, J. F., *Profiles in Courage – 50th Anniversary Edition* (New York: Harper Perennial, 2003)

Kilcullen, D., *The Accidental Guerrilla: Fighting Small Wars in the Midst of a Big One* (London: Hurst & Company, 2009)

Kitson, F., *Low Intensity Operations: Subversion, Insurgency, Peacekeeping* (London: Faber and Faber, 1971)

Kolko, G., *Anatomy of War: Vietnam, the United States and the Modern Historical Experience* (New York: The New Press, 1985)

Komer, W., *Impact of Pacification on Insurgency in South Vietnam* (Santa Monica: RAND Corporation, 1970)

Komer, R. W., *The Malayan Emergency in Retrospect: The Organization of a Successful Counterinsurgency Effort* (Santa Monica: RAND Corporation, 1972)

Lanning, M.L., & Cragg, D., *Inside the VC and the NVA. The Real Story of North Vietnam's Armed Forces* (New York: Fawcett Columbine, 1992)

Law, R.D., *Terrorism: A History* (Cambridge: Polity Press, 2009)

Lawrence, M., *Assuming the Burden: Europe and the American Commitment to War in Vietnam* (Berkeley: University of California Press, 2005)

Laqueur, W., *A History of Terrorism* (New York: Transaction Publishers, 2001)

Lembbcke, J., *The Spitting Image: Myth, Memory, and the Legacy of Vietnam* (New York: New York University Press, 1998)

Leffler, M.P., & Painter, D.S., *Origins of the Cold War* (London: Routledge, 1994)

Levy, D., *The Debate Over Vietnam* (Baltimore: Johns Hopkins University Press, 1991)

Lewy, G., *America in Vietnam* (New York: Oxford University Press, USA, 1978)

Logevall, F., *Choosing War – The Lost Chance for Peace and the Escalation of War in Vietnam* (Berkeley: University of California Press, 1999)

Logevall, F., *The Origins of the Vietnam War* (New York: Longman, 2001)

Long, A., *On 'Other War': Lessons from Five Decades of RAND Counterinsurgency Research* (Santa Monica: Rand Corporation, 2006)

Lynn, J.A., *Battle: A History of Combat and Culture from Ancient Greece to Modern America* (Cambridge: Westview, 2004)

Mackay, A., & Tatham, S., *Behavioural Conflict – Why Understanding People and their Motivations will Provide Decisive in Future Conflict* (Saffron Walden: Military Studies Press, 2011)

Mackinlay, J., & Al-Baddawy, A., *Rethinking Counterinsurgency* (Santa Monica: Rand, 2007)

Manwaring, M.G., *Shadows of Things Past and Images of the Future: Lessons for the Insurgencies in our Midst* (Carlisle, PA: Strategic Studies Institute, 2004)

Martin, G., *Understanding Terrorism: Challenges, Perspectives and Issues* (Thousand Oaks: Sage Publications, 2006)

McCauley, M., *Russia, America and the Cold War* (Harlow: Pearson Education, 2004)

McCauley, M., *The Origins of the Cold War* (New York: Longman, 1983)

McDonough, F., *The British Empire* (Bedford: Hodder and Stoughton, 1994)

McMahon, R.J. (ed.), *Major Problems in the History of the Vietnam War* (Boston: Houghton Mifflin Company, 2003)

McMahon, R.J., & Paterson, T.G., *Problems in American Civilisation: The Origins of the Cold War* (Boston: Houghton Mifflin, 1999)

McMahon, R., *Major Problems in the History of the Vietnam War* (Lexington, Mass: DC Heath & Co, 2008)

McNamara, R.S., Blight, J.G., & Brigham, R.K., *Argument without End – in Search of Answers to the Vietnam Tragedy* (New York: Public Affairs, 1999)

Mead, W.R., *God and Gold: Britain, America and the Making of the Modern World* (New York: Random House, 2007)

Merom, G., *How Democracies Lose Small Wars: State, Society and the Failures of France in Algeria, Israel in Lebanon and the United States in Vietnam* (New York: Cambridge University Press, 2003)

Metz, S., & Millen, R., *Insurgency and Counterinsurgency in the 21st Century: Reconceptualising Threat and Response* (Washington: Strategic Studies Institute, 2004)

Metz, S., & Millen, R., *Insurgency in Iraq and Afghanistan: Change and Continuity* (Washington: Strategic Studies Institute, 2007)

Miller, E., *Misalliance: Ngo Dinh Diem, the United States, and the Fall of South Vietnam* (Cambridge: Harvard University Press, 2013)

Moore, H., & Galloway, J., *We Were Soldiers Once … and Young: Ia Drang – the Battle that Changed the War in Vietnam* (Novato: Presidio Press, 2004)

Moyar, M., *A Question of Command: Counterinsurgency from the Civil War to Iraq* (New Haven: Yale University Press, 2009)

Moyar, M., *Phoenix and the Birds of Prey: Counterinsurgency and Counterterrorism in Vietnam* (Lincoln: University of Nebraska, 1997)

Moyar, M., *Triumph Forsaken: The Vietnam War, 1954–1965* (Cambridge: Cambridge University Press, 2006)

Mumford, A., *Puncturing the Counterinsurgency Myth: Britain and Irregular Warfare in the Past, Present, and Future* (Carlisle: US Army War College, 2011)

Mumford, A., *The Counter-insurgency Myth: The British Experience of Irregular Warfare. Cass Military Studies.* (London: Routledge, 2012)

Murray, W., & Mansoor, P.R. (eds), *Hybrid Warfare: Fighting Complex Opponents from the Ancient World to the Present* (Cambridge: Cambridge University Press, 2012)

Nagl, J.A., *Learning to Eat Soup with a Knife: Counterinsurgency Lessons from Malaya and Vietnam* (Chicago: University of Chicago Press, 2002)

Nalty, B.C., *The Vietnam War. The History of America's Conflict in Southeast Asia* (New York: Salamander Books, 1996)

Neale, J., *The American War: Vietnam 1960–1975* (London: Bookmarks, 2001)

Newman, J.M., *JFK and Vietnam* (New York: Warner Books, 1993)

Newsinger, J., *British Counterinsurgency: From Palestine to Northern Ireland* (Chippenham: Palgrave, 2002)

Nielson, K., & Kennedy, G. (eds), *The British Way in Warfare: Power and the International System, 1856–1956* (Farnham: Ashgate, 2006)

Nighswonger, W.A., *Rural Pacification in Vietnam* (New York: Praeger, 1966)

Nye, J.S., *Understanding International Conflicts: An Introduction to Theory and History* (New York: Pearson / Longman, 2007)

O'Brien, T., *The Things they Carried* (London: Flamingo, 1991)

Osborne, M., *Strategic Hamlets in South Vietnam: A Survey and Comparison* (New York: Cornell University, 1965)

Phillips, S., *The Cold War* (Oxford: Heinemann, 2001)

Pillar, P.R., *Terrorism and U.S. Foreign Policy* (Washington: Brookings Institution, 2001)

Pike, D., *PAVN: People's Army of Vietnam* (Novato, California: Presidio Press, 1986)

Pike, D., *Viet Cong – The Organization and Techniques of the National Liberation Front of South Vietnam* (Cambridge, Massachusetts: MIT Press, 1966)

Porch, D., *Counterinsurgency: Exposing the Myths of the New Way of War* (Cambridge: Cambridge University Press, 2013)

Prados, J., & Pratt-Porter, M. (eds), *Inside the Pentagon Papers* (Lawrence, Kansas: University of Kansas Press, 2004)

Preston, A., *The War Council. McGeorge Bundy, The NSC and Vietnam* (Cambridge: Harvard University Press, 2006)

Rabasa, A., Warner, L.A., Chalk, P., Khilko, I., & Shukla, P., *Money in the Bank: Lessons Learned from Past Counterinsurgency (COIN) Operations* (Santa Monica: RAND, 2007)

Record, J., *The Wrong War: Why we lost in Vietnam* (Annapolis, Maryland: Naval Institute Press, 1998)

Rich, P.B., & Duyvesteyn, I. (eds), *The Routledge Handbook of Insurgency and Counterinsurgency* (London: Routledge, 2012)

Rid, T., & Keaney, T. (eds), *Understanding Counterinsurgency: Doctrine, Operations and Challenges* (Oxford: Routledge, 2010)

Rose, G.D., *Operational Analysis in Support of Recent Military Operations* (Farnborough: DSTL, 2004)

Rosenau, W., *Subversion and Insurgency* (Santa Monica: RAND, 2007)

Rosenau, W., & Long, A., *The Phoenix Program and Counterinsurgency* (Santa Monica: RAND, 2009)

Ruane, K. (ed.), *The Vietnam Wars* (Manchester: Manchester University Press, 2000)

Ruane, K., *War and Revolution in Vietnam, 1930–75* (London: UCL Press, 1998)

Sams, K., *Command and Control 1965* (Christiansburg: Dalley Book Services, 1966)

Samson, J. (ed.), *The British Empire – Oxford Readers* (Oxford: Oxford University Press, 2001)

Sanders, V., *The USA and Vietnam 1945–75* (Abingdon: Hodder Murray, 2007)

Sarkasian, S., *Unconventional Conflicts in a New Security Era: Lessons from Malaya and Vietnam* (Westport: Greenwood Press, 1993)

Sauvain, P., *Vietnam* (Cheltenham: Stanley Thornes, 1997)

Scanlon. P., *The Tree Wants to be still but the Wind won't let it* (Bloomington, IN: the 1st Books Library, 2000)

Schlesinger, A.M., *A Thousand Days: John F. Kennedy in the White House* (Greenwich: Fawcett Crest, 1965)

Schleisinger, A.M., *Robert Kennedy and his Times* (New York: Mariner Books, 1979)

Schulinzger, R.D., *A Time for War: The United States and Vietnam, 1941–1975* (New York: Oxford University Press, USA 1997)

Schwab, O., *Defending the Free World. John F. Kennedy, Lyndon Johnson, and the Vietnam War; 1961–1965* (West Port, Connecticut: Praeger, 1998)

Selverstone, M.J. (ed.), *A Companion to John F. Kennedy* (Chichester: Wiley Blackwell, 2014)

Sevy, G. (ed.), *The American Experience in Vietnam* (Norman: University of Oklahoma Press, 1989)

Shay, J., *Achilles in Vietnam. Combat Trauma and the Undoing of Character* (New York: Touchstone, 1994)

Shaw, G.D.T., *The Lost Mandate of Heaven: The American Betrayal of Ngo Dinh Diem, President of Vietnam* (San Francisco: Ignatius Press, 2013)

Short, A., *The Origins of the Vietnam War* (London: Longman, 1989)

Smith, E.D., *Counter-insurgency Operations 1: Malaya and Borneo* (London: Ian Allen Ltd, 1985)

Smith, M.L.R., & Martin Jones, D., *The Political Impossibility of Modern Counterinsurgency. Strategic Problems, Puzzles and Paradoxes* (New York: Columbia University Press, 2015)

Smith, R., *An International History of the Vietnam War: The Kennedy Strategy* (New York: Palgrave Macmillan, 1985)

Smith, R., *The Utility of Force: The Art of War in the Modern World* (New York: Penguin, 2006)

Solomon, Z., *Combat Stress Reaction: The Enduring Toll of War* (New York: Plenum Press, 1993)

Sorensen, T.C., *Kennedy* (London: Pan Books, 1965)

Spector, R.H., *After Tet: The Bloodiest Year in Vietnam* (New York: The Free Press, 1993)

Stewart, G., *Vietnam's Lost Revolution: Ngo Dinh Diem's Failure to Build An Independent Nation, 1955–1963* (Cambridge: Cambridge University Press, 2017)

Stewart, N., *The Changing Nature of Warfare 1700–1945* (Oxford: Hodder Murray, 2001)
Strachan, H., *The Direction of War: Contemporary Strategies in Historical Perspective* (Cambridge: Cambridge University Press, 2013)
Taber, R., *The War of the Flea: Guerrilla Warfare – Theory and Practice* (St. Albans: Paladin Press, 1970)
Tanham, G.K., *Communist Revolutionary Warfare: From the Vietminh to the Viet Cong,* 2nd edition (Westport: Praeger Security International, 2006)
Tatham, S., & Mackay, A., *Behavioural Conflict: Why Understanding People and Their Motives Will Prove Decisive in Future Conflict* (London: Military Studies Press, 2011)
Thayer, C.W., *Guerrilla* (London: Michael Joseph Ltd, 1964)
Thompson, L., *The Counter – Insurgency Handbook* (London: Greenhill Books, 2002)
Thornton, R., *Asymmetric Warfare* (Cambridge: Polity Press, 2007)
Trinquier, R., *Modern Warfare: A French View of Counterinsurgency,* 3rd edition (Westport: Praeger Security International, 2006)
Trullinger, J.W., *Village at War: An Account of the Conflict in Vietnam* (Stanford: Stanford University Press, 1994)
Tse–Tung, M., *On Guerrilla Warfare* (Chicago: University of Illinois Press, 1961)
Tzu, S., *The Art of War* (Ware: Wordsworth Edition, 1998)
Valentine, D., *The Phoenix Program* (Lincoln: William Morrow and Co, 1990)
Vien, N.K. (ed.), *Vietnam Studies N° 20 – 'American Failure'* (Xunhasaba, Hanoi: 1968)
Warren, J.A., *Giap.The General who defeated America in Vietnam* (New York: Palgrave Macmillan, 2013)
Wiest, A., & Doidge, M.J. (eds), *Triumph Revisited: Historians Battle for the Vietnam War* (New York: Routledge, 2010)
Williams, W.A. (ed.), *America in Vietnam – A Documentary History* (New York: W.W. Norton and Company, 1975)
Wolf, C., *Insurgency and Counterinsurgency: New Myths and Old Realities* (Santa Monica: RAND Corporation, 1965)
Wolf, E.R., *Peasant Wars of the Twentieth Century* (London: Faber and Faber, 1971)
Woodruff, M.W., *Unheralded Victory. Who Won the Vietnam War?* (London: Harper Collins, 1999)

JOURNALS AND ARTICLES

Adloff, V.T., 'Britain's Policy in Malaya', *Far Eastern Survey*, 16 (1947), p.112
Adloff, V.T., 'Opposition in Malaya', *Far Eastern Survey*, 16 (1947), pp.130–131
Ahmed, S., 'The United States and Terrorism in Southwest Asia: September 11 and Beyond', *International Security,* 26 (2001/02), pp.79–93
Alexander, J., & McGregor, J., 'War Stories: Guerrilla Narratives of Zimbabwe's Liberation War', *History Workshop Journal*, 57 (2004), pp.79–100
Ambert, A.M., Adler, P.A., Adler, P., & Detzner, D.F., 'Understanding and Evaluating Qualitative Research', *Journal of Marriage and Family*, 57 (1995), pp.879–893
Andrade, D., 'Westmoreland was right: learning the wrong lessons from the Vietnam War', *Small Wars & Insurgencies*, 19 (2008), pp.145–181
Anderson, D., et al, 'Interchange: Legacies of the Vietnam War', *The Journal of American History*, 93 (2006), pp.452–490
Anderson, D.M., 'British Abuse and Torture in Kenya's Counter-insurgency, 1952–1960', *Small Wars & Insurgencies*, 23 (2012), pp.700–719
Andrade, D. & Willbanks, J.H., 'CORDS / Phoenix: Counterinsurgency Lessons from Vietnam for the Future', *Military Review*, March–April (2006), pp.9 – 23
Anonymous, 'An Interview with Bernard Fall', *Marine Corps Gazette*, 51 (1964), pp.10–11
Arquilla, J., 'The end of war as we knew it? Insurgency, counterinsurgency and lessons from the forgotten history of early terror networks', *Third World Quarterly*, 28 (2007), pp.369–386
Arreguin-Toft, I., 'How the Weak Win Wars – A Theory of Asymmetric Conflict', *International Security*, 26 (2001), pp.93–12
Aylwin–Foster, N., 'Changing the Army for Counterinsurgency Operations', *Military Review*, November–December (2005), pp.2–15
Barnes, T., 'War by Numbers: Another Quantitative Revolution', *Geopolitics*, 00 (2015), pp.1–6
Bass, T.A., 'Counterinsurgency and Torture', *American Quarterly*, 60 (2008), pp.233–240
Beckett, I.F., 'British Counter-insurgency: a Historiographical Reflection', *Small Wars & Insurgencies*, 23 (2012), pp.781–798
Bell, M., 'In Afghanistan, Memories of Vietnam', *New Statesman*, 20/08 (2007)
Bender, G.J., 'The Limits of Counterinsurgency: An African Case', *Comparative Politics*, 4 (1972), pp.331–360
Bennett, H., 'A Very Salutary Effect': The Counter–Terror Strategy in the Early Malayan Emergency, June 1948 to December 1949', *Journal of Strategic Studies*, 32 (2009), pp.415–444
Bennett. H., 'Minimum Force in British Counterinsurgency', *Small Wars & Insurgencies*, 21 (2010), pp.459–475
Benvenuti, A., 'The British Military Withdrawal from Southeast Asia and its Impact on Australia's Cold War Strategic Interests', *Cold War History*, 5 (2005), pp.189–210
Berger, M.T., & Borer, D.A., 'The Long War: insurgency, counterinsurgency and collapsing states', *Third World Quarterly*, 28 (2007), pp.197–215
Berger, M.T., Burgess, K., Mauldin, J., & Sullivan, M.P., '"Déjà Vu All Over Again": Counterinsurgency and the 'American Way of War', *Intelligence and National Security*, 22 (2007), pp.910–931
Betts, R.K., 'Is Strategy an Illusion?', *International Security*, 25 (2000), pp.5–50
Blanken, L., & Overbaugh, J., 'Looking for Intel? … or Looking for Answers? Reforming Military Intelligence for a Counterinsurgency Environment', *Intelligence and National Security*, 27 (2012), pp.559–575
Blanken, L.J., & Lepore, J.J., 'Performance measurement in military operations: information versus incentives', *Defence and Peace Economics*, 26 (2015), pp.516–535
Bortree, J.R., 'IO During the Malayan Emergency', *IO Sphere*, Spring (2007), pp.24–32
Breede, Captain C.H., 'Intelligence Lessons and The Emerging Canadian Counter-insurgency Doctrine', *Canadian Army Journal*, 9 (2006), pp.24–40
Brown, A., 'Perestroika and the End of the Cold War', *Cold War History*, 7 (2007), pp.1–17
Bryant, G.J., 'Asymmetric Warfare: The British Experience in Eighteenth-Century India', *The Journal of Military History*, 68 (2004), pp.431–469
Bulloch, G., 'Military Doctrine and Counterinsurgency: A British Perspective', *Parameters*, Summer (1996), pp.4–16
Burleigh, M., 'Britain's Brutal Battles for Hearts and Minds', *BBC History,* 14 (2013) no page number
Busch, P., 'Killing the 'Vietcong: The British Advisory Mission and the Strategic Hamlet Programme', *Journal of Strategic Studies*, 25 (2002), pp.135–162
Busch, P., 'Supporting the War: Britain's Decision to send the Thompson Mission to Vietnam, 1960–61', *Cold War History*, 2 (2001), pp.69–94
Byman, D., 'Death Solves All Problems': The Authoritarian Model of Counterinsurgency', *Journal of Strategic Studies*, No Volume (2015), pp.1–36
Carland, J.M., 'Winning the Vietnam War: Westmoreland's Approach in Two Documents', *The Journal of Military History*, 68 (2004), pp.553–574
Casebeer, W.D., 'The Importance of Treating Culture as a System: Lessons on Counter-insurgency Strategy from the British Iraqi Mandate', *Strategic Insights*, IV (2005)
Cassidy, R.M., 'Back to the Street without Joy: Counterinsurgency Lessons from Vietnam and Other Small Wars', *Parameters*, Summer (2004), pp.73–83
Cassidy, R.M., 'The British Army and Counterinsurgency: The Salience of Military Culture', *Military Review*, May–June (2005), pp.53–59
Cassidy, R.M., 'The Long Small War: Indigenous Forces for Counterinsurgency', *Parameters*, Summer (2006), pp.47–62
Cassidy, R.M., 'Winning the War of the Flea – Lessons from Guerilla Warfare', *Military Review*, September–October (2004), pp.41–46
Catton, P.E., 'Counter-insurgency and Nation Building: The Strategic Hamlet Programme in South Vietnam, 1961–1963', *The International History Review*, 21 (1999), pp.918–940
Catton, P.E., 'Refighting Vietnam in the History Books: The Historiography of the War', *OAH Magazine of History,* 18 (2004), pp.7–11
Caverley, J.D., 'The Myth of Military Myopia: Democracy, Small Wars, and Vietnam', *International Security*, 34 (2009/2010), pp.119–157
Celeski, J.D., 'Strategic Aspects of Counterinsurgency', *Military Review*, March–April (2005), pp.35–41
Chen, K.C., 'Hanoi's Three Decisions and the Escalation of the Vietnam War', *Political Science Quarterly*, 90 (1975), pp.239–259
Chin, W., 'Examining the Application of British Counterinsurgency Doctrine by the American Army in Iraq', *Small Wars & Insurgencies*, 18 (2007), pp.1–26
Clemis, M.G., 'Crafting non–kinetic warfare: the academic–military nexus in US counterinsurgency doctrine', *Small Wars & Insurgencies*, 20 (2009), pp.160–184
Cohen, E., Crane, C., Horvath, J., & Nagl, J., 'Principles, Imperatives, and Paradoxes of Counterinsurgency', *Military Review*, March–April (2006), pp.49–53
Cohen, M.A., 'The Myth of a Kinder, Gentler War', *World Policy Journal*, 27 (2010), pp.75–86
Cohen, R.S., 'Just How Important Are 'Hearts and Minds' Anyway? Counterinsurgency Goes to the Polls', *Journal of Strategic Studies*, 37 (2014), pp.609–636
Comber, L., 'The Malayan Special Branch on the Malayan–Thai frontier during the Malayan Emergency (1948–60)', *Intelligence & National Security*, 21 (2006), pp.77–99
Connolly, C., 'The American Factor: Sino–American Rapprochement and Chinese Attitudes to the Vietnam War, 1968–72', *Cold War History*, 5 (2005), pp.501–527
Cornish, P., 'The United States and Counterinsurgency: 'Political First, Political Last, Political Always', *International Affairs*, 85 (2009), pp.61–79
Cull, N.J., 'The Man who Invented Truth: The Tenure of Edward R. Murrow as Director of the United States Information Agency during the Kennedy years', *Cold War History*, 4 (2003), pp.23–48

Darley, W.M. (ed.), 'Counterinsurgency Reader: Special Edition', *Military Review*, October (2006), pp.2–195

Deery, P., 'The Terminology of Terrorism: Malaya, 1948–52', *Journal of Southeast Asian Studies*, 34 (2003), pp.231–247

Desai, R., & Eckstein, H., 'Insurgency: The Transformation of Peasant Rebellion', *World Politics*, 42 (1990), pp.441–465

de Sola–Pool, I., 'Political Alternatives to the Viet Cong', *Asian Survey*, 7 (1967), pp.555–566

Dixon, P., (2009): 'Hearts and Minds'? British Counter-insurgency from Malaya to Iraq', *Journal of Strategic Studies*, 32 (2009), pp.353–381

Donnell, J.C., 'Pacification Reassessed', *Asian Survey*, 7 (1967), pp.567–576

Dorussen, H., 'Mixing Carrots with Sticks: Evaluating the Effectiveness of Positive Incentives', *Journal of Peace Research*, 38 (2001), pp.251–262

Downes, A.B., 'Draining the Sea by Filling the Graves: Investigating the Effectiveness of Indiscriminate Violence as a Counterinsurgency Strategy', *Civil Wars*, 9 (2007), pp.420–444

Doyle, M.W., & Sambanis, N., 'International Peacebuilding: A Theoretical and Quantitative Analysis', *The American Political Science Review*, 94 (2000), pp.779–801

Duncanson, D., '"Symbiotic Insurgency" in Vietnam Ten Years after', *International Affairs (Royal Institute of International Affairs 1944–)*, 54 (1978), pp.589–601

Egnell, R., 'Lessons from Helmand, Afghanistan: what now for British counterinsurgency?', *International Affairs*, 87 (2011), pp.297–315

Egnell, R., 'Winning "Hearts and Minds"? A Critical Analysis of Counter-insurgency Operations in Afghanistan', *Civil Wars*, 12 (2010), pp.282–303

Fahey, J.J., 'A Peace Pilgrimage: From Total War to World Community', *U.S. Catholic Historian*, 27 (2009), pp.45–60

Fall, B.B., 'The Theory and Practice of Insurgency and Counterinsurgency', *Military Review*, September–October (2015), pp.40–48

Fall, B.B., 'The Theory and Practice of Insurgency and Counterinsurgency', *Naval War College Review*, Winter (1998), pp.1–11

Fearon, J.D., & Laitin, D.D., 'Ethnicity, Insurgency, and Civil War', *The American Political Science Review*, 97 (2003), pp.75–90

Findley, M.G., & Young, J.K., 'Fighting Fire with Fire? How (Not) to Neutralize an Insurgency', *Civil Wars*, 9 (2007), pp.378–401

Fitzgerald, D., 'Sir Robert Thompson, Strategic Patience and Nixon's War in Vietnam', *Journal of Strategic Studies*, 37 (2014), pp.998–1026

Fitzgerald, D., 'Vietnam, Iraq and the Rebirth of Counter-insurgency', *Irish Studies in International Affairs*, 21 (2010), pp.149–159

Ford, C.M., 'Speak No Evil: Targeting a Population's Neutrality to Defeat an Insurgency', *Parameters*, Summer (2005), pp.51–66

Friedman, J.A., 'Manpower and Counterinsurgency: Empirical Foundations for Theory and Doctrine', *Security Studies*, 20 (2011), pp.556–591

Gates, J.M., 'Two American Wars in Asia: Successful Colonial Warfare in the Philippines and Cold War Failure in Vietnam', *War in History*, 8 (2001), pp.47–71

Gentile, G.P., 'The Selective Use of History in the Development of American Counterinsurgency Doctrine', *Army History*, Summer (2009), pp.21–35

Ginty, R.M., 'Social network analysis and counterinsurgency: a counterproductive strategy?', *Critical Studies on Terrorism*, 3 (2010), pp.209–226

Gonzalez, R.J., 'Human Terrain', *Anthropology Today*, 24 (2008), pp.21–26

Gortzak, Y., 'The prospects of combined action: Lessons from Vietnam', *Small Wars & Insurgencies*, 25 (2014), pp.137–160

Gortzak, Y., 'Using Indigenous Forces in Counterinsurgency Operations: The French in Algeria, 1954–1962', *Journal of Strategic Studies*, 32 (2009), pp.307–333

Greenhill, K.M., & Staniland, P., 'Ten Ways to Lose at Counterinsurgency', *Civil Wars*, 9 (2007), pp.402–419

Griffin, A.L., Hall, B., & Ross, A.T., 'The Australian counterinsurgency campaign in the Vietnam war: the ambush battle', *Journal of Maps*, 10 (2014), pp.61–64

Grinter, L.E., 'How They Lost: Doctrines, Strategies and Outcomes of the Vietnam War', *Asian Survey*, 15 (1975), pp.1114–1132

Grossheim, M., 'Revisionism in the Democratic Republic of Vietnam: New Evidence from the East German Archives', *Cold War History*, 5 (2005), pp.451–477

Grubbs, L.K., 'Is There a Deep Fight in a Counterinsurgency?', *Military Review*, July–August (2005), pp.28–31

Guan, A.C., 'Khe Sanh – from the Perspective of the North Vietnamese Communists', *War in History*, 8 (2001) pp.87–98

Guan, A.C., 'The Vietnam War, 1962–64: The Vietnamese Communist Perspective', *Journal of Contemporary History*, 35 (2000), pp.601–618

Gventer, C.W., 'Counterinsurgency and its Critics', *Journal of Strategic Studies*, 37 (2014), pp.637–663

Hack, K., 'Everyone Lived in Fear: Malaya and the British Way of Counterinsurgency', *Small Wars & Insurgencies*, 23 (2012) pp.671–699

Hack, K., 'The Malayan Emergency as Counter-insurgency Paradigm', *Journal of Strategic Studies*, 32 (2009), pp.383–414

Hall, B., & Ross, A., 'Kinetics in counterinsurgency: some influences on soldier combat performance in the 1st Australian Task Force in the Vietnam War', *Small Wars & Insurgencies*, 21 (2010), pp.498–518

Hammes, T.X., 'The Future of Counterinsurgency', *Foreign Policy Research Institute*, Fall (2012), pp.565–587

Hannah, M., 'Torture and the Ticking Bomb: The War on Terrorism as a Geographical Imagination of Power/Knowledge', *Annals of the Association of American Geographers*, 96 (2006), pp.622–640

Hasik, J., 'Learning in counterinsurgency: what do we really know?', *Defense & Security Analysis*, 29 (2013), pp.203–217

Hassan, M.H.B., 'Key Considerations in Counter–ideological Work against Terrorist Ideology', *Studies in Conflicts and Terrorism*, 29 (2006), pp.531–558

Hendry, J.B., 'Economic Development under Conditions of Guerrilla Warfare: The Case of Viet Nam', *Asian Survey*, 2 (1962), pp.1–12

Heuser, B., 'The Cultural Revolution in Counter-insurgency', *Journal of Strategic Studies*, 30 (2007), pp.153–171

Hochmüller, M., & Müller, M.M., 'Locating Guatemala in Global Counterinsurgency', *Globalizations*, (2015), pp.1–17

Hoffman, F.G., 'Neo-Classical Counterinsurgency?', *Parameters*, Summer (2007), pp.71–87

Hoffmann, S, Huntington, S.P., May, E.R., Neustadt, R.N., & Schelling, TC., 'Vietnam Reappraised', *International Security*, 6 (1981), pp.3–26

Homan, R., 'The Ethics of Covert Methods', *The British Journal of Sociology*, 31 (1980), pp.46–59

Hooks, G., & Mosher, C., 'Outrages against Personal Dignity: Rationalizing Abuse and Torture in the War on Terror', *Social Forces*, 83 (2005), pp.1627–1645

Hopkins, B.D., 'The Problem with "Hearts and Minds" in Afghanistan', *Middle East Report*, 255 (2010), pp.24–29

Hughes, J., 'Frank Kitson in Northern Ireland and the British Way of Counterinsurgency', *History Ireland*, 22 (2014), pp.44–48

Hughes, M., 'Introduction: British Ways of Counter-insurgency', *Small Wars & Insurgencies*, 23 (2012), pp.580–590

Jackson, B.A., 'Counterinsurgency Intelligence in a Long War: The British Experience in Northern Ireland', *Military Review*, January–February (2007), pp.74–85

Jackson, A., 'British Counterinsurgency in History: A Useful Precedent?', *British Army Review*, 139 (2006) p.12

Jackson, M., General, 'British Counter-insurgency from Malaya to Iraq', *Journal of Strategic Studies*, 32 (2007), pp.347–351

Jardine, E., 'Population centric counterinsurgency and the movement of peoples', *Small Wars & Insurgencies*, 23 (2012), pp.264–294

Johnson, L.K., & Caruson, K., 'The Seven Sins of American Foreign Policy', *Political Science and Politics*, 36 (2003), pp.5–10

Joiner, C.A., 'The Ubiquity of the Administrative Role in Counterinsurgency', *Asian Survey*, August (1967), pp.1–23

Jones, D.M., Smith, M.L.R., & Stone, J., 'Counter–COIN: Counterinsurgency and the Pre-emption of Strategy', *Studies in Conflict & Terrorism*, 35 (2012), pp.597–617

Jones, D.M., & Smith, M.L.R., 'Myth and the Small War Tradition: Reassessing the discourse of British counter-insurgency', *Small Wars & Insurgencies*, 24 (2013), pp.436–464

Jones, D.M., & Smith, M.L.R., 'Whose Hearts and Whose Minds? The Curious Case of Global Counter-insurgency', *Journal of Strategic Studies*, 33 (2010), pp.81–121

Jorgensen, J.G., 'On Ethics and Anthropology', *Current Anthropology*, 12 (1971), pp.321–334

Jumper, R., 'The Communist Challenge to South Viet Nam', *Far Eastern Survey*, 25 (1956), pp.161–168

Jundanian, B.F., 'Resettlement Programs: Counterinsurgency in Mozambique',*Comparative Politics*, 6 (1974), pp.519–540

Kane, P., 'Renewal and Transformation: The Historian as How-to Guide', *U.S. Catholic Historian*, 25 (2007), pp.69–78

Kanet, R.E., 'The Superpower Quest for Empire: The Cold War and Soviet Support for "Wars of National Liberation"', *Cold War History*, 6 (2006), pp.331–352

Kalyvas, S.N., & Kocher, M.A., 'The Dynamics of Violence in Vietnam: An Analysis of the Hamlet Evaluation System (HES)', *Journal of Peace Research*, 46 (2009), pp.335–355

Katagiri, N., 'Winning hearts and minds to lose control: exploring various consequences of popular support in counterinsurgency missions', *Small Wars & Insurgencies*, 22 (2011), pp.170–195

Kebede, M., 'The Rehabilitation of Violence and the Violence of Rehabilitation: Fanon and Colonialism', *Journal of Black Studies*, 31 (2001), pp.539–562

Kennedy, R., 'Malaya: Colony without Plan', *Far Eastern Survey*, 14 (1945), pp.225–26

Khalili, L., 'The New (and Old) Classics of Counterinsurgency', *Middle East Report*, 255 (2010), pp.14–23

Khalili, L., 'Thinking about Violence', *International Journal of Middle East Studies*, 45 (2013), pp.791–794
Kirk-Greene, A., 'Decolonization: The Ultimate Diaspora', *Journal of Contemporary History*, 36 (2001), pp.133–151
Kocher, M.A., Pepinsky, T.B., & Kalyvas, S.N., 'Aerial Bombing and Counterinsurgency in the Vietnam War', *American Journal of Political Science*, 55 (2011), pp.201–218
Kollars, N.A., 'War's Horizon: Soldier-Led Adaptation in Iraq and Vietnam', *Journal of Strategic Studies*, 38 (2015), pp.529–553
Kovats-Bernat, J.C., 'Negotiating Dangerous Fields: Pragmatic Strategies for Fieldwork Amid Violence and Terror', *American Anthropologist*, New Series, 104 (2002), pp.208–222
Kiszely, J., 'Learning About Counterinsurgency', *RUSI Journal*, December (2006), pp.17–21
Kramer, M., 'The Perils of Counterinsurgency: Russia's War in Chechnya', *International Security*, 29 (2004/2005), pp.5–63
Kuzmarov, J., 'From Counter-insurgency to Narco-Insurgency: Vietnam and the International War on Drugs', *The Journal of Policy History*, 20 (2008), pp.344–378
Kydd, A.H., & Straus, S., 'The Road to Hell? Third-Party Intervention to Prevent Atrocities', *American Journal of Political Science*, 57 (2013), pp.673–684
Ladwig, W.C., 'Managing Counterinsurgency: Lessons from Malaya', *Military Review*, May–June (2007), pp.56–66
Latham, M.E., 'Redirecting the revolution? The USA and the failure of nation-building in South Vietnam', *Third World Quarterly*, 27:1 (2006), pp.27–41
Levine, D.H., 'Care and Counterinsurgency', *Journal of Military Ethics*, 9 (2010), pp.139–159
Liên, T.T., (2005) 'The Catholic Question in North Vietnam: From Polish Sources, 1954–56', *Cold War History*, 5 (2005), pp.427–449
Lomperis, T.J., 'Giap's Dream, Westmoreland's Nightmare', *Parameters*, June (1988), pp.18–31
Lyall, J., 'Are Coethnics More Effective Counterinsurgents? Evidence from the Second Chechen War', *American Political Science Review*, 104 (2010), p.1–20
Lyall, J., 'Do Democracies Make Inferior Counterinsurgents? Reassessing Democracy's Impact on War Outcomes and Duration', *International Organization*, 64 (2010), pp.167–192
Lyall, J., & Wilson, I., 'Rage against the Machines: Explaining Outcomes in Counterinsurgency Wars', *International Organization*, 63 (2009), pp.67–106
Lynn, J.A., 'Patterns of Insurgency and Counterinsurgency', *Military Review*, July–August (2005), pp.22–27
Luttwak, E.N., 'Dead End: Counterinsurgency Warfare as Military Malpractice', *Harper's Magazine*, February (2007), pp.33–42
Long, A., 'The Quiet Americans: CIA, NSA, and Counterinsurgency', *Journal of Cold War Studies*, 13 (2011), pp.149–184
MacDonald, P.K., '"Retribution Must Succeed Rebellion": The Colonial Origins of Counterinsurgency Failure', *International Organization*, 67 (2013), pp.253–286
Magno, J.P.Jr., & Gregor, A.J., 'Insurgency and Counterinsurgency in the Philippines', *Asian Survey*, 26 (1986), pp.501–517
Major, P., & Mitter, R., 'East is East and West is West? Towards a comparative socio-cultural history of the Cold War', *Cold War History*, 4 (2003), pp.1–22
Malkasian, C., 'Toward a Better Understanding of Attrition: The Korean and Vietnam Wars', *The Journal of Military History*, 68 (2004), pp.911–942
Maranto, R., & Tuchman, P.S., 'Knowing the Rational Peasant: The Creation of Rival Incentive Structures in Vietnam', *Journal of Peace Research*, 29 (1992), pp.249–264
Mack, A., 'Counterinsurgency in the Third World: theory and practice', British *Journal of International Studies*, 1 (1975), pp.226–253
Markel, W., 'Draining the Swamp: The British Strategy of Population Control', *Parameters*, Spring (2006), pp.35–48
Marks, T.A., 'Evaluating insurgent/counterinsurgent Performance', *Small Wars & Insurgencies*, 11 (2000), pp.21–45
Marr, D., 'Political Attitudes and Activities of Young Urban Intellectuals in South Viet-Nam', *Asian Survey*, 6 (1966), pp.249–263
Marshall, A. 'Imperial Nostalgia, the Liberal Lie, and the Perils of Postmodern Counterinsurgency', *Small Wars & Insurgencies*, 21 (2010), pp.233–258
Matthews, W.C., 'The Kennedy Administration, Counterinsurgency, and Iraq's First Bathist Regime', *International Journal of Middle East Studies*, 43 (2011), pp.635–653
McAdam, D., 'Tactical Innovation and the Pace of Insurgency', *American Sociological Review*, 48 (1983), pp.735–754
McAllister, J., 'Who Lost Vietnam: Soldiers, Civilians, and U.S Military Strategy', *International Security*, 35 (Winter 2010/11), pp.95–123
McAllister, J., & Schulte, I., 'The Limits of Influence in Vietnam: Britain, the United States and the Diem Regime, 1959–63', *Small Wars & Insurgencies*, 17:1 (2006), pp.22–43
McFadden, E.M., 'Contemporary Counterinsurgency Operations: History as a Guide to Assist in the Development of the Joint Interagency Task Force', *Comparative Strategy*, 24 (2005), pp.361–378
McFate, M., 'Anthropology and Counterinsurgency: The Strange Story of their Curious Relationship', *Military Review*, March–April (2005), pp.24–38
McFate, M., 'The Military Utility of Understanding Adversary Culture', *Joint Force Quarterly*, 38 (2005), pp.42–48
McFate, M., & Jackson, A.V., 'The Object Beyond War: Counterinsurgency and the Four Tools of Political Competition', *Military Review*, January–February (2006), pp.13–26
Merom, G., 'Strong Powers in Small Wars: The Unnoticed Foundations of Success', *Small Wars & Insurgencies*, 9 (1998), pp.38–63
Metz, S., 'A Flame Kept Burning: Counterinsurgency Support after the Cold War', *Parameters*, Autumn (1995), pp.31–41
Metz, S., 'Insurgency and Counterinsurgency in Iraq', *The Washington Quarterly*, 27 (2003–04), pp.25–36
Miakinkov, E., 'The Agency of Force in Asymmetrical Warfare and Counterinsurgency: The Case of Chechnya', *Journal of Strategic Studies*, 34 (2011), pp.647–680
Michaels, J.H., 'Agents for Stability or Chaos: Conceptualizing Intelligence "Relevance" in Counterinsurgency', *Studies in Conflict & Terrorism*, 34 (2011), pp.212–227
Michaels, J.H., 'Managing Global Counterinsurgency: The Special Group (CI) 1962–1966', *Journal of Strategic Studies*, 35 (2012), pp.33–61
Michaels, J.H., & Gawthorpe, A.J., 'Spies, advisors, and grunts: Film portrayals of counterinsurgency in Vietnam', *Small Wars & Insurgencies*, 26 (2015), pp.668–687
Mockaitis, T.R., 'The Minimum Force Debate: Contemporary Sensibilities meet Imperial Practice', *Small Wars & Insurgencies*, 23 (2012), pp.762–780
Moore, R.M., 'Counterinsurgency force ratio: strategic utility or nominal necessity', *Small Wars & Insurgencies*, 24 (2013), pp.857–878
Morales, O.P., The Evolution of Counterinsurgency Warfare: A Historical Overview', *Revista de Relaciones Internacionales*, 6 (2011), pp.195–220
Mueller, J., 'Six Rather Unusual Propositions about Terrorism', *Terrorism and Political Violence*, 17 (2005), pp.487–505
Mumford, A., 'Minimum Force meets Brutality: Detention, Interrogation and Torture in British Counter-insurgency Campaigns', *Journal of Military Ethics*, 11 (2012), pp.10–25
Murshed, S.M., 'Conflict, Civil War and Underdevelopment: An Introduction', *Journal of Peace Research*, 39 (2002), pp.387–393
Nadzhafov, D.G., 'The Beginning of the Cold War between East and West: The aggravation of ideological confrontation', *Cold War History*, 4 (2004), pp.140–174
Nicole, L., 'Torture: The Need for a Dialogue with Its Victims and Its Perpetrators', *Journal of Peace Research*, 24 (1987), pp.315–322
North, J., 'General Hoche and Counterinsurgency', *The Journal of Military History*, 67 (2003), pp.529–540
O'Brien, S.P., 'Anticipating the Good, the Bad, and the Ugly: An Early Warning Approach to Conflict and Instability Analysis', *The Journal of Conflict Resolution*, 46 (2002), pp.791–811
O'Dowd, E.C., 'What Kind of War is This?', *Journal of Strategic Studies*, 37 (2014), pp.1027–1049
Odgaard, L., & Nielsen, T.G., 'China's Counterinsurgency Strategy in Tibet and Xinjiang', *Journal of Contemporary China*, 23 (2014), pp.535–555
Osornprasop, S., 'Amidst the Heat of the Cold War in Asia: Thailand and the American Secret War in Indochina (1960–74)', *Cold War History*, 7 (2007), pp.349–371
Ouellet, E., & Pahlavi, P.V., 'Institutional Analysis and Irregular Warfare: A Case Study of the French Army in Algeria 1954–1960', *Journal of Strategic Studies*, 34 (2011), pp.799–824
Painter, D., 'A Partial History of the Cold War', *Cold War History*, 6 (2006), pp.527–534
Parker, T., 'Fighting an Antaean Enemy: How Democratic States Unintentionally Sustain the Terrorist Movements they Oppose', *Terrorism and Political Violence*, 19 (2007), pp.155–179
Payne, K., 'Some Principles for Influence in Counterinsurgency', *The British Army Review*, 150 (2010/2011), pp.23–30
Peic, G., 'Civilian Defense Forces, State Capacity, and Government Victory in Counterinsurgency Wars', *Studies in Conflict & Terrorism*, 37 (2014), pp.162–184
Pieper, H., 'The German Approach to Counterinsurgency in the Second World War', *The International History Review*, 37 (2015), pp.631–642
Plakoudas, S., 'Strategy in Counterinsurgency: A Distilled Approach', *Studies in Conflict & Terrorism*, 38 (2015), pp.132–145
Porch, D., (2011) 'The Dangerous Myths and Dubious Promise of COIN', *Small Wars & Insurgencies*, 22 (2011), pp.239–257
Pottier, P., (2005) 'A French Experience in Counterinsurgency during the French Indochina War', *Small Wars & Insurgencies*, 16 (2005), pp.125–146
Protheroe, G.J., 'Limiting America's Engagement: Roger Hilsman's Vietnam War, 1961–1963', *Diplomacy & Statecraft*, 19 (2008), pp.263–288
Quackenbush, S.L., & Murdie, A., 'We Always Fight the Last War? Prior Experiences in Counterinsurgency and Conventional Warfare and War Outcomes', *International Interactions*, 41 (2015), pp.183–200

Quester. G.H., The Guerrilla Problem in Retrospect, *Military Affairs*, 39 (1975), pp.192–196
Ramakrishna, K., 'Bribing the Reds to Give Up': Rewards Policy in the Malayan Emergency', *War in History*, 9 (2002), pp.332–353
Ravlo, H., Gleditsch, N.P, & Dorussen, H., 'Colonial War and the Democratic Peace', *The Journal of Conflict Resolution*, 47 (2003), pp.520–548
Regan, J.M., 'The "O'Brien Ethic" as an Interpretative Problem', *Journal of British Studies*, 52 (2013), pp.908–939
Reis, B. C., 'The Myth of British Minimum Force in Counterinsurgency Campaigns during Decolonisation (1945–1970)', *Journal of Strategic Studies*, 34 (2011), pp.245–279
Rid, T., 'The Nineteenth Century Origins of Counterinsurgency Doctrine', *Journal of Strategic Studies*, 33 (2010), pp.727–758
Ridler, J.S., 'A lost work of El Lobo: Lieutenant-Colonel Charles T.R. Bohannan's unpublished study of guerrilla warfare and counterinsurgency in the Philippines, 1899–1955', *Small Wars & Insurgencies*, 26 (2015), pp.292–312
Rogers, B.L., 'Teaching and Social Reform in the 1960s: Lessons from National Teacher Corps Oral Histories', *Oral History Review*, 35 (2008), pp.39–67
Rosen, S.P., 'Vietnam and the American Theory of Limited War', *International Security*, 7 (1982), pp.83–113
Roxborough, I., 'Learning and Diffusing the Lessons of Counterinsurgency: The U.S. Military from Vietnam to Iraq', *Sociological Focus*, 39 (2006), pp.319–346
Ruane, K., 'Refusing to Pay the Price: British Foreign Policy and the Pursuit of Victory in Vietnam, 1952–4', *The English Historical Review*, 110 (1995), pp.70–92
Rubin, B., 'The October War and US Counter-insurgency Strategy', *MERIP Reports*, 22 (1973), pp.22–24
Russell, J.A., 'Counterinsurgency American style: Considering David Petraeus and twenty-first century irregular war', *Small Wars & Insurgencies*, 25 (2014), pp.69–90
Savage Brosman, C., 'Torture and Terrorism', *The French Review*, 59 (1986), pp.723–729
Scigliano, R.G., 'Political Parties in South Vietnam under the Republic', *Pacific Affairs*, 33, (1960), pp.327–346
Scigliano, R., 'Vietnam: A Country at War', *Asian Survey*, 3 (1963), pp.48–54
Scigliano, R., 'Vietnam: Politics and Religion', *Asian Survey*, 4 (1964), pp.666–673
Schaffer, M.B., 'A Model of 21st Century Counterinsurgency Warfare', *The Journal of Defense Modeling and Simulation: Applications, Methodology and Technology*, 4 (2007) p.380
Schaffer, R., 'The 1940 Small Wars Manual and the "Lessons of History"', *Military Affairs*, 36 (1972), pp.46–51
Scheipers, S., 'Counterinsurgency or irregular warfare? Historiography and the study of "small wars"', *Small Wars & Insurgencies*, 25 (2014), pp.879–899
Schroden, J., 'A best practice for assessment in counterinsurgency', *Small Wars & Insurgencies*, 25 (2014), pp.479–486
Schroden, J.J., 'Measures for Security in a Counterinsurgency', *Journal of Strategic Studies*, 32 (2009), pp.715–744
Sepp, K.I., 'Best Practices in Counterinsurgency', *Military Review*, May–June (2005), pp.8–12
Shafer, M.D., 'The Unlearned Lessons of Counterinsurgency', *Political Science Quarterly*, 103 (1988), pp.57–80
Shultz, R., 'Breaking the Will of the Enemy during the Vietnam War: The Operationalization of the Cost-Benefit Model of Counterinsurgency Warfare', *Journal of Peace Research*, 15 (1978), pp.109–129
Silcock, T.H., 'Policy for Malaya 1952', *International Affairs (Royal Institute of International Affairs 1944–)*, 28 (1952), pp.445–451
Simpson, J.G., 'Not by Bombs Alone: Lessons from Malaya', *JFQ*, Summer (1999), pp.91–98
Smith, S.C., (2001) 'General Templer and Counter-insurgency in Malaya: Hearts and Minds, Intelligence, and Propaganda', *Intelligence & National Security*, 16 (2001), pp.60–78
Soderlund, W.C., 'An Analysis of the Guerrilla Insurgency and Coup D'Etat as Techniques of Indirect Aggression', *International Studies Quarterly*, 14 (1970), pp.335–360
Statler, K., 'Triumph Imagined', *Diplomatic History*, January (2008), pp.153–157
Strachan, H., 'British Counter-insurgency from Malaya to Iraq', *The RUSI Journal*, 152 (2007), pp.8–11
Strachan, H., 'The British Way in Warfare Revisited', *The Historical Journal*, 26 (1983), pp.447–461
Strachan, H., 'The Lost Meaning of Strategy', *Survival: Global Politics and Strategy*, 47 (2005), pp.33–54
Strachan, H., 'Training, Morale and Modern War', *Journal of Contemporary History*, 41 (2006), pp.211–227
Strickland, Maj A., 'Reinventing the Counterinsurgency Wheel', *Small Wars Journal*, July (2005), pp.13–17
Stringer, K.D., 'Global counterinsurgency and US Army expansion: the case for recruiting foreign troops', *Small Wars & Insurgencies*, 22 (2011), pp.142–169
Sullivan, P.L., 'War Aims and War Outcomes: Why Powerful States Lose Limited Wars', *The Journal of Conflict Resolution*, 51 (2007), pp.496–524
Suri, J., 'The Cold War, Decolonization, and Global Social Awakenings: Historical Intersections', *Cold War History*, 6 (2006), pp.353–363
Szalontai, B., 'Political and Economic Crisis in North Vietnam, 1955–56', *Cold War History*, 5 (2005), pp.395–426
Thomas, M., 'Silent Partners: SOE's French Indo-China Section, 1943–1945', *Modern Asian Studies*, 34 (2000), pp.943–976
Tilman, R.O., 'The Non-Lessons of the Malayan Emergency', *Asian Survey*, 6 (1966), pp.407–419
Tomes, R., 'Relearning Counterinsurgency Warfare', *Parameters*, Spring (2004), pp.16–28
Tovy, T., 'Peasants and Revolutionary Movements: The Viet Cong as a Case Study', *War in History*, 17 (2010), pp.217–230
Tovy, T., 'The Theoretical Aspect of Targeted Killings: The Phoenix Program as a Case Study', *Journal of Military and Strategic Studies*, 11 (2009), pp.1–24
Ucko, D., 'Countering Insurgents through Distributed Operations: Insights from Malaya 1948–1960', *Journal of Strategic Studies*, 30 (2007), pp.47–72
Varsori, A., 'Britain and US Involvement in the Vietnam War during the Kennedy Administration, 1961–63', *Cold War History*, 3 (2003), pp.83–112
Weaver, E., 'Strategic Hamlets', *Fortnight*, 293 (1991), p.19
White, N.J., 'Capitalism and Counter-insurgency? Business and Government in the Malayan Emergency1948–57', *Modern Asian Studies*, 32 (1998), pp.149–177
Whittingham, D., 'Savage Warfare': C.E. Callwell, the Roots of Counter-insurgency, and the Nineteenth Century Context', *Small Wars & Insurgencies*, 23 (2012), pp.591–607
Wilson, Major, I., 'Strategy Revisited', *Military Review*, January–February (2003), pp.42–49
Witty, D.M., 'A Regular Army in Counterinsurgency Operations: Egypt in North Yemen, 1962– 1967', *The Journal of Military History*, 65 (2001), pp.401–439
Young, J. W., 'Britain and 'LBJ's War', 1964–68', *Cold War History*, 2 (2002), pp.63–92
Young, M.B., 'Two, Three, Many Vietnams', *Cold War History*, 6 (2006), pp.413–424
Zambernardi, L., 'Counterinsurgency's Impossible Trilemma', *The Washington Quarterly*, 33 (2010), pp.21–34
Zasloff, J., 'Rural Resettlement in South Viet Nam: The Agroville Program', *Pacific Affairs*, 35 (1962–1963), pp.327–340

UNPUBLISHED PAPERS, PRESENTATIONS AND THESES

Papers

Conover, G.B., 'The Impact of Operational Void: The Strategic Hamlet Program, 1961–1963', (Paper, School of Advanced Military Studies United States Army Command and General Staff College, Fort Leavenworth, Kansas, 1989)
Cordesman, A.H., 'The Long War: The United States as a Self-Inflicted Wound', (Paper, The Center for Strategic and International Studies, Washington, 2007)
Findley, M.G., & Young, J.K., 'Swatting Flies with Pile Drivers? Modeling Insurgency and Counterinsurgency', (Paper, University of Illinois, 2006)
Mumford, A., 'Rethinking the Malayan Emergency: Counter-insurgency Lessons for Iraq', (Conference Papers, University of Sheffield, 2006)
Young, J.K., 'Iron Fist or Velvet Glove?: Evaluating Competing Approaches to Counterinsurgency', (Meeting Paper, International Studies Association, Chicago, 2007)

Presentations

Cordesman, A.H., 'Rethinking the Challenge of Counterinsurgency Warfare', (Presentation, The Centre for Strategic and International Studies, Washington, 2005)
Farmer, J., 'Counter-insurgency: Principles and Practice in Vietnam', (Lecture, RAND Corporation, Santa Monica, 1964)
O'Donnell, J.B., 'The Strategic Hamlet Program in Kien Hoa Province, South Vietnam: A Case Study in Counter-insurgency', (Conference Presentation, Princeton University Center of International Studies, Princeton, New Jersey, May 11, 1965)
Phillips, R., 'Rufus Phillips on Why Vietnam Matters: An Eyewitness Account of Lessons Not Learned', (Lecture, Arlington Learning in Retirement Institute, Arlington, VA, May 23, 2012)
Senlis, Countering the Insurgency in Afghanistan: Losing Friends and Making Enemies (Conference, London, 2007)
Wells, S.F. & Braestrup, P., 'Some Lessons and Non-Lessons of Vietnam: Ten Years After the Paris Peace Accords', (Conference Report, Woodrow Wilson International Center for Scholars, 1983)

Theses

Chong, O.W., 'War as they knew it: Revolutionary War and Counterinsurgency', (Thesis,
S. Rajaratnam School of International Studies, Nanyang Technological University, Singapore, 2007)

Cushman, J.H., 'External Support of the Viet Cong: An Analysis and Proposal', (Thesis, National War College, Washington D.C., 1965)
Farmer, J., 'Counter-insurgency: Vietnam 1962–1963', (Thesis, RAND Corporation, Santa Monica, 1963)
Higgins, J.M., 'The Misapplication of the Malayan Counterinsurgency Model to the Strategic Hamlet Program', (M.A. Thesis, Faculty of the U.S. Army Command and General Staff College, Fort Leavenworth, Kansas, 2001)
Kilcullen, D.J., 'The Political Consequences of Military Operations in Indonesia 1945 – 99: A fieldwork Analysis of the Power Diffusion effects of Guerrilla Conflict', (PhD, University of New South Wales, 2000)
Leahy, P.F., 'Why Did the Strategic Hamlets Program Fail?', (Thesis, Fort Leavenworth, Kansas, 1990)
Lovering, R. S., 'Sir Robert Thompson's Better War: The British Advisory Mission and the South Vietnamese Strategic Hamlet Program, 1961–1963', (Thesis, The University of Southern Mississippi, 2017)
Pelli, F.D., 'Insurgency, Counterinsurgency and the Marines in Vietnam' (Thesis, USMC, 1990)
Sepp, K.I., 'Resettlement, Regroupment, Reconcentration: Deliberate Government Directed Population Relocation in Support of Counter-insurgency Operations', (M.A. Thesis, U.S. Army Command and General Staff College, Fort Leavenworth, Kansas, 1975)

Miscellaneous Documentation

Kilcullen, D.J., *'Countering Global Insurgency'*, (Australian Government Department of Defence, 2004)
Kilcullen, D.J., *'Three Pillars of Counterinsurgency'*, (Washington D.C.: U.S. Government Counterinsurgency Conference, 2006)

WORLDWIDE WEB SOURCES

Video Primary Sources

Moyar, M., *Triumph Forsaken: The Vietnam War, 1954–1965* (US Army Heritage and Education Centre – Perspectives: December 12, 2007). Available: https://www.youtube.com/watch?v=Am7a–R2EsUs (accessed March 20, 2008)

Online Articles

Anthony Cordesman & Arleigh Burke, 'The Long War: The United States as a Self-inflicted Wound', *The Centre for Strategic and International Studies*, (2007), [Online]. Available: <www.csis.org/burke>(accessed March 20, 2008). Please note that as of 12/12/2018 this article has been removed from the website.
Daivd Kilcullen, 'A6 – Counterinsurgency in Iraq: Theory and Practice 2007', *Small Wars Journal*, (2007), [Online]. Available: <www.smallwarsjournal.com/documents/kilcullencoinbrief 26sept07.ppt>(accessed March 20, 2008), Please note that as of 12/12/2018 this article has been removed from the website.
Mark Moyar, 'Vietnam: Historians at War', *US Army Research – Paper 33*, (2008), [Online]. Available: <http://digitalcommons.unl.edu/cgi/ viewcontent.cgi?article= 1042&context= usarmyresearch> (accessed March 20, 2008)

NOTES

Introduction

1 *Foreign Relations of the United States 1961–63, Volume III: No 41. Letter from the Commander, Military Assistance Command, Vietnam (Harkins) to President Diem Saigon, February 23, 1963.*

2 John F. Kennedy Presidential Library and Museum (hereafter referred to as JFK), Report on Visit to Delta Provinces, 1962–1963, RKG Thompson March 13, 1963, British Advisory Mission, Saigon. Roger Hilsman Papers, Countries, Philippines – Vietnam 8/30/63–8/31/63, Box 003, Folder 14. See also, for example, Thompson, *Defeating Communist Insurgency: Experiences from Malaya and Vietnam* (London: Chatto and Windus, 1966) and Thompson, *Make for the Hills.*.

3 The initial counterinsurgency strategy was based upon the 'Counterinsurgency Plan' of 1961. This was modified and amended several times throughout this period and several versions were proposed from 1961–1963. These will be discussed at relevant points in the book. The initial plan contained measures in the Political, Economic, Military and Psychological fields. The plan can be located at The Vietnam Center and Archive, Texas Tech University (hereafter referred to as TTU), 2130112001, Basic Counterinsurgency Plan for Vietnam, 04 January 1961, Folder 12, Box 01, Douglas Pike Collection: Unit 02 – Military Operations. Additional details of the plan can be found in *Foreign Relations of the United States* (hereafter referred to as FRUS) *1961–63, Volume I: No 1. Paper Prepared by the Country Team Staff Committee, Saigon, January 4, 1961* (Washington DC: US Department of State, 1988).

4 Preston was discussing the interaction between Diem and the American government but the point is transferrable and valid to the Strategic Hamlet Programme. See A. Preston, 'Vietnam' in *A Companion to John F. Kennedy*, ed. M.J. Selverstone, (Chichester: Wiley Blackwell, 2014), p.280.

5 Some of the main items used in this study include interviews with Viet Cong prisoners conducted by the RAND Corporation and are located at the Miami University Library, Ohio, OCLC Number: 1658815, Microfilm – Rand Vietnam Interview Series V: Viet Cong Organizational Activities at Hamlet/Village Level (Santa Monica: RAND Corporation, 1968). Viet Cong responses to the Strategic Hamlet Programme are contained in documents located at TTU, for example, 2120207002, NLF Anti-Strategic Hamlet Programme, 1962, Folder 07, Box 02, Douglas Pike Collection: Unit 01 – Assessment and Strategy. The American counterinsurgency strategy is contained in several archive files at the Kennedy Library and includes items such as The Gilpatric Report located at the John F. Kennedy Presidential Library and Museum, JFKNSF–330–002, National Security Action Memoranda [NSAM]: NSAM 52, re: Report of the Vietnam Task Force, Papers of John F. Kennedy. Presidential Papers, National Security Files, Meetings and Memoranda, Box 330 and Roger Hilsman's A Strategic Concept for South Vietnam located at JFK, RHPP–003–006, Vietnam: "A Strategic Concept for South Vietnam, 2 February 1962", Roger Hilsman Personal Papers. Countries Files, 1961–1964. Series 1, Box 3. Sir Robert Thompson's attempt to influence counterinsurgency strategy through a version of the so-called Delta Plan can be read at JFK, RHPP–003–009, Roger Hilsman Personal Papers, Countries Files, 1961–1964, Series 1, Box 3, Folder 5 and also in *FRUS 1961–63, Volume II: No 51. Draft Paper by the Head of the British Advisory Mission in Vietnam (Thompson),* Saigon (undated) (Washington DC: US Department of State, 1988). In contrast, Diem's official Delta Plan can be accessed in *FRUS 1961–63, Volume II: No 13. Decree by the President of the Republic of Vietnam, Saigon, March 16, 1962* (Washington DC: US Department of State, 1988). See also Thompson's initial plan for Delta pacification in TTU, 2120203029, Letter from Sir Robert Thompson to Ngo Dinh Diem (With Attachment), 13 November 1961, Folder 03, Box 02, Douglas Pike Collection: Unit 01 – Assessment and Strategy, Enclosure No 2, Dispatch 205.

6 W. Davison, *R–1024–ARPA – User's Guide to the Rand Interviews in Vietnam* (Rand, Santa Monica, 1972), Davison, *R–1024–ARPA*, p.9; Davison, *R–1024–ARPA*, p.9.

7 R. Phillips, 'Rufus Phillips on Why Vietnam Matters: An Eyewitness Account of Lessons Not Learned', (Lecture, Arlington Learning in Retirement Institute, Arlington, VA, May 23, 2012), Time 47:40.

8 These works include R.S. McNamara, *In Retrospect: The Tragedy and Lessons of Vietnam* (New York: Random House, 1995); R.S. McNamara, J.G. Blight, & R.K. Brigham, *Argument without End – in Search of Answers to the Vietnam Tragedy* (New York: Public Affairs, 1999); L.H. Addington, *America's War in Vietnam – A Short Narrative History* (Bloomington: Indiana University Press, 2000); D. Halberstam, *The Making of a Quagmire: America and Vietnam during the Kennedy Era,* Revised Edition (Lanham, Maryland: Rowman & Littlefield Publishers, 2008).

9 See for example, P. E. Catton, *Diem's Final Failure: Prelude to America's War in Vietnam* (Lawrence: University of Kansas, 2002), D.W.P. Elliott, *The Vietnamese War: Revolution and Social Change in the Mekong Delta, 1930–1975.* New York: East Gate Books, 2003, E. Miller, *Misalliance: Ngo Dinh Diem, the United States, and the Fall of South Vietnam* (Cambridge: Harvard University Press, 2013) or R. Phillips, *Why Vietnam Matters: An Eyewitness Account of Lessons not Learned* (Annapolis, Naval Institute Press, 2008). Also of interest is M. Osborne, *Strategic Hamlets in South Vietnam: A Survey and Comparison* (New York: Cornell University, 1965) and the CIA's own analysis of this time period in CIA, *Analysis of the Strategic Hamlets' Programme and of the Montagnard situation in South Vietnam, July 11, 1962* (Publication Site Unknown, 1962). Further studies also include work such as P.F. Leahy, 'Why Did the Strategic Hamlet Programme Fail?', (Thesis, Fort Leavenworth, Kansas, 1990); P.E. Catton, 'Counter-insurgency and Nation Building: The Strategic Hamlet Programme in South Vietnam, 1961–1963', *The International History Review*, 21 (1999), pp.918–940; G.B. Conover, 'The Impact of Operational Void: The Strategic Hamlet Program, 1961–1963', (Paper, School of Advanced Military Studies United States Army Command and General Staff College, Fort Leavenworth, Kansas, 1989); J.M. Higgins, 'The Misapplication of the Malayan Counterinsurgency Model to the Strategic Hamlet Program', (M.A. Thesis, Faculty of the US Army Command and General Staff College, Fort Leavenworth, Kansas, 2001); R. Clutterbuck, *The Long, Long War: Counterinsurgency in Malaya and Vietnam* (Westport: Praeger, 1966); W.C. Ladwig III, 'Managing Counterinsurgency: Lessons from Malaya', *Military Review*, May–June (2007), pp.56–66; S. Sarkasian, *Unconventional Conflicts in a New Security Era: Lessons from Malaya and Vietnam* (Westport: Greenwood Press, 1993).

10 D. Hunt, *Vietnam's Southern Revolution: From Peasant Insurrection to Total War* (Amherst: University of Massachusetts Press, 2008).

11 A.C. Guan, 'The Vietnam War, 1962–64: The Vietnamese Communist Perspective', *Journal of Contemporary History*, Vol. 35 (2000), p.601.

12 F. Kitson, *Low Intensity Operations: Subversion, Insurgency, Peacekeeping* (London: Faber and Faber, 1971), p.35.

13 For further details see P.B. Rich, & I. Duyvesteyn (eds), *The Routledge Handbook of Insurgency and Counterinsurgency* (London: Routledge, 2012), p.14.

14 D. Kilcullen, 'Intelligence' in *Understanding Counterinsurgency: Doctrine, Operations and Challenges*, ed. T. Rid and T. Keaney (Oxford: Routledge, 2010), p.144.

15 B.B. Fall, 'The Theory and Practice of Insurgency and Counterinsurgency', *Naval War College Review*, Winter, (1998), p.2.
16 For more on this see French, *The British Way in Counter-insurgency, 1945–1967* (Oxford: Oxford University Press, 2011), p.9.
17 French, *The British Way in Counter-insurgency*, p.9.
18 See for example, TTU, 23970129002, Summary, An Informal Appreciation of The Status of The Strategic Hamlet Programme – Prepared by USOM Rural Affairs, 01 June 1963, Folder 29, Box 01, Rufus Phillips Collection.
19 JFK, RHPP-003-009, Memorandum From the Director of the Bureau of Intelligence and Research (Hilsman) and Michael V. Forrestal of the National Security Council Staff to the President, Washington, January 25, 1963. Vietnam: Hilsman trip, December 1962–January 1963: Basic report and "Eyes Only" annex. Roger Hilsman Personal Papers, Countries Files, 1961–1964, Series 1, Box 3, pp.6–7.
20 JFK, RHPP-003-009, Memorandum From the Director of the Bureau of Intelligence and Research (Hilsman) and Michael V. Forrestal of the National Security Council Staff to the President, Washington, January 25, 1963. Vietnam: Hilsman trip, December 1962–January 1963: Basic report and "Eyes Only" annex. Roger Hilsman Personal Papers, Countries Files, 1961–1964, Series 1, Box 3, p.7.
21 R. Thompson, *Make for the Hills: Memories of Far Eastern Wars* (London: Leo Cooper, 1989), p.143.
22 R.S. McNamara, *In Retrospect: The Tragedy and Lessons of Vietnam* (New York: Random House, 1995), pp.323–324.

Chapter 1

1 Lyndon B. Johnson Presidential Library and Museum (hereafter referred to as LBJ), Transcript, Douglas Pike Oral History, Interview I (by Ted Gittinger), June 02, 1981, Internet Copy, p.11.
2 See, for example, Thompson, *Defeating Communist Insurgency*; Thompson, *Make for the Hills*; Clutterbuck, *The Long, Long War: Counter-insurgency in Malaya and Vietnam*; Higgins, 'The misapplication of the Malayan Counterinsurgency Model to the Strategic Hamlet Programme'; Ladwig III, 'Managing Counterinsurgency: Lessons from Malaya'; Sarkasian, *Unconventional Conflicts in a New Security Era: Lessons from Malaya and Vietnam*.
3 Again, see for example, Thompson, *Defeating Communist Insurgency*; Thompson, *Make for the Hills*; Clutterbuck, *The Long, Long War: Counterinsurgency in Malaya and Vietnam*; Higgins, 'The misapplication of the Malayan Counterinsurgency Model to the Strategic Hamlet Programme'; Ladwig III, 'Managing Counterinsurgency: Lessons from Malaya'; Sarkasian, *Unconventional Conflicts in a New Security Era*.
4 JFK, JFKNSF-203-003, Letter From the President's Military Representative (Taylor) to the President, [Attachment 2] Paper Prepared by the Members of the Taylor Mission Washington, Vietnam: Subjects: Taylor Report, 3 November 1961: Rostow Working Copy. Papers of John F. Kennedy, Presidential Papers, National Security Files, Countries, Vietnam, Box 203, Tab C, p.6; JFK, JFKNSF-203-003, Letter From the President's Military Representative (Taylor) to the President, [Attachment 2], p.6; Thompson wrote a report to President Kennedy in 1963 noting the many successes of the counterinsurgency strategy. See JFK, Report on Visit to Delta Provinces, 1962–1963, RKG Thompson March 13, 1963, British Advisory Mission, Saigon. Roger Hilsman Papers, Countries, Philippines – Vietnam 8/30/63–8/31/63, Box 003, Folder 14.
5 *FRUS 1961–63, Volume I: No 1. Paper Prepared by the Country Team Staff Committee, Saigon, January 4, 1961.*
6 JFK, JFKNSF-203-003, Letter From the President's Military Representative (Taylor) to the President, [Attachment 2] Paper Prepared by the Members of the Taylor Mission Washington, Vietnam: Subjects: Taylor Report, 3 November 1961, Tab C, p.7.
7 SNIE, *50–61 Outlook in Mainland Southeast Asia* (Washington DC: Director of Central Intelligence, No 364, 28 March 1961), p.7; SNIE, *50–61 Outlook in Mainland Southeast Asia*, p.8.
8 SNIE, *50–61 Outlook in Mainland Southeast Asia*, p.7; SNIE, *10–62 Communist Objectives, Capabilities, and Intentions in Southeast Asia* (Washington DC: Director of Central Intelligence, No 352, 21 February 1962), p.9.
9 SNIE, *50–61 Outlook in Mainland Southeast Asia*, p.10.
10 SNIE, *50–61 Outlook in Mainland Southeast Asia*, p.10.
11 SNIE, *14.3 / 53–61 Prospects for North and South Vietnam* (Washington DC: Director of Central Intelligence, No 370, 15 August 1961), p.12.
12 JFK, JFKPOF-128-010, Address by George W. Ball April 30 1962 Veterans Memorial Building Civic Center, Detroit, Michigan, Papers of John F Kennedy. Presidential Papers, President's Office Files, Country Files Vietnam, General, Box 128, p.3; SNIE, *14.3 / 53–61 Prospects for North and South Vietnam*, p.13.
13 Phase 1: Build political strength. Limit military action. Phase 2: Gain strength and consolidate. 'Govern' small areas. Phase 3: Commit regular forces. See T.X. Hammes, *The Sling and the Stone: On War in the 21st Century* (St.Paul: Zenith Press, 2006), p.52; Ho Chi Minh declared his plan in 1951 – 'In the first stage… all we did was to preserve and increase our main forces. In the second stage, we have actively contended with the enemy and prepared for the general counter-offensive. The third stage is the general offensive' – see Hammes, *The Sling and the Stone*, p.59.
14 JFK, JFKNSF-203-003, Letter From the President's Military Representative (Taylor) to the President, [Attachment 2] Paper Prepared by the Members of the Taylor Mission Washington, Vietnam: Subjects: Taylor Report, 3 November 1961, Tab C, p.1; JFK, JFKNSF-203-003, Letter From the President's Military Representative (Taylor) to the President, [Attachment 2] Paper Prepared by the Members of the Taylor Mission Washington, Vietnam: Subjects: Taylor Report, 3 November 1961, Tab C, p.1.
15 JFK, JFKNSF-203-003, Letter From the President's Military Representative (Taylor) to the President, [Attachment 2] Paper Prepared by the Members of the Taylor Mission Washington, Vietnam: Subjects: Taylor Report, 3 November 1961, Tab C, p.1.
16 JFK, RHPP-003-006, A Strategic Concept for South Vietnam, p.1; SNIE, *10–62 Communist Objectives, Capabilities, and Intentions in Southeast Asia*, p.2
17 SNIE, *14.3 / 53–61 Prospects for North and South Vietnam*, p.10;
18 JFK, JFKNSF-203-003, Letter From the President's Military Representative (Taylor) to the President, [Attachment 2] Paper Prepared by the Members of the Taylor Mission Washington, Vietnam: Subjects: Taylor Report, 3 November 1961, Tab C, p.2.
19 SNIE, *10–62 Communist Objectives, Capabilities, and Intentions in Southeast Asia*, p.2.
20 SNIE, *14.3 / 53–61 Prospects for North and South Vietnam*, p.10; SNIE, *14.3 / 53–61 Prospects for North and South Vietnam*, p.10.
21 *FRUS 1961–63, Volume II: No 328. Report by the Deputy Director of the Vietnam Working Group (Heavner) Washington, December 11, 1962.*
22 JFK, RHPP-003-006, A Strategic Concept for South Vietnam, p.3; *FRUS 1961–63, Volume II: No 328. Report by the Deputy Director of the Vietnam Working Group (Heavner) Washington, December 11, 1962.*
23 JFK, JFKNSF-203-003, Letter From the President's Military Representative (Taylor) to the President, [Attachment 2] Paper Prepared by the Members of the Taylor Mission Washington, Vietnam: Subjects: Taylor Report, 3 November 1961, Tab C, p.7; JFK, JFKNSF-203-003, Letter From the President's Military Representative (Taylor) to the President, [Attachment 2], p.7.
24 *FRUS 1961–63, Volume I: 223. Note From the Deputy Assistant Secretary of Defense for International Security Affairs (Bundy) to the Secretary of Defense (McNamara) Washington, November 7, 1961. [Attachment 1] Draft Paper Prepared by the Deputy Assistant Secretary of Defense for International Security Affairs (Bundy); FRUS 1961–63, Volume I: 223. Note From the Deputy Assistant Secretary of Defense for International Security Affairs (Bundy) to the Secretary of Defense (McNamara) Washington, November 7, 1961. [Attachment 1] Draft Paper Prepared by the Deputy Assistant Secretary of Defense for International Security Affairs (Bundy).*
25 *FRUS 1961–63, Volume I: 223. Note From the Deputy Assistant Secretary of Defense for International Security Affairs (Bundy) to the Secretary of Defense (McNamara) Washington, November 7, 1961. [Attachment 1] Draft Paper Prepared by the Deputy Assistant Secretary of Defense for International Security Affairs (Bundy).*
26 JFK, JFKNSF-193-004, Memorandum From the President's Deputy Special Assistant for National Security Affairs (Rostow) to the President's Special Assistant for National Security Affairs (Bundy), Washington, January 30, 1961, Papers of John F Kennedy. Presidential Papers, National Security Files, Country Files, Vietnam, General, 1961: January–March, Box 193, p.3.
27 JFK, JFKNSF-193-004, Memorandum From the President's Deputy Special Assistant for National Security Affairs (Rostow) to the President's Special Assistant for National Security Affairs (Bundy), p.3.
28 JFK, JFKNSF-330-002, NSAM 52, re: Report of the Vietnam Task Force, p.8.
29 *FRUS 1961–63, Volume I: No 1. Paper Prepared by the Country Team Staff Committee, Saigon, January 4, 1961.*
30 JFK, JFKNSF-203-003, Letter From the President's Military Representative (Taylor) to the President, [Attachment 2] Paper Prepared by the Members of the Taylor Mission Washington, Vietnam: Subjects: Taylor Report, 3 November 1961, Tab C, p.7; JFK, JFKNSF-203-003, Letter From the President's Military Representative (Taylor) to the President, [Attachment 2] Paper Prepared by the Members of the Taylor Mission Washington, Vietnam: Subjects: Taylor Report, 3 November 1961, Tab C, p.7.
31 JFK, JFKNSF-203-003, Letter From the President's Military Representative (Taylor) to the President, [Attachment 2] Paper Prepared by the Members of the Taylor Mission Washington, Vietnam: Subjects: Taylor Report, 3 November 1961, Tab C, p.7.
32 JFK, JFKNSF-203-003, Letter From the President's Military Representative (Taylor) to the President, [Attachment 2] Paper Prepared by the Members of the Taylor Mission Washington, Vietnam: Subjects: Taylor Report, 3 November 1961, Tab C, p.7.
33 JFK, JFKNSF-203-003, Letter From the President's Military Representative (Taylor) to the President Appendix B Memorandum From the Chairman of the Vietnam Task Force (Cottrell) to the President's Military Representative (Taylor) Washington, October 27, 1961. Vietnam: Subjects: Taylor Report, 3 November 1961: Rostow Working Copy. Papers of John F. Kennedy, Presidential Papers, National Security Files, Countries, Vietnam, Box 203, p.4.
34 JFK, JFKNSF-193-004, Memorandum From the President's Deputy Special Assistant for National Security Affairs (Rostow) to the President's Special Assistant for National Security Affairs (Bundy), Washington, January 30, 1961, p.2.
35 JFK, JFKNSF-193-004, Memorandum From the President's Deputy Special Assistant for National Security Affairs (Rostow) to the President's Special Assistant for National Security Affairs (Bundy), Washington, January 30, 1961, pp.2–3.
36 JFK, JFKNSF-193-004, Memorandum From the President's Deputy Special Assistant for National Security Affairs (Rostow) to the President's Special Assistant for National Security Affairs (Bundy), Washington, January 30, 1961, pp.2–3.
37 JFK, JFKNSF-193-004, Memorandum From the President's Deputy Special Assistant for National Security Affairs (Rostow) to the President's Special Assistant for National Security Affairs (Bundy), Washington, January 30, 1961, pp.2–3.
38 SNIE, *14.3 / 53–61 Prospects for North and South Vietnam*, p.10.
39 TTU, 6-20-15A5-116-UA17-149_000001, A Threat to the Peace: North Vietnam's Effort to Conquer South Vietnam – Part II, The Appendices, Vietnam Center and Sam Johnson Vietnam Archive. 1961, Box 1693, Folder 48; Michigan State University Archives & Historical Collections, Ralph F. Turner Papers, Appendix N, p.78.

40 SNIE, *50–61 Outlook in Mainland Southeast Asia*, p.7; *FRUS 1961–63, Volume I: No 274. Memorandum From the President's Deputy Special Assistant for National Security Affairs (Rostow) to the President, Washington, November 24, 1961.*
41 SNIE, *14.3 / 53–61 Prospects for North and South Vietnam*, p.10.
42 *FRUS 1961–63, Volume I: No 274. Memorandum From the President's Deputy Special Assistant for National Security Affairs (Rostow) to the President, Washington, November 24, 1961.*
43 SNIE, *14.3 / 53–61 Prospects for North and South Vietnam*, p.10.
44 JFK, JFKNSF–330–002, NSAM 52, re: Report of the Vietnam Task Force, p.4.
45 *FRUS 1961–63, Volume I: No 1. Paper Prepared by the Country Team Staff Committee, Saigon, January 4, 1961.*
46 JFK, JFKNSF–330–002, NSAM 52, re: Report of the Vietnam Task Force, Annex 1, p.1; JFK, JFKNSF–330–002, NSAM 52, re: Report of the Vietnam Task Force, Annex 1, pp.1–2.
47 JFK, JFKNSF–330–002, NSAM 52, re: Report of the Vietnam Task Force, Annex 1, p.2.
48 SNIE, *14.3 / 53–61 Prospects for North and South Vietnam*, 15 August 1961, pp.10–11.
49 SNIE, *10–62 Communist Objectives, Capabilities, and Intentions in Southeast Asia*, p.9.
50 SNIE, *10–62 Communist Objectives, Capabilities, and Intentions in Southeast Asia*,, p.9; SNIE, *10–62 Communist Objectives, Capabilities, and Intentions in Southeast Asia*, p.9.
51 *FRUS 1961–63, Volume I: No 1. Paper Prepared by the Country Team Staff Committee, Saigon, January 4, 1961.*
52 TTU, 2390711005, A Threat to the Peace, p.8.
53 *FRUS 1961–63, Volume I: No 1. Paper Prepared by the Country Team Staff Committee, Saigon, January 4, 1961.*
54 *FRUS 1961–63, Volume I: No 21. Memorandum of a Conversation, Embassy Residence, March 27, 1961.*
55 *FRUS 1961–63, Volume I: No 1. Paper Prepared by the Country Team Staff Committee, Saigon, January 4, 1961.*
56 TTU, 2293801019, A Study Viet Cong Use of Terror, March 1967, Folder 01, Box 38, Douglas Pike Collection: Unit 03 – War Atrocities, p.84.
57 TTU, 2120208019, Experiences in the Antistrategic Hamlet Programme, October–November 1962, p.3.
58 JFK, RHPP–003–006, A Strategic Concept for South Vietnam, p.2; CIA Documents, *Counter Insurgency Critical List* (Washington DC: Director of Central Intelligence, 25 July 1962), p.8.
59 SNIE, *14.3 / 53–61 Prospects for North and South Vietnam*, p.10.
60 JFK, JFKPOF–128–010, Address by George W. Ball April 30 1962 Veterans Memorial Building Civic Center, Detroit, Michigan, Papers of John F Kennedy. Presidential Papers, President's Office Files, Country Files Vietnam, General, Box 128, p.7.
61 JFK, RHPP–003–006, A Strategic Concept for South Vietnam, p.3; JFK, RHPP–003–006, A Strategic Concept for South Vietnam, p.3
62 JFK, RHPP–003–006, A Strategic Concept for South Vietnam, p.22.
63 JFK, RHPP–003–006, A Strategic Concept for South Vietnam, p.22.
64 Donnell & Hickey, *RM–3208–ARPA – The Vietnamese 'Strategic Hamlets': A Preliminary Report*, pp.17–18.
65 TTU, 2390711005, A Threat to the Peace, p.11.
66 JFK, RHPP–003–006, A Strategic Concept for South Vietnam, p.1; JFK, RHPP–003–006, A Strategic Concept for South Vietnam, p.1.
67 SNIE, *14.3 / 53–61 Prospects for North and South Vietnam*, p.10; SNIE, *14.3 / 53–61 Prospects for North and South Vietnam*, p.10.
68 TTU, 2120203029, Letter from Sir Robert Thompson to Ngo Dinh Diem (With Attachment), 13 November 1961, Enclosure No 2, Dispatch 205, p.1/347; TTU, 2120203029, Letter from Sir Robert Thompson to Ngo Dinh Diem (With Attachment), 13 November 1961, Enclosure No 2, Dispatch 205, p.1/347.
69 JFK, RHPP–003–006, A Strategic Concept for South Vietnam, p.9.
70 JFK, RHPP–003–011, Memorandum From the Assistant Secretary of State for Far Eastern Affairs (Hilsman) to the Secretary of State Washington, April 1963. Vietnam: Hilsman trip, December 1962–January 1963: Basic report and "Eyes Only" annex: Related Papers. Roger Hilsman Personal Papers, Countries Files, 1961–1964, Series 1, Box 3, p.2.
71 *FRUS 1961–63, Volume I: No 119. Telegram From the Embassy in Vietnam to the Department of State, Saigon, August 14, 1961, 11 a.m.*
72 JFK, RHPP–003–011, Memorandum From the Assistant Secretary of State for Far Eastern Affairs (Hilsman) to the Secretary of State Washington, April 1963. Vietnam: Hilsman trip, December 1962–January 1963: Basic report and "Eyes Only" annex: Related Papers. Roger Hilsman Personal Papers, Countries Files, 1961–1964, Series 1, Box 3, p.2.
73 TTU, 2120203029, Letter from Sir Robert Thompson to Ngo Dinh Diem (With Attachment), 13 November 1961, Enclosure No 2, Dispatch 205, p.3/349; TTU, 2120203029, Letter from Sir Robert Thompson to Ngo Dinh Diem (With Attachment), 13 November 1961, Enclosure No 2, Dispatch 205, p.4/350.
74 *FRUS 1961–63, Volume III: No 197. Research Memorandum From the Deputy Director of the Bureau of Intelligence and Research (Denney) to the Acting Secretary of State RFE–58 Washington, July 1, 1963.*
75 D. Galula in D.J. Kilcullen 'A6 – Counterinsurgency in Iraq: Theory and Practice 2007', *Small Wars Journal* (2007), p.40. [Online], Available: http://www.smallwarsjournal.com/documents/kilcullencoinbrief 26sept07.ppt.
76 Brigham, *Is Iraq another Vietnam?*, p.54.
77 TTU, 23970130054, Booklet – Vietnam's Strategic Hamlets, February 1963, Folder 30, Box 01, Rufus Phillips Collection, p.3.
78 CIA Telegram, *Strategic Hamlets* (Washington DC: Director of Central Intelligence 20 February 1962), p.2.
79 TTU, 2120101001, Vietnam Counterinsurgency – The Diem Era: Strategic Hamlet (5 pages) [No Date], folder 01, Box 01, Douglas Pike Collection: Unit 01 – Assessment and Strategy.
80 TTU, 2120101001, Vietnam Counterinsurgency – The Diem Era: Strategic Hamlet, p.177.
81 TTU, 2120101001, Vietnam Counterinsurgency – The Diem Era: Strategic Hamlet, p.178.
82 Catton, *Diem's Final Failure*, p.92.
83 Catton, *Diem's Final Failure*, p.92.
84 TTU, 2120101001, Vietnam Counterinsurgency – The Diem Era: Strategic Hamlet, p.178; TTU, 23970131052, Memo for Record – Operation Sunrise, p.1.
85 *FRUS 1961–63, Volume II: No 205. Memorandum of Conversation Between the Vietnamese Secretary of State at the Presidency (Thuan) and the Charge in Vietnam (Trueheart), Saigon, May 24, 1962*; See Department of Defense, US–Vietnam Relations 1945–1967, Volume IV. B. 2, Evolution of the War, Strategic Hamlet Programme 1961–1963, Box 3, 270/80/9/7 (Washington DC: National Archives and Records Administration, declassified 2011), pp.22–27 for further details.
86 Bragg, *Vietnam, Korea and US Foreign Policy 1945 – 75*, p.105.
87 See Phillips, *Why Vietnam Matters*, pp.126–139 for further details.
88 As noted previously details of the plan can be found in *FRUS 1961–63, Volume I: No 1. Paper Prepared by the Country Team Staff Committee, Saigon, January 4, 1961.*
89 As noted previously, The Gilpatric Report can be found at the JFK, JFKNSF–330–002, National Security Action Memoranda [NSAM]: NSAM 52, re: Report of the Vietnam Task Force, Papers of John F. Kennedy. Presidential Papers, National Security Files, Meetings and Memoranda, Box 330.
90 The Staley Plan can be located, amongst other places, at Texas Tech University – the citation being: TTU, 2120202011, Joint Action Programme Proposed by the Vietnam–United States Special Financial Group, 25 July 1961, Folder 02, Box 02, Douglas Pike Collection: Unit 01 – Assessment and Strategy.
91 Details of the *Geographically Phased National Level Operation Plan for Counterinsurgency* can be found in Department of Defense, US–Vietnam Relations 1945–1967, Volume IV. B. 2, Evolution of the War, Strategic Hamlet Programme 1961–1963, Box 3, 270/80/9/7 (Washington DC: National Archives and Records Administration, declassified 2011), p.24.
92 JFK, RHPP–003–006, A Strategic Concept for South Vietnam.
93 JFK, RHPP–003–006, A Strategic Concept for South Vietnam; Hilsman drew upon Thompson's plans given to Diem in 1961. See for example, Thompson's version of the so-called Delta Plan which can be read in the JFK, RHPP–003–009, Roger Hilsman Personal Papers, Countries Files, 1961–1964, Series 1, Box 3, Folder 5 and also in *FRUS 1961–63, Volume II: No 51. Draft Paper by the Head of the British Advisory Mission in Vietnam (Thompson)*, Saigon (undated). In contrast, Diem's official Delta Plan can be accessed in *FRUS 1961–63, Volume II: No 13. Decree by the President of the Republic of Vietnam, Saigon, March 16, 1962.* See also Thompson's initial plan for Delta pacification in TTU, 2120203029, Letter from Sir Robert Thompson to Ngo Dinh Diem (With Attachment), 13 November 1961, Enclosure No 2, Dispatch 205.
94 Some specific plans included the so-called Delta Plan which can be read in the JFK, RHPP–003–009, Roger Hilsman Personal Papers, Countries Files, 1961–1964, Series 1, Box 3, Folder 5; Diem's official Delta Plan can be accessed in *FRUS 1961–63, Volume II: No 13. Decree by the President of the Republic of Vietnam, Saigon, March 16, 1962.* See also Thompson's initial plan for Delta pacification in TTU, 2120203029, Letter from Sir Robert Thompson to Ngo Dinh Diem (With Attachment), 13 November 1961, Enclosure No 2, Dispatch 205 and TTU, 23970206004, Booklet – South Vietnam CPSVN Comprehensive Plan, No Date, Folder 06, Box 02, Rufus Phillips Collection for further details.
95 See *FRUS 1961–63, Volume II: No 235. Letter From the Director of the Vietnam Working Group (Wood) to the Ambassador in Vietnam (Nolting) Washington, July 6, 1962 [Enclosure] Draft Action Plan Vietnam* (Washington DC: US Department of State, 1988) for the initial draft and *FRUS 1961–63, Volume III: No 18. Memorandum From the Commander in Chief, Pacific (Felt) to the Joint Chiefs of Staff – CINCPAC 3010 Ser 0079, Honolulu, January 25, 1963 – Comprehensive Plan for South Vietnam (CPSVN)* (Washington DC: US Department of State, 1988) or TTU, 23970206004, Booklet – South Vietnam CPSVN Comprehensive Plan, No Date, Folder 06, Box 02, Rufus Phillips Collection for further details.
96 *FRUS 1961–63, Volume III: No 18. Memorandum From the Commander in Chief, Pacific (Felt) to the Joint Chiefs of Staff – CINCPAC 3010 Ser 0079, Honolulu, January 25, 1963* (Washington DC: US Department of State, 1988) or TTU, 23970206004, Booklet – South Vietnam CPSVN Comprehensive Plan, No Date, Folder 06, Box 02, Rufus Phillips Collection for further details.
97 *FRUS 1961–63, Volume II: No 257. Memorandum From the Deputy Director of the Vietnam Working Group (Heavner) to the Director (Wood) Washington, August 3, 1962.*
98 JFK, RHPP–003–009, Memorandum From the Director of the Bureau of Intelligence and Research (Hilsman) and Michael V. Forrestal of the National Security Council Staff to the President, Washington, January 25, 1963. Vietnam: Hilsman trip, December 1962–January 1963: Basic report and "Eyes Only" annex. Roger Hilsman Personal Papers, Countries Files, 1961–1964, Series 1, Box 3, pp.6–7.
99 JFK, RHPP–003–009, Memorandum From the Director of the Bureau of Intelligence and Research (Hilsman) and Michael V. Forrestal of the National Security Council Staff to the President, Washington, January 25, 1963. Vietnam: Hilsman trip, December 1962–January 1963: Basic report and "Eyes Only" annex. Roger Hilsman Personal Papers, Countries Files, 1961–1964, Series 1, Box 3, p.7.
100 *FRUS 1961–63, Volume III: No 197. Research Memorandum From the Deputy Director of the Bureau of Intelligence and Research (Denney) to the Acting Secretary of State RFE–58 Washington, July 1, 1963.*
101 TTU, 23970201051, Extract – Interministerial Committee for Strategic Hamlets Criteria for Completed Hamlets, 19 July 1962, Folder 01, Box 02, Rufus Phillips Collection.
102 Donnell & Hickey, *RM–3208–ARPA, – The Vietnamese 'Strategic Hamlets': A Preliminary Report*, p.4.
103 Donnell & Hickey, *RM–3208–ARPA, – The Vietnamese 'Strategic Hamlets': A Preliminary Report*, p.5.

104 Donnell & Hickey, *RM–3208–ARPA – The Vietnamese 'Strategic Hamlets': A Preliminary Report*, p.4.
105 *FRUS 1961–63, Volume III: No 197. Research Memorandum From the Deputy Director of the Bureau of Intelligence and Research (Denney) to the Acting Secretary of State RFE–58 Washington, July 1, 1963.*
106 *FRUS 1961–63, Volume III: No 197. Research Memorandum From the Deputy Director of the Bureau of Intelligence and Research (Denney) to the Acting Secretary of State RFE–58 Washington, July 1, 1963.*
107 JFK, RHPP–003–006, A Strategic Concept for South Vietnam, p.18.
108 JFK, RHPP–003–006, A Strategic Concept for South Vietnam, p.18.
109 JFK, RHPP–003–006, A Strategic Concept for South Vietnam, p.16.
110 JFK, RHPP–003–006, A Strategic Concept for South Vietnam, p.23
111 JFK, RHPP–003–006, A Strategic Concept for South Vietnam, p.23
112 JFK, RHPP–003–006, A Strategic Concept for South Vietnam, p.22.
113 JFK, RHPP–003–006, A Strategic Concept for South Vietnam, p.22.
114 JFK, RHPP–003–006, A Strategic Concept for South Vietnam, p.22.
115 TTU, 23970201051, Extract – Interministerial Committee for Strategic Hamlets Criteria for Completed Hamlets, 19 July 1962, Folder 01, Box 02, Rufus Phillips Collection.
116 Donnell & Hickey, *RM–3208–ARPA – The Vietnamese 'Strategic Hamlets': A Preliminary Report*, p.5.
117 JFK, RHPP–003–006, A Strategic Concept for South Vietnam, p.23; JFK, RHPP–003–006, A Strategic Concept for South Vietnam, p.23.
118 JFK, RHPP–003–006, A Strategic Concept for South Vietnam, p.15; JFK, RHPP–003–006, A Strategic Concept for South Vietnam, p.15.
119 JFK, RHPP–003–006, A Strategic Concept for South Vietnam, p.23.
120 These successes will be discussed in detail later in the book but indications of progress can found in documents such as TTU, 23970128002, Report, A Report on Counter-insurgency in Vietnam, 20 July 1962 or TTU, 2120207002, NLF Anti-Strategic Hamlet Programme, 1962.
121 TTU, 23970128002, Report, A Report on Counter-insurgency in Vietnam, 20 July 1962, p.3.
122 LBJ, Transcript, William E. Colby Oral History, Interview II (by Ted Gittinger), March 01, 1982, Internet Copy, p.6.
123 *FRUS 1961–63, Volume II: No 297. Paper Prepared in the Department of State Washington, undated.*
124 *FRUS 1961–63, Volume II: No 297. Paper Prepared in the Department of State Washington, undated.*125TTU, 23970128002, Report, A Report on Counter-insurgency in Vietnam, 20 July 1962, p.11.
126 TTU, 23970128002, Report, A Report on Counter-insurgency in Vietnam, 20 July 1962, p.11.
127 TTU, 23970128002, Report, A Report on Counter-insurgency in Vietnam, 20 July 1962, p.11; TTU, 23970128002, Report, A Report on Counter-insurgency in Vietnam, 20 July 1962, p.11.
128 *FRUS 1961–63, Volume II: No 332. Memorandum From the Director of the Bureau of Intelligence and Research (Hilsman) to the Assistant Secretary of State for Far Eastern Affairs (Harriman), Washington, December 19, 1962.*
129 *FRUS 1961–63, Volume II: No 328. Report by the Deputy Director of the Vietnam Working Group (Heavner), Washington, December 11, 1962; FRUS 1961–63, Volume II: No 297. Paper Prepared in the Department of State Washington, undated.*
130 JFK, RHPP–003–009, Memorandum From the Director of the Bureau of Intelligence and Research (Hilsman) and Michael V. Forrestal of the National Security Council Staff to the President, Washington, January 25, 1963, p.3.
131 JFK, RHPP–003–009, Memorandum From the Director of the Bureau of Intelligence and Research (Hilsman) and Michael V. Forrestal of the National Security Council Staff to the President, Washington, January 25, 1963, p.6.
132 JFK, RHPP–003–009, Memorandum From the Director of the Bureau of Intelligence and Research (Hilsman) and Michael V. Forrestal of the National Security Council Staff to the President, Washington, January 25, 1963, p.1.
133 *FRUS 1961–63, Volume III: No 26. Report by an Investigative Team Headed by the Chief of Staff, United States Army (Wheeler), to the Joint Chiefs of Staff, Washington, January 1963.*
134 SNIE, *53–63 Prospects in South Vietnam* (Washington DC: Director of Central Intelligence, No 361, 17 April 1963), p.1.
135 TTU, 23970210004, Memo from Earl J. Young to Rufus Phillips – re: Mid-Year Progress Report, 06 September 1963, Folder 10, Box 02, Rufus Phillips Collection, p.7.
136 *FRUS 1961–63, Volume II: No 332. Senator Mansfield's Visit to Vietnam and Subsequent Report; Visits and Reports by Johnson and Heavner December 1962. Memorandum From the Director of the Bureau of Intelligence and Research (Hilsman) to the Assistant Secretary of State for Far Eastern Affairs (Harriman).*
137 *FRUS 1961–63, Volume II: No180. Memorandum for the Record Washington, May 3, 1962.*
138 TTU, 23970201037, Report – The Situation in Vietnam, 14 September 1963, p.1; TTU, 23970201037, Report – The Situation in Vietnam, 14 September 1963, p.1.
139 *FRUS 1961–63, Volume III: No 102. Memorandum From the Assistant Director for Rural Affairs, United States Operations Mission in Vietnam (Phillips), to the Director of the Mission (Brent) Saigon, May 1,1963;* SNIE, *53–63 Prospects in South Vietnam*, p.9.
140 *FRUS 1961–63, Volume III: No 102. Memorandum From the Assistant Director for Rural Affairs, United States Operations Mission in Vietnam (Phillips), to the Director of the Mission (Brent) Saigon, May 1,1963;* SNIE, *53–63 Prospects in South Vietnam*, p.9.
141 JFK, RHPP–003–009, Memorandum From the Director of the Bureau of Intelligence and Research (Hilsman) and Michael V. Forrestal of the National Security Council Staff to the President, Washington, January 25, 1963, p.2.
142 *FRUS 1961–63, Volume II: No 187. Paper Prepared in the Department of Defense, Washington, undated.*
143 *FRUS 1961–63, Volume II: No 139. Memorandum From the Director of the Bureau of Intelligence and Research (Hilsman) to the Assistant Secretary of State for Far Eastern Affairs (Harriman) Washington, April 3, 1962.*
144 *FRUS 1961–63, Volume III: No 102. Memorandum From the Assistant Director for Rural Affairs, United States Operations Mission in Vietnam (Phillips), to the Director of the Mission (Brent) Saigon, May 1,1963;* SNIE, *53–63 Prospects in South Vietnam*, p.9.
145 JFK, Report on Visit to Delta Provinces, 1962–1963, RKG Thompson March 13, 1963, British Advisory Mission, Saigon. Roger Hilsman Papers, Countries, Philippines – Vietnam 8/30/63–8/31/63, Box 003, Folder 14, p.7.
146 JFK, Report on Visit to Delta Provinces, 1962–1963, RKG Thompson March 13, 1963, British Advisory Mission, Saigon. Roger Hilsman Papers, Countries, Philippines – Vietnam 8/30/63–8/31/63, Box 003, Folder 14, p.7.
147 JFK, Report on Visit to Delta Provinces, 1962–1963, RKG Thompson March 13, 1963, British Advisory Mission, Saigon. Roger Hilsman Papers, Countries, Philippines – Vietnam 8/30/63–8/31/63, Box 003, Folder 14, p.6; JFK, Report on Visit to Delta Provinces, 1962–1963, RKG Thompson March 13, 1963, British Advisory Mission, Saigon. Roger Hilsman Papers, Countries, Philippines – Vietnam 8/30/63–8/31/63, Box 003, Folder 14, p.2.
148 JFK, Memorandum, March 11, 1963 British Advisory Mission, Saigon. Roger Hilsman Papers, Countries, Philippines – Vietnam 8/30/63–8/31/63, Box 003, Folder 14, p.2.
149 *FRUS 1961–63, Volume III: No 77. Memorandum of Conversation, White House Washington, April 4, 1963, 10 a.m.*
150 *FRUS 1961–63, Volume II: No 332. Senator Mansfield's Visit to Vietnam and Subsequent Report; Visits and Reports by Johnson and Heavner December 1962. Memorandum From the Director of the Bureau of Intelligence and Research (Hilsman) to the Assistant Secretary of State for Far Eastern Affairs (Harriman) RFE–66 Washington, December 19, 1962.*
151 *FRUS 1961–63, Volume II: No 173. Memorandum From the Officer in Charge of Vietnam Affairs (Heavner) to the Ambassador in Vietnam (Nolting), Saigon, April 27, 1962; FRUS 1961–63, Volume II: No 173. Memorandum From the Officer in Charge of Vietnam Affairs (Heavner) to the Ambassador in Vietnam (Nolting), Saigon, April 27, 1962.*
152 *FRUS 1961–63, Volume II: No 319. Memorandum From the Chairman of the Joint Chiefs of Staff (Taylor) to the Secretary of Defense (McNamara) CM–117–62 Washington, November 17, 1962.*
153 TTU, 0720406007, Studies of the National Liberation Front of South Vietnam, 15–16 April 1965, Folder 06, Box 04, John Donnell Collection p.2; TTU, 0720406008, Studies of the National Liberation Front of South Vietnam Interviews 139, 12–14 April 1966, Folder 06, Box 04, John Donnell Collection p.5.
154 J. Farmer, 'Counter-insurgency: Principles and Practice in Vietnam', (Lecture, RAND Corporation, Santa Monica, 1964), p.6.
155 Farmer, 'Counter-insurgency: Principles and Practice in Vietnam', (Lecture, RAND Corporation, Santa Monica, 1964), p.7.
156 TTU, 23970129002, Summary, An Informal Appreciation of The Status of The Strategic Hamlet Programme – Prepared by USOM Rural Affairs, 01 June 1963, Folder 29, Box 01, Rufus Phillips Collection, p.1.
157 TTU, 23970129002, Summary, An Informal Appreciation of The Status of The Strategic Hamlet Programme – Prepared by USOM Rural Affairs, 01 June 1963, Folder 29, Box 01, Rufus Phillips Collection, p.1.
158 JFK, Report on Visit to Delta Provinces, 1962–1963, RKG Thompson March 13, 1963, p.4.
159 JFK, Report on Visit to Delta Provinces, 1962–1963, RKG Thompson March 13, 1963, p.6.
160 JFK, Memorandum, March 11, 1963 British Advisory Mission, Saigon. Roger Hilsman Papers, Countries, Philippines – Vietnam 8/30/63–8/31/63, Box 003, Folder 14, p.2.
161 JFK, Memorandum, March 11, 1963 British Advisory Mission, Saigon. Roger Hilsman Papers, Countries, Philippines – Vietnam 8/30/63–8/31/63, Box 003, Folder 14, p.2.
162 JFK, Memorandum, March 11, 1963 British Advisory Mission, Saigon. Roger Hilsman Papers, Countries, Philippines – Vietnam 8/30/63–8/31/63, Box 003, Folder 14, p.4; JFK, Report on Visit to Delta Provinces, 1962–1963, RKG Thompson March 13, 1963, p.3.
163 JFK, Report on Visit to Delta Provinces, 1962–1963, RKG Thompson March 13, 1963, pp.3–4; JFK, Report on Visit to Delta Provinces, 1962–1963, RKG Thompson March 13, 1963, pp.3–4.
164 JFK, Report on Visit to Delta Provinces, 1962–1963, RKG Thompson March 13, 1963, p.1.
165 TTU, 23970129001, Summary, Second Informal Appreciation of The Status of The Strategic Hamlet Programme – Prepared by USOM Rural Affairs, 01 September 1963, Folder 29, Box 01, Rufus Phillips Collection, p.5.
166 TTU, 23970129001, Summary, Second Informal Appreciation of The Status of The Strategic Hamlet Programme – Prepared by USOM Rural Affairs, 01 September 1963, Folder 29, Box 01, Rufus Phillips Collection, p.21.
167 TTU, 23970128002, Report, A Report on Counter-insurgency in Vietnam, 20 July 1962, p.13.
168 JFK, RHPP–003–009, Memorandum From the Director of the Bureau of Intelligence and Research (Hilsman) and Michael V. Forrestal of the National Security Council Staff to the President, Washington, January 25, 1963, p.2.
169 JFK, RHPP–003–009, Memorandum From the Director of the Bureau of Intelligence and Research (Hilsman) and Michael V. Forrestal of the National Security Council Staff to the President, Washington, January 25, 1963, p.2.
170 TTU, 2120301025, Department of State Research Memorandum: Statistics on the War Effort in South Vietnam Show Unfavorable Trends, 22 October 1963, Folder 01, Box 03, Douglas Pike Collection: Unit 01 – Assessment and Strategy, p.1; TTU, 2120301025, Department of State Research Memorandum: Statistics on the War Effort in South Vietnam Show Unfavorable Trends, 22 October 1963, Folder 01, Box 03, Douglas Pike Collection: Unit 01 – Assessment and Strategy, p.1.

171 TTU, 2120301025, Department of State Research Memorandum: Statistics on the War Effort in South Vietnam Show Unfavorable Trends, 22 October 1963, Folder 01, Box 03, Douglas Pike Collection: Unit 01 – Assessment and Strategy, p.5.
172 TTU, 2120301025, Department of State Research Memorandum: Statistics on the War Effort in South Vietnam Show Unfavorable Trends, 22 October 1963, Folder 01, Box 03, Douglas Pike Collection: Unit 01 – Assessment and Strategy, p.2.
173 Miami University Library, Ohio, OCLC Number: 1658815, Interview 97 – Member of Hamlet Propaganda, Culture and Indoctrination Section, Microfilm – Rand Vietnam Interview Series V: Viet Cong Organizational Activities at Hamlet/Village Level (Santa Monica: RAND Corporation, 1968), p.1; Miami University Library, Ohio, OCLC Number: 1658815, Interview 7 – Village Party Chapter Member, Microfilm – Rand Vietnam Interview Series V: Viet Cong Organizational Activities at Hamlet/Village Level (Santa Monica: RAND Corporation, 1968), p.2.
174 TTU, 2120207002, NLF Anti-Strategic Hamlet Programme, 1962, p.23.
175 TTU, 2120208019, Experiences in the Antistrategic Hamlet Programme, October–November 1962, p.3.
176 TTU, 0720804001, Studies of the National Liberation Front of South Vietnam Interviews, 05 March 1966, Folder 04, Box 08, John Donnell Collection, p.12.
177 JFK, RHPP–003–009, Memorandum From the Director of the Bureau of Intelligence and Research (Hilsman) and Michael V. Forrestal of the National Security Council Staff to the President, Washington, January 25, 1963, p.3.
178 *FRUS 1961–63, Volume III: No 11. Current Intelligence Memorandum Prepared in the Office of Current Intelligence, Central Intelligence Agency, Washington, January 11, 1963; FRUS 1961–63, Volume III: No 26. Report by an Investigative Team Headed by the Chief of Staff, United States Army (Wheeler), to the Joint Chiefs of Staff, Washington, January 1963.*
179 *FRUS 1961–63, Volume III: No 11. Current Intelligence Memorandum Prepared in the Office of Current Intelligence, Central Intelligence Agency, Washington, January 11, 1963; FRUS 1961–63, Volume III: No 26. Report by an Investigative Team Headed by the Chief of Staff, United States Army (Wheeler), to the Joint Chiefs of Staff, Washington, January 1963.*
180 *FRUS 1961–63, Volume III: No 11. Current Intelligence Memorandum Prepared in the Office of Current Intelligence, Central Intelligence Agency, Washington, January 11, 1963; FRUS 1961–63, Volume III: No 26. Report by an Investigative Team Headed by the Chief of Staff, United States Army (Wheeler), to the Joint Chiefs of Staff, Washington, January 1963.*
181 *FRUS 1961–63, Volume III: No 11. Current Intelligence Memorandum Prepared in the Office of Current Intelligence, Central Intelligence Agency, Washington, January 11, 1963; FRUS 1961–63, Volume III: No 26. Report by an Investigative Team Headed by the Chief of Staff, United States Army (Wheeler), to the Joint Chiefs of Staff, Washington, January 1963.*
182 *FRUS 1961–63, Volume III: No 26. Report by an Investigative Team Headed by the Chief of Staff, United States Army (Wheeler), to the Joint Chiefs of Staff, Washington, January 1963*; SNIE, *53–63 Prospects in South Vietnam*, p.11.
183 TTU, 2120207002, NLF Anti-Strategic Hamlet Programme, 1962, p.21; TTU, 2120207002, NLF Anti-Strategic Hamlet Programme, 1962., p.20.
184 TTU, 2120207007, Report on Struggle Efforts to Destroy Strategic Hamlet in Bien Hoa Province, January 1962, Folder 07, Box 02, Douglas Pike Collection: Unit 01 – Assessment and Strategy, p.2.
185 TTU, 2120207002, NLF Anti-Strategic Hamlet Programme, 1962, p.21; TTU, 2120207002, NLF Anti-Strategic Hamlet Programme, 1962, p.21; TTU, 2120207002, NLF Anti-Strategic Hamlet Programme, 1962, p.21.
186 *FRUS 1961–63, Volume III: No 26. Report by an Investigative Team Headed by the Chief of Staff, United States Army (Wheeler), to the Joint Chiefs of Staff, Washington, January 1963.*
187 *FRUS 1961–63, Volume III: No 207. Report by the Joint Chiefs of Staff's Special Assistant for Counterinsurgency and Special Activities (Krulak), Washington, undated.*
188 *FRUS 1961–63, Volume III: No 26. Report by an Investigative Team Headed by the Chief of Staff, United States Army (Wheeler), to the Joint Chiefs of Staff, Washington, January 1963; FRUS 1961–63, Volume II: No 13. Memorandum for the Record Saigon, January 12, 1962.*
189 *FRUS 1961–63, Volume II: No 13. Memorandum for the Record Saigon, January 12, 1962; FRUS 1961–63, Volume IV: No 158. Memorandum of Conversation, Saigon, September 29, 1963, 2:30–5:30 p.m.*
190 *FRUS 1961–63, Volume II: No 13. Memorandum for the Record Saigon, January 12, 1962; FRUS 1961–63, Volume IV: No 158. Memorandum of Conversation, Saigon, September 29, 1963, 2:30–5:30 p.m.*
191 *FRUS 1961–63, Volume IV: No 158. Memorandum of Conversation, Saigon, September 29, 1963, 2:30–5:30 p.m.*
192 Donnell, *14436–IBA/ARPA – Viet Cong Recruitment: Why and How Men Join*, p.17.
193 Donnell, *14436–IBA/ARPA – Viet Cong Recruitment: Why and How Men Join*, p.10.
194 Donnell, *14436–IBA/ARPA – Viet Cong Recruitment: Why and How Men Join*, p.10; Donnell, *14436–IBA/ARPA – Viet Cong Recruitment: Why and How Men Join*, p.10.
195 Donnell, *14436–IBA/ARPA – Viet Cong Recruitment: Why and How Men Join*, p.10A; Donnell, *14436–IBA/ARPA – Viet Cong Recruitment: Why and How Men Join*, p.11.
196 Donnell, *14436–IBA/ARPA – Viet Cong Recruitment: Why and How Men Join*, p.12; Donnell, *14436–IBA/ARPA – Viet Cong Recruitment: Why and How Men Join*, p.11.
197 Donnell, *14436–IBA/ARPA – Viet Cong Recruitment: Why and How Men Join*, p.12.
198 Donnell, *14436–IBA/ARPA – Viet Cong Recruitment: Why and How Men Join*, p.11; Donnell, *14436–IBA/ARPA – Viet Cong Recruitment: Why and How Men Join*, p.11.
199 *FRUS 1961–63, Volume III: No 26. Report by an Investigative Team Headed by the Chief of Staff, United States Army (Wheeler), to the Joint Chiefs of Staff, Washington, January, 1963; FRUS 1961–63, Volume III: No 26. Report by an Investigative Team Headed by the Chief of Staff, United States Army (Wheeler), to the Joint Chiefs of Staff, Washington, January, 1963.*
200 TTU, 23970134024, Booklet – Notes on Strategic Hamlets, 15 August 1963, Folder 34, Box 01, Douglas Pike Collection: Unit 05 – National Liberation Front, p.2
201 TTU, 23970134024, Booklet – Notes on Strategic Hamlets, 15 August 1963, Folder 34, Box 01, Douglas Pike Collection: Unit 05 – National Liberation Front, p.2
202 TTU, 23970128002, Report, A Report on Counter-insurgency in Vietnam, 20 July 1962, p.4.
203 *FRUS 1961–63, Volume II: No 328. Report by the Deputy Director of the Vietnam Working Group (Heavner), Washington, December 11, 1962.*
204 *FRUS 1961–63, Volume II: No 328. Report by the Deputy Director of the Vietnam Working Group (Heavner), Washington, December 11, 1962.*
205 TTU, 23970134024, Booklet – Notes on Strategic Hamlets, 15 August 1963, p.4; TTU, 23970134024, Booklet – Notes on Strategic Hamlets, p.4.
206 *FRUS 1961–63, Volume II: No 328. Report by the Deputy Director of the Vietnam Working Group (Heavner), Washington, December 11, 1962.*
207 *FRUS 1961–63, Volume II: No 328. Report by the Deputy Director of the Vietnam Working Group (Heavner), Washington, December 11, 1962.*
208 Donnell & Hickey, *RM–3208–ARPA – The Vietnamese 'Strategic Hamlets': A Preliminary Report*, p.7.
209 Donnell & Hickey, *RM–3208–ARPA – The Vietnamese 'Strategic Hamlets': A Preliminary Report*, p.7.
210 Donnell & Hickey, *RM–3208–ARPA – The Vietnamese 'Strategic Hamlets': A Preliminary Report*.
211 TTU, 23970128002, Report, A Report on Counter-insurgency in Vietnam, 20 July 1962, p.4.
212 Donnell & Hickey, *RM–3208–ARPA – The Vietnamese 'Strategic Hamlets': A Preliminary Report*, p.8.
213 Donnell & Hickey, *RM–3208–ARPA – The Vietnamese 'Strategic Hamlets': A Preliminary Report*, p.9.
214 Donnell & Hickey, *RM–3208–ARPA – The Vietnamese 'Strategic Hamlets': A Preliminary Report*, p.9.
215 Donnell & Hickey, *RM–3208–ARPA – The Vietnamese 'Strategic Hamlets': A Preliminary Report*, p.9.
216 Donnell & Hickey, *RM–3208–ARPA – The Vietnamese 'Strategic Hamlets': A Preliminary Report*, pp.9–10.
217 TTU, 23970134024, Booklet – Notes on Strategic Hamlets, 15 August 1963, p .11.
218 *FRUS 1961–63, Volume II: No 297. Paper Prepared in the Department of State Washington, undated; FRUS 1961–63, Volume II: No 297. Paper Prepared in the Department of State Washington, undated.*
219 TTU, 23970129001, Summary, Second Informal Appreciation of The Status of The Strategic Hamlet Programme, 01 September 1963, 01 September 1963, p.7.
220 Farmer, 'Counter-insurgency: Principles and Practice in Vietnam', p.6.
221 Phillips, 'Rufus Phillips on Why Vietnam Matters: An Eyewitness Account of Lessons Not Learned', Time 50:00.
222 TTU, 2120208020, Policy Instructions from "Chin Nam" to the South, 27 September 1962, Folder 08, Box 02, Douglas Pike Collection: Unit 01 – Assessment and Strategy, p.4.
223 TTU, 23970128002, Report, A Report on Counter-insurgency in Vietnam, 20 July 1962, p.16.
224 TTU, 23970128002, Report, A Report on Counter-insurgency in Vietnam, 20 July 1962, p.16.
225 JFK, Memorandum, March 11, 1963 British Advisory Mission, Saigon. Roger Hilsman Papers, Countries, Philippines – Vietnam 8/30/63–8/31/63, Box 003, p.1.
226 JFK, Memorandum, March 11, 1963 British Advisory Mission, Saigon. Roger Hilsman Papers, Countries, Philippines – Vietnam 8/30/63–8/31/63, Box 003, p.1.
227 TTU, 2120208019, Experiences in the Antistrategic Hamlet Programme, October–November 1962, p.2.
228 TTU, 2120208019, Experiences in the Antistrategic Hamlet Programme, October–November 1962, p.2.
229 *FRUS 1961–63, Volume III: No 26. Report by an Investigative Team Headed by the Chief of Staff, United States Army (Wheeler), to the Joint Chiefs of Staff, Washington, January 1963.*

Chapter 2

1 LBJ, Transcript, William E. Colby Oral History, Interview II, March 01, 1982, p.6.
2 TTU, 2120207002, NLF Anti-Strategic Hamlet Programme, 1962, Folder 07, Box 02, Douglas Pike Collection: Unit 01 – Assessment and Strategy.
3 TTU, 2120102007, Assessment of the Status of the Revolution in Vietnam (Probably by the Western Nambo Central Committee), 25 September 1962; TTU, 2120207003, Viet Cong Study Document on Strategic Hamlets, 1962; TTU, 2120208019, Experiences in the Antistrategic Hamlet Programme, October–November 1962, Folder 08, Box 02, Douglas Pike Collection: Unit 01 – Assessment and Strategy.
4 See, for example, JFK, RHPP–003–011, Memorandum From the Assistant Secretary of State for Far Eastern Affairs (Hilsman) to the Secretary of State Washington, April 1963. Vietnam: Hilsman trip, December 1962–January 1963: Basic report and "Eyes Only" annex. Roger Hilsman Personal Papers, Countries Files, 1961–1964, Series 1, Box 3; JFK, Report on Visit to Delta Provinces, 1962–1963, RKG Thompson March 13, 1963, British Advisory Mission, Saigon. Roger Hilsman Papers, Countries, Philippines – Vietnam 8/30/63–8/31/63, Box 003, Folder 14; *FRUS 1961–63, Volume II: No 149.*

Memorandum From the Director of the Vietnam Task Force (Cottrell) to the Assistant Secretary of State for Far Eastern Affairs (Harriman), Washington, April 6, 1962; See also Thompson, *Defeating Communist Insurgency*; Thompson, *Make for the Hills.*

5 TTU, 2120207002, NLF Anti-Strategic Hamlet Programme, 1962, p.23.

6 TTU, 2120207003, Viet Cong Study Document on Strategic Hamlets, 1962, p.2; TTU, 2120207003, Viet Cong Study Document on Strategic Hamlets, 1962, p.2.

7 TTU, 2120207002, NLF Anti-Strategic Hamlet Programme, 1962, p.23; TTU, 2120207002, NLF Anti-Strategic Hamlet Programme, 1962, p.23.

8 Osborne, *Strategic Hamlets in South Vietnam*, p.47.

9 Osborne, *Strategic Hamlets in South Vietnam*, p.48 – quote taken from Clandestine Liberation Front Radio, 17 April, 1963.

10 TTU, 23130005003, Communist assessment of South Vietnam scene: 1/62–6/63, 01 January 1963, Folder 005, Box 30, Douglas Pike Collection: Unit 05 – National Liberation Front, p.13.

11 TTU, 23130005003, Communist assessment of South Vietnam scene: 1/62–6/63, 01 January 1963, Folder 005, Box 30, Douglas Pike Collection: Unit 05 – National Liberation Front, p.13.

12 TTU, 23130005003, Communist assessment of South Vietnam scene: 1/62–6/63, 01 January 1963, Folder 005, Box 30, Douglas Pike Collection: Unit 05 – National Liberation Front, p.13.

13 TTU, 23130005003, Communist assessment of South Vietnam scene: 1/62–6/63, 01 January 1963, Folder 005, Box 30, Douglas Pike Collection: Unit 05 – National Liberation Front, p.13; TTU, 23130005003, Communist assessment of South Vietnam scene: 1/62–6/63, 01 January 1963, Folder 005, Box 30, Douglas Pike Collection: Unit 05 – National Liberation Front, p.14.

14 TTU, 2120207002, NLF Anti-Strategic Hamlet Programme, 1962, p.20.

15 TTU, 2120102007, Assessment of the Status of the Revolution in Vietnam, 25 September 1962, p.4.

16 TTU, 2121610016, Captured Documents, VC Measures Against the Strategic Hamlet Programme, May 1970, p.11; TTU, 2121610016, Captured Documents, VC Measures Against the Strategic Hamlet Programme, May 1970, p.11.

17 TTU, 23130005003, Communist assessment of South Vietnam scene: 1/62–6/63, 01 January 1963, p.11.

18 TTU, 23130005003, Communist assessment of South Vietnam scene: 1/62–6/63, 01 January 1963, p.13; TTU, 23130005003, Communist assessment of South Vietnam scene: 1/62–6/63, 01 January 1963, p.16.

19 TTU, 2120208020, Policy Instructions from "Chin Nam" to the South, 27 September 1962, p.22.

20 TTU, 2120310008, NLF Study of War History, 1961 Thru 1964 – Translation of Captured Enemy Document, 28 March 1970, Folder 10, Box 03, Douglas Pike Collection: Unit 01 – Assessment and Strategy, p.8.

21 TTU, 2120310008, NLF Study of War History, 1961 Thru 1964 – Translation of Captured Enemy Document, 28 March 1970, Folder 10, Box 03, Douglas Pike Collection: Unit 01 – Assessment and Strategy, p.8; TTU, 2120310008, NLF Study of War History, 1961 Thru 1964 – Translation of Captured Enemy Document, 28 March 1970, Folder 10, Box 03, Douglas Pike Collection: Unit 01 – Assessment and Strategy, p.8; TTU, 2120310008, NLF Study of War History, 1961 Thru 1964 – Translation of Captured Enemy Document, 28 March 1970, Folder 10, Box 03, Douglas Pike Collection: Unit 01 – Assessment and Strategy, p.8.

22 TTU, 2120310008, NLF Study of War History, 1961 Thru 1964 – Translation of Captured Enemy Document, 28 March 1970, Folder 10, Box 03, Douglas Pike Collection: Unit 01 – Assessment and Strategy, p.11.

23 TTU, 23118026001, Kinh nghiem chong pha ap chien luoc cua dong bao xa H (Khu II) (Experiences of Struggle with and Elimination of Strategic Hamlets of H Villagers), 01 October 1962, Folder 026, Box 18, Douglas Pike Collection: Unit 05 – National Liberation Front, p.2.

24 TTU, 23118026001, Kinh nghiem chong pha ap chien luoc cua dong bao xa H (Khu II) (Experiences of Struggle with and Elimination of Strategic Hamlets of H Villagers), 01 October 1962, Folder 026, Box 18, Douglas Pike Collection: Unit 05 – National Liberation Front, p.3; TTU, 23118026001, Kinh nghiem chong pha ap chien luoc cua dong bao xa H (Khu II) (Experiences of Struggle with and Elimination of Strategic Hamlets of H Villagers), 01 October 1962, Folder 026, Box 18, Douglas Pike Collection: Unit 05 – National Liberation Front, p.3.

25 TTU, 23130005003, Communist assessment of South Vietnam scene: 1/62–6/63, 01 January 1963, p.14.

26 TTU, 23130005003, Communist assessment of South Vietnam scene: 1/62–6/63, 01 January 1963, p.15; TTU, 23130005003, Communist assessment of South Vietnam scene: 1/62–6/63, 01 January 1963, p.17.

27 TTU, 2120207002, NLF Anti-Strategic Hamlet Programme, 1962, p.21.

28 *Ib* TTU, 2120207002, NLF Anti-Strategic Hamlet Programme, 1962, p.21.

29 TTU, 23130005003, Communist assessment of South Vietnam scene: 1/62–6/63, 01 January 1963, p.14.

30 TTU, 23130005003, Communist assessment of South Vietnam scene: 1/62–6/63, 01 January 1963, p.17.

31 See Karnow, *Vietnam: A History*, p.274; Thompson, *Defeating Communist Insurgency*, p.137.

32 TTU, 2120207002, NLF Anti-Strategic Hamlet Programme, 1962, p.20; TTU, 2120207002, NLF Anti-Strategic Hamlet Programme, 1962, p.21.

33 TTU, 2120102007, Assessment of the Status of the Revolution in Vietnam, 25 September 1962, p.6.

34 TTU, 23130005003, Communist assessment of South Vietnam scene: 1/62–6/63, 01 January 1963, p.15; TTU, 23130005003, Communist assessment of South Vietnam scene: 1/62–6/63, 01 January 1963, p.16.

35 *FRUS 1961–63, Volume III: No 41. Letter From the Commander, Military Assistance Command, Vietnam (Harkins) to President Diem Saigon, February 23, 1963.*

36 S. Tzu, *The Art of War* (Ware: Wordsworth Edition, 1998).

37 TTU, 2120207002, NLF Anti-Strategic Hamlet Programme, 1962, p.23.

38 Higgins, 'The Misapplication of the Malayan Counterinsurgency Model to the Strategic Hamlet Programme', p.43.

39 TTU, 2121610016, Captured Documents, VC Measures Against the Strategic Hamlet Programme, May 1970, p.11.

40 TTU, 23130005003, Communist assessment of South Vietnam scene: 1/62–6/63, 01 January 1963, p.3.

41 TTU, 2121610016, Captured Documents, VC Measures Against the Strategic Hamlet Programme, May 1970, p.6

42 TTU, 2121610016, Captured Documents, VC Measures Against the Strategic Hamlet Programme, May 1970, p.6; TTU, 0720216027, The CRIMP Documents, 1963, Folder 16, Box 02, John Donnell Collection, p.28.

43 The colours were used to denote the level of perceived threat and government control. See also TTU, 23130005003, Communist assessment of South Vietnam scene: 1/62–6/63, 01 January 1963, p.10.

44 TTU, 2121610016, Captured Documents, VC Measures Against the Strategic Hamlet Programme, May 1970, p.6.

45 TTU, 23130005003, Communist assessment of South Vietnam scene: 1/62–6/63, 01 January 1963, p.10.

46 TTU, 23130005003, Communist assessment of South Vietnam scene: 1/62–6/63, 01 January 1963, p.10.

47 TTU, 2121610016, Captured Documents, VC Measures Against the Strategic Hamlet Programme, May 1970, p.6.

48 TTU, 23130005003, Communist assessment of South Vietnam scene: 1/62–6/63, 01 January 1963, Folder 005, Box 30, Douglas Pike Collection: Unit 05 – National Liberation Front, p.10.

49 TTU, 2121610016, Captured Documents, VC Measures Against the Strategic Hamlet Programme, May 1970, p.6.

50 TTU, 2121610016, Captured Documents, VC Measures Against the Strategic Hamlet Programme, May 1970, p.6.

51 TTU, 2121610016, Captured Documents, VC Measures Against the Strategic Hamlet Programme, May 1970, p.6.

52 TTU, 2121610016, Captured Documents, VC Measures Against the Strategic Hamlet Programme, May 1970, p.7.

53 TTU, 2121610016, Captured Documents, VC Measures Against the Strategic Hamlet Programme, May 1970, p.7.

54 TTU, 2121610016, Captured Documents, VC Measures Against the Strategic Hamlet Programme, May 1970, p.11; TTU, 2121610016, Captured Documents, VC Measures Against the Strategic Hamlet Programme, May 1970, p.11; TTU, 2121610016, Captured Documents, VC Measures Against the Strategic Hamlet Programme, May 1970, p.12.

55 See for example, documents such as the Communist assessment of South Vietnam scene held at TTU, 23130005003, Communist assessment of South Vietnam scene: 1/62–6/63, 01 January 1963, Folder 005, Box 30, Douglas Pike Collection: Unit 05 – National Liberation Front, the NLF Anti-Strategic Hamlet Programme held at TTU, 2120207002, NLF Anti-Strategic Hamlet Programme, 1962, Folder 07, Box 02, Douglas Pike Collection: Unit 01 – Assessment and Strategy and The Destruction of the Enemy's Strategic Hamlet Programme also held at TTU, 2120208021, The Destruction of the Enemy's Strategic Hamlet Programme, November 1962, Folder 08, Box 02, Douglas Pike Collection: Unit 01 – Assessment and Strategy.

56 TTU, 23130005003, Communist assessment of South Vietnam scene: 1/62–6/63, 01 January 1963, p.17.

57 TTU, 2120207002, NLF Anti-Strategic Hamlet Programme, 1962, p.20.

58 TTU, 2120208021, The Destruction of the Enemy's Strategic Hamlet Programme, November 1962, p.2.

59 TTU, 2120207002, NLF Anti-Strategic Hamlet Programme, 1962, p.20.

60 TTU, 2120207002, NLF Anti-Strategic Hamlet Programme, 1962, p.31.

61 TTU, 2120207002, NLF Anti-Strategic Hamlet Programme, 1962, p.31.

62 TTU, 2120207002, NLF Anti-Strategic Hamlet Programme, 1962, p.32; TTU, 2120207002, NLF Anti-Strategic Hamlet Programme, 1962, p.33.

63 TTU, 23118026001, Kinh nghiem chong pha ap chien luoc cua dong bao xa H, 01 October 1962, p.2; TTU, 23118026001, Kinh nghiem chong pha ap chien luoc cua dong bao xa H, 01 October 1962, p.2.

64 TTU, 2120207002, NLF Anti-Strategic Hamlet Programme, 1962, p.20.

65 TTU, 2120207002, NLF Anti-Strategic Hamlet Programme, 1962, 1962, p.20.

66 TTU, 23130005003, Communist assessment of South Vietnam scene: 1/62–6/63, 01 January 1963, p.19.

67 TTU, 23130005003, Communist assessment of South Vietnam scene: 1/62–6/63, 01 January 1963, p.17; TTU, 23130005003, Communist assessment of South Vietnam scene: 1/62–6/63, 01 January 1963, p.17.

68 TTU, 23130005003, Communist assessment of South Vietnam scene: 1/62–6/63, 01 January 1963, p.19; TTU, 23130005003, Communist assessment of South Vietnam scene: 1/62–6/63, 01 January 1963, p.19.

69 TTU, 23118026001, Kinh nghiem chong pha ap chien luoc cua dong bao xa H, 01 October 1962, p.2; TTU, 2120207002, NLF Anti-Strategic Hamlet Programme, 1962, p.32.

70 TTU, 2120207002, NLF Anti-Strategic Hamlet Programme, 1962, p.21.

71 TTU, 2120207002, NLF Anti-Strategic Hamlet Programme, 1962, p.21.

72 TTU, 23130005003, Communist assessment of South Vietnam scene: 1/62–6/63, 01 January 1963, p.2; TTU, 23130005003, Communist assessment of South Vietnam scene: 1/62–6/63, 01 January 1963, p.3.

73 TTU, 23130005003, Communist assessment of South Vietnam scene: 1/62–6/63, 01 January 1963, p.3.

74 TTU, 2120207002, NLF Anti-Strategic Hamlet Programme, 1962, p.21.

75 TTU, 2120207002, NLF Anti-Strategic Hamlet Programme, 1962, p.23.

76 TTU, 2120207002, NLF Anti-Strategic Hamlet Programme, 1962, p.23.

77 TTU, 2120102007, Assessment of the Status of the Revolution in Vietnam, 25 September 1962, p.7.

78 TTU, 0720216027, The CRIMP Documents, 1963, p.23.

79 TTU, 23130005003, Communist assessment of South Vietnam scene: 1/62–6/63, 01 January 1963, p.18.

80 TTU, 0720216027, The CRIMP Documents, 1963, p.10.

81 TTU, 2120208011, Needs of the Revolution, July 1962, Folder 08, Box 02, Douglas Pike Collection: Unit 01 – Assessment and Strategy, p.15.

82 TTU, 2120207002, NLF Anti-Strategic Hamlet Programme, 1962, p.33.
83 TTU, 2120207002, NLF Anti-Strategic Hamlet Programme, 1962, p.33.
84 TTU, 2121610016, Captured Documents, VC Measures Against the Strategic Hamlet Programme, May 1970, p.15.
85 TTU, 0720216027, The CRIMP Documents, 1963, p.16.
86 TTU, 2120207002, NLF Anti-Strategic Hamlet Programme, 1962, p.38.
87 TTU, 2121610016, Captured Documents, VC Measures Against the Strategic Hamlet Programme, May 1970, p.16.
88 TTU, 2120207002, NLF Anti-Strategic Hamlet Programme, 1962, p.38.
89 TTU, 2121610016, Captured Documents, VC Measures Against the Strategic Hamlet Programme, May 1970, May 1970, p.15.
90 TTU, 2120208020, Policy Instructions from "Chin Nam" to the South, 27 September 1962, p.9.
91 TTU, 2120208020, Policy Instructions from "Chin Nam" to the South, 27 September 1962, p.9.
92 TTU, 0720216027, The CRIMP Documents, 1963, p.14.
93 TTU, 0720216027, The CRIMP Documents, 1963, p.14.
94 TTU, 23130005003, Communist assessment of South Vietnam scene: 1/62–6/63, 01 January 1963, p.16.
95 TTU, 23130005003, Communist assessment of South Vietnam scene: 1/62–6/63, 01 January 1963, p.16; TTU, 23130005003, Communist assessment of South Vietnam scene: 1/62–6/63, 01 January 1963, p.16.
96 TTU, 2120102007, Assessment of the Status of the Revolution in Vietnam, 25 September 1962, p.16.
97 TTU, 2121610016, Captured Documents, VC Measures Against the Strategic Hamlet Programme, May 1970, p.15.
98 TTU, 0720216027, The CRIMP Documents, 1963, p.12; TTU, 0720216027, The CRIMP Documents, 1963, p.12.
99 TTU, 23130001021, Translation of a mimeographed training bulletin captured in Vinh Long province in November 1963, probably written in 1962, Folder 001, Box 30, Douglas Pike Collection: Unit 05 – National Liberation Front, p.38.
100 TTU, 2121610016, Captured Documents, VC Measures Against the Strategic Hamlet Programme, May 1970, p.15.
101 R.M. Pearce, *RM–4692–1–ARPA – Evolution of a Vietnamese Village – Part II: The Past, August 1945 to April 1965* (Santa Monica: Rand Corporation, 1966), p.42.
102 Pearce, *RM–4692–1–ARPA*, p.42.
103 TTU, 2121610016, Captured Documents, VC Measures Against the Strategic Hamlet Programme, May 1970, p.14.
104 TTU, 2121610016, Captured Documents, VC Measures Against the Strategic Hamlet Programme, May 1970, p.14.
105 TTU, 2120102007, Assessment of the Status of the Revolution in Vietnam, 25 September 1962, p.7.
106 TTU, 2120207002, NLF Anti-Strategic Hamlet Programme, 1962, p.33.
107 TTU, 2121610016, Captured Documents, VC Measures Against the Strategic Hamlet Programme, May 1970, p.9.
108 TTU, 2121610016, Captured Documents, VC Measures Against the Strategic Hamlet Programme, May 1970, p.10.
109 TTU, 2120207002, NLF Anti-Strategic Hamlet Programme, 1962, p.34.
110 TTU, 23118026001, Kinh nghiem chong pha ap chien luoc cua dong bao xa H, 01 October 1962, p.6.
111 TTU, 2120207002, NLF Anti-Strategic Hamlet Programme, 1962, p.42.
112 TTU, 2120207002, NLF Anti-Strategic Hamlet Programme, p.42.
113 TTU, 2120207002, NLF Anti-Strategic Hamlet Programme, p.42.
114 TTU, 2120207002, NLF Anti-Strategic Hamlet Programme, p.42.
115 TTU, 2120207002, NLF Anti-Strategic Hamlet Programme, p.42.
116 TTU, 2120208019, Experiences in the Antistrategic Hamlet Programme, October–November 1962, p.3.
117 TTU, 2120208019, Experiences in the Antistrategic Hamlet Programme, October–November 1962, p.3; TTU, 23118026001, Kinh nghiem chong pha ap chien luoc cua dong bao xa H, 01 October 1962, p.3.
118 TTU, 2121610016, Captured Documents, VC Measures Against the Strategic Hamlet Programme, May 1970, p.17.
119 TTU, 23118026001, Kinh nghiem chong pha ap chien luoc cua dong bao xa H, 01 October 1962, p.3.
120 TTU, 2121610016, Captured Documents, VC Measures Against the Strategic Hamlet Programme, May 1970, p.17; TTU, 2120208011, Needs of the Revolution, July 1962, p.16.
121 TTU, 23118026001, Kinh nghiem chong pha ap chien luoc cua dong bao xa H, 01 October 1962, p.3.
122 TTU, 2130208015, VCD 34 – The People Should Support the Resistance Struggle Against the Enemy's Strategic Hamlet and Army Draft Schemes, 01 January 1962, Folder 08, Box 02, Douglas Pike Collection: Unit 02 – Military Operations.
123 TTU, 2130208015, VCD 34 – The People Should Support the Resistance Struggle Against the Enemy's Strategic Hamlet and Army Draft Schemes, 01 January 1962, Folder 08, Box 02, Douglas Pike Collection: Unit 02 – Military Operations.
124 TTU, 2130208015, VCD 34 – The People Should Support the Resistance Struggle Against the Enemy's Strategic Hamlet and Army Draft Schemes, 01 January 1962, Folder 08, Box 02, Douglas Pike Collection: Unit 02 – Military Operations, p.1.
125 TTU, 2130208015, VCD 34 – The People Should Support the Resistance Struggle Against the Enemy's Strategic Hamlet and Army Draft Schemes, 01 January 1962, Folder 08, Box 02, Douglas Pike Collection: Unit 02 – Military Operations, p.2.
126 TTU, 2121610016, Captured Documents, VC Measures Against the Strategic Hamlet Programme, May 1970, p.10.
127 TTU, 2121610016, Captured Documents, VC Measures Against the Strategic Hamlet Programme, May 1970, p.10.
128 TTU, 2120208019, Experiences in the Antistrategic Hamlet Programme, October–November 1962, p.2.
129 TTU, 2120208019, Experiences in the Antistrategic Hamlet Programme, October–November 1962, p.2; TTU, 2120208019, Experiences in the Antistrategic Hamlet Programme, October–November 1962, p.2.
130 TTU, 2120208011, Needs of the Revolution, July 1962, p.25; TTU, 2120208011, Needs of the Revolution, July 1962, p.25; TTU, 2120208011, Needs of the Revolution, July 1962, p.25; TTU, 2120208011, Needs of the Revolution, July 1962, p.25.
131 TTU, 2120208011, Needs of the Revolution, July 1962, p.25; TTU, 2120208011, Needs of the Revolution, July 1962, p.25; TTU, 2120208011, Needs of the Revolution, July 1962, p.25; TTU, 2120208011, Needs of the Revolution, July 1962, p.25.
132 TTU, 23130001021, Translation of a mimeographed training bulletin captured in Vinh Long province in November 1963, probably written in 1962, p.38/21.
133 TTU, 0720804001, Studies of the National Liberation Front of South Vietnam Interviews, 05 March 1966, p.12.
134 TTU, 0720804001, Studies of the National Liberation Front of South Vietnam Interviews, 05 March 1966, p.12
135 TTU, 0720804001, Studies of the National Liberation Front of South Vietnam Interviews, 05 March 1966, p.12.
136 TTU, 2120207002, NLF Anti-Strategic Hamlet Programme, 1962, p.39.
137 TTU, 2121610016, Captured Documents, VC Measures Against the Strategic Hamlet Programme, May 1970, p.16; TTU, 2121610016, Captured Documents, VC Measures Against the Strategic Hamlet Programme, May 1970, p.16.
138 Miami University Library, Ohio, OCLC Number: 1658815, Interview 93 – Finance Member, Microfilm – Rand Vietnam Interview Series V: Viet Cong Organizational Activities at Hamlet/Village Level (Santa Monica: RAND Corporation, 1968), p.1.
139 TTU, 2120207002, NLF Anti-Strategic Hamlet Programme, 1962, p.41
140 TTU, 2120207002, NLF Anti-Strategic Hamlet Programme, 1962, p.41.
141 TTU, 2120211017, Viet Cong Instructions on Military Defenses, April 1963, Folder 11, Box 02, Douglas Pike Collection: Unit 01 – Assessment and Strategy, p.1.
142 TTU, 23130001021, Translation of a mimeographed training bulletin captured in Vinh Long province in November 1963, probably written in 1962, p.38/21; TTU, 2120208011, Needs of the Revolution, July 1962, p.11; TTU, 2120208011, Needs of the Revolution, July 1962, p.12.
143 S.W. Cochran, *16157–ISA/ARPA – Motivation and Morale: Some Questions – Some Answers* (Santa Monica: RAND Corporation, 1967), p.24.
144 TTU, 2120207002, NLF Anti-Strategic Hamlet Programme, 1962, p.33.
145 Donnell, *14436–IBA/ARPA – Viet Cong Recruitment: Why and How Men Join*, p.109.
146 Donnell, *14436–IBA/ARPA – Viet Cong Recruitment: Why and How Men Join*, p.109.
147 Donnell, *14436–IBA/ARPA – Viet Cong Recruitment: Why and How Men Join*, p.110.
148 TTU, 2120208011, Needs of the Revolution, July 1962, p.17; TTU, 2120208011, Needs of the Revolution, July 1962, p.17.
149 TTU, 2310104001, Let Us Develop The Fighting Spirit To Destroy The Americano–Diem Strategic Alliance, 20 July 1962, Folder 04, Box 01, Douglas Pike Collection: Unit 05 – National Liberation Front.
150 TTU, 2310104001, Let Us Develop The Fighting Spirit To Destroy The Americano–Diem Strategic Alliance, 20 July 1962, Folder 04, Box 01, Douglas Pike Collection: Unit 05 – National Liberation Front, p.4.
151 TTU, 2310104001, Let Us Develop The Fighting Spirit To Destroy The Americano–Diem Strategic Alliance, 20 July 1962, Folder 04, Box 01, Douglas Pike Collection: Unit 05 – National Liberation Front, p.4.
152 TTU, 2310104001, Let Us Develop The Fighting Spirit To Destroy The Americano–Diem Strategic Alliance, 20 July 1962, Folder 04, Box 01, Douglas Pike Collection: Unit 05 – National Liberation Front.
153 Miami University Library, Ohio, OCLC Number: 1658815, Interview 21 – Medical Cadre, Microfilm – Rand Vietnam Interview Series V: Viet Cong Organizational Activities at Hamlet/Village Level (Santa Monica: RAND Corporation, 1968), p.2.
154 Miami University Library, Ohio, OCLC Number: 1658815, Interview 21 – Medical Cadre, Microfilm – Rand Vietnam Interview Series V: Viet Cong Organizational Activities at Hamlet/Village Level (Santa Monica: RAND Corporation, 1968), p.2.
155 TTU, 2120207002, NLF Anti-Strategic Hamlet Programme, 1962, pp.39–40.
156 TTU, 2120207002, NLF Anti-Strategic Hamlet Programme, 1962, pp.39–40.
157 TTU, 2120207002, NLF Anti-Strategic Hamlet Programme, 1962, p.41.
158 TTU, 2120207002, NLF Anti-Strategic Hamlet Programme, 1962, p.41.
159 TTU, 2120207002, NLF Anti-Strategic Hamlet Programme, 1962, p.41.
160 TTU, 2120207002, NLF Anti-Strategic Hamlet Programme, 1962, p.41.
161 TTU, 2120207002, NLF Anti-Strategic Hamlet Programme, 1962, p.39.
162 TTU, 2120207002, NLF Anti-Strategic Hamlet Programme, 1962, p.39 TTU, 2120207002, NLF Anti-Strategic Hamlet Programme, 1962, p.39.
163 TTU, 2120207003, Viet Cong Study Document on Strategic Hamlets, 1962, p.1.
164 TTU, 2120207002, NLF Anti-Strategic Hamlet Programme, 1962, p.39.
165 TTU, 0720216027, The CRIMP Documents, 1963, p.13.
166 TTU, 2120207002, NLF Anti-Strategic Hamlet Programme, 1962, p.34.
167 TTU, 2120207002, NLF Anti-Strategic Hamlet Programme, 1962, p.33.
168 TTU, 2120207002, NLF Anti-Strategic Hamlet Programme, 1962, pp.33–34.
169 TTU, 2120207002, NLF Anti-Strategic Hamlet Programme, 1962, p.34.
170 TTU, 2390711005, A Threat to the Peace, p.2.
171 TTU, 0720216027, The CRIMP Documents, 1963, p.36; *Ib* TTU, 0720216027, The CRIMP Documents, 1963, p.36.
172 TTU, 2120208011, Needs of the Revolution, July 1962, p.10.
173 TTU, 2120208011, Needs of the Revolution, July 1962, p.18.

Chapter 3

1 Phillips, 'Rufus Phillips on Why Vietnam Matters: An Eyewitness Account of Lessons Not Learned', Time 49:05.
2 Phillips, 'Rufus Phillips on Why Vietnam Matters: An Eyewitness Account of Lessons Not Learned', Time 49:45.
3 K.I. Sepp, 'Best Practices in Counterinsurgency', *Military Review*, May–June (2005), p..10.
4 TTU, 2120207002, NLF Anti-Strategic Hamlet Programme, 1962, pp.26–27.
5 TTU, 23970128002, Report, A Report on Counter-insurgency in Vietnam, 20 July 1962, p.6.
6 Phillips and O'Donnell give an excellent account of their time in Vietnam in H. Neese, & J. O'Donnell, (eds), *Prelude to Tragedy: Vietnam 1960–1965* (Annapolis: Naval Institute Press, 2001). Phillips also discussed this time period in detail in his memoirs *Why Vietnam Matters: An Eyewitness Account of Lessons not Learned,* which were discussed in the introduction.
7 Unknown Correspondent, Saigon, 'Lessons of the War in South Vietnam', *The Times,* 21 January 1963.
8 Unknown Correspondent, Saigon, 'Lessons of the War in South Vietnam', *The Times,* 21 January 1963.
9 *FRUS 1961–63, Volume 3: No 97. Memorandum From the Director of the Vietnam Working Group (Wood) to the Assistant Secretary of State for Far Eastern Affairs (Hilsman), April 18, 1963.*
10 *FRUS 1961–63, Volume I: No 3. Summary Record of a Meeting, The White House, Washington, January 28, 1961, 10 a.m–12:15 p.m.;* S. Phillips, *The Cold War* (Oxford: Heinemann, 2001), p.221.
11 TTU, 2120102007, Assessment of the Status of the Revolution in Vietnam, 25 September 1962, p.4.
12 TTU, 23130001021, Translation of a mimeographed training bulletin captured in Vinh Long province in November 1963, probably written in 1962, p.38–8; TTU, 23130001021, Translation of a mimeographed training bulletin captured in Vinh Long province in November 1963, probably written in 1962, p.38–8.
13 TTU, 23130005003, Communist assessment of South Vietnam scene: 1/62–6/63, 01 January 1963, p.12; TTU, 23130005003, Communist assessment of South Vietnam scene: 1/62–6/63, 01 January 1963, p.12.
14 TTU, 2120208011, Needs of the Revolution, July 1962, p.3; TTU, 2120207002, NLF Anti-Strategic Hamlet Programme, 1962, p.12; TTU, 2120208011, Needs of the Revolution, July 1962, p.3; TTU, 2120207002, NLF Anti-Strategic Hamlet Programme, 1962, p.12; TTU, 2120208011, Needs of the Revolution, July 1962, p.3; TTU, 2120207002, NLF Anti-Strategic Hamlet Programme, 1962, p.13.
15 TTU, 23130010017, Programme of the South Vietnam National Front for liberation, 01 January 1961, Folder 010, Box 30, Douglas Pike Collection: Unit 05 – National Liberation Front, p.22.
16 See the general tone and examples given in TTU, 2120207002, NLF Anti-Strategic Hamlet Programme, 1962, for evidence of this type of propaganda.
17 Farmer, 'Counter-insurgency: Principles and Practice in Vietnam: 1962–1963', p.3.
18 Miami University Library, Ohio, OCLC Number: 1658815, Interview 72 – Village Security, Microfilm – Rand Vietnam Interview Series V: Viet Cong Organizational Activities at Hamlet/Village Level (Santa Monica: RAND Corporation, 1968), p.2.
19 Pearce, *RM–4692–1–ARPA – Evolution of a Vietnamese Village – Part II: The Past, August 1945 to April 1965,* p.23; Pearce, *RM–4692–1–ARPA – Evolution of a Vietnamese Village,* p.23.
20 JFK, JFKPOF–128–009, Letter from Theodore H. White to the President October 11, 1961, Papers of John F Kennedy. Presidential Papers, President's Office Files, Country Files, Vietnam: General, 1960–1961, Box 128, p.1.
21 JFK, JFKPOF–128–009, Letter from Theodore H. White to the President October 11, 1961, Papers of John F Kennedy. Presidential Papers, President's Office Files, Country Files, Vietnam: General, 1960–1961, Box 128, p.1.
22 TTU, 0720806003, Studies of the National Liberation Front of South Vietnam, 23 April 1965, Folder 06, Box 08, John Donnell Collection, p.5.
23 TTU, 2120207002, NLF Anti-Strategic Hamlet Programme, 1962, p.30.
24 TTU, 2120207002, NLF Anti-Strategic Hamlet Programme, 1962, p.31.
25 TTU, 2120207002, NLF Anti-Strategic Hamlet Programme, 1962, p.29.
26 Miami University Library, Ohio, OCLC Number: 1658815, Interview 72 – Village Security, Microfilm – Rand Vietnam Interview Series V: Viet Cong Organizational Activities at Hamlet/Village Level (Santa Monica: RAND Corporation, 1968), p.2.
27 TTU, 2120208011, Needs of the Revolution, July 1962, p.13.
28 TTU, 2120207002, NLF Anti-Strategic Hamlet Programme, 1962, p.25; TTU, 2120207002, NLF Anti-Strategic Hamlet Programme, 1962, p.25.
29 Donnell, *14436–IBA/ARPA – Viet Cong Recruitment: Why and How Men Join,* p.68.
30 Miami University Library, Ohio, OCLC Number: 1658815, Interview 4 – Civilian Prisoner, Microfilm – Rand Vietnam Interview Series V: Viet Cong Organizational Activities at Hamlet/Village Level (Santa Monica: RAND Corporation, 1968), p.5.
31 TTU, The Vietnam Center and Archive, Texas Tech University, 23130001021, Translation of a mimeographed training bulletin captured in Vinh Long province in November 1963, p.38–1.
32 Donnell, *14436–IBA/ARPA – Viet Cong Recruitment: Why and How Men Join,* p.xv.
33 Miami University Library, Ohio, OCLC Number: 1658815, Interview 8 – Deputy Head of the village Economic and Finance Section, Microfilm – Rand Vietnam Interview Series V: Viet Cong Organizational Activities at Hamlet/Village Level (Santa Monica: RAND Corporation, 1968), p.18.
34 Miami University Library, Ohio, OCLC Number: 1658815, Interview 75 – Village Party Committee Member, Microfilm – Rand Vietnam Interview Series V: Viet Cong Organizational Activities at Hamlet/Village Level (Santa Monica: RAND Corporation, 1968), p.1.
35 Donnell, *14436–IBA/ARPA – Viet Cong Recruitment: Why and How Men Join,* p.48.
36 Donnell, *14436–IBA/ARPA – Viet Cong Recruitment: Why and How Men Join,* p.47.
37 Miami University Library, Ohio, OCLC Number: 1658815, Interview 87 – Civilian Prisoner, Microfilm – Rand Vietnam Interview Series V: Viet Cong Organizational Activities at Hamlet/Village Level (Santa Monica: RAND Corporation, 1968), p.1.
38 TTU, 0720804001, Studies of the National Liberation Front of South Vietnam, 23 April 1965, p.17; TTU, 0720804001, Studies of the National Liberation Front of South Vietnam, 23 April 1965, p.17.
39 TTU, 0720804001, Studies of the National Liberation Front of South Vietnam, 23 April 1965, p.17.
40 TTU, 0720804001, Studies of the National Liberation Front of South Vietnam, 23 April 1965, p.17.
41 Miami University Library, Ohio, OCLC Number: 1658815, Interview 31 – Refugee Farmer, Microfilm – Rand Vietnam Interview Series V: Viet Cong Organizational Activities at Hamlet/Village Level (Santa Monica: RAND Corporation, 1968), p.5.
42 Miami University Library, Ohio, OCLC Number: 1658815, Interview 26 – Hamlet Cadre in self-defense Platoon, Microfilm – Rand Vietnam Interview Series V: Viet Cong Organizational Activities at Hamlet/Village Level (Santa Monica: RAND Corporation, 1968), p.8.
43 *FRUS 1961–63, Volume I: No 1. Paper Prepared by the Country Team Staff Committee, Saigon, January 4, 1961.*
44 TTU, 2120102007, Assessment of the Status of the Revolution in Vietnam, 25 September 1962, p.6; TTU, 2120207002, NLF Anti-Strategic Hamlet Programme, 1962, p.8.
45 A good description of Personalism can be found in 'Vietnam Dilutes its Democracy', *The Times,* 1 July 1963. Catton also expands in detail about the origins and nature of this philosophy in *Diem's Final Failure,* pp.38–50.
46 TTU, 23118026001, Kinh nghiem chong pha ap chien luoc cua dong bao xa H, 01 October 1962, p.1.
47 TTU, 2120207002, NLF Anti-Strategic Hamlet Programme, 1962, pp.15–16.
48 TTU, 2120207002, NLF Anti-Strategic Hamlet Programme, 1962, p.18.
49 TTU, 2120207002, NLF Anti-Strategic Hamlet Programme, 1962, p.15.
50 Pearce, *RM–4692–1–ARPA – Evolution of a Vietnamese Village – Part II: The Past, August 1945 to April 1965,* p.42.
51 JFK, JFKPOF–128–010, Address by George W. Ball April 30 1962 Veterans Memorial Building Civic Center, Detroit, Michigan, Papers of John F Kennedy. Presidential Papers, President's Office Files, Country Files, Vietnam, General, Box 128, p.7.
52 JFK, JFKPOF–128–010, Address by George W. Ball April 30 1962 Veterans Memorial Building Civic Center, Detroit, Michigan, Papers of John F Kennedy. Presidential Papers, President's Office Files, Country Files, Vietnam, General, Box 128, p.7.
53 Phillips, 'Rufus Phillips on Why Vietnam Matters: An Eyewitness Account of Lessons Not Learned', Time 1:02:00.
54 SNIE, *14.3 / 53–61 Prospects for North and South Vietnam,* 15 August 1961, p.11.
55 TTU, 23970128002, Report, A Report on Counter-insurgency in Vietnam, 20 July 1962, p.2; TTU, 23970128002, Report, A Report on Counter-insurgency in Vietnam, 20 July 1962, p.1; SNIE, *14.3 / 53–61 Prospects for North and South Vietnam,* 15 August 1961, p.12.
56 Donnell & Hickey, *RM–3208–ARPA – The Vietnamese 'Strategic Hamlets': A Preliminary Report,* p.1; See Miami University Library, Ohio, OCLC Number: 1658815, Microfilm – Rand Vietnam Interview Series V: Viet Cong Organizational Activities at Hamlet/Village Level (Santa Monica: RAND Corporation, 1968).
57 Miami University Library, Ohio, OCLC Number: 1658815, Interview 7 – Village Party Chapter Member, Microfilm – Rand Vietnam Interview Series V: Viet Cong Organizational Activities at Hamlet/Village Level (Santa Monica: RAND Corporation, 1968), p.1.
58 Miami University Library, Ohio, OCLC Number: 1658815, Interview 97 – Member of Hamlet Propaganda, Culture and Indoctrination Section, Microfilm – Rand Vietnam Interview Series V: Viet Cong Organizational Activities at Hamlet/Village Level (Santa Monica: RAND Corporation, 1968), p.1.
59 TTU, 1610101001, Vietnamese Ranger Operations in War Zone D, 1962–63, August 1965, Folder 01, Box 01, Charles (Bob) Nulsen Collection, p.3.
60 TTU, 1610101001, Vietnamese Ranger Operations in War Zone D, 1962–63, August 1965, Folder 01, Box 01, Charles (Bob) Nulsen Collection, p.14.
61 TTU, 1610101001, Vietnamese Ranger Operations in War Zone D, 1962–63, August 1965, Folder 01, Box 01, Charles (Bob) Nulsen Collection, p.3.
62 JFK, RHPP–003–006, A Strategic Concept for South Vietnam, p.2.
63 TTU, 1610101001, Vietnamese Ranger Operations in War Zone D, 1962–63, August 1965, Folder 01, Box 01, Charles (Bob) Nulsen Collection, p.2.
64 Miami University Library, Ohio, OCLC Number: 1658815, Interview 97 – Member of Hamlet Propaganda, Culture and Indoctrination Section, Microfilm – Rand Vietnam Interview Series V: Viet Cong Organizational Activities at Hamlet/Village Level (Santa Monica: RAND Corporation, 1968), p.4.
65 SNIE, *10–62 Communist Objectives, Capabilities, and Intentions in Southeast Asia,* 21 February 1962, p.3.
66 SNIE, *10–62 Communist Objectives, Capabilities, and Intentions in Southeast Asia,* 21 February 1962, p.3.
67 TTU, 0720804001, Studies of the National Liberation Front of South Vietnam, 23 April 1965, p.76.
68 Miami University Library, Ohio, OCLC Number: 1658815, Interview 9 – Village Party Committee Member, Microfilm – Rand Vietnam Interview Series V: Viet Cong Organizational Activities at Hamlet/Village Level (Santa Monica: RAND Corporation, 1968), p.10.

69 Miami University Library, Ohio, OCLC Number: 1658815, Interview 9 – Village Party Committee Member, Microfilm – Rand Vietnam Interview Series V: Viet Cong Organizational Activities at Hamlet/Village Level (Santa Monica: RAND Corporation, 1968), p.10.
70 TTU, 2390711005, A Threat to the Peace, p.9.
71 TTU, 0720406006, Studies of the National Liberation Front of South Vietnam Interviews 142, 16 April 1966, p.5.
72 JFK, RHPP–003–006, A Strategic Concept for South Vietnam, p.2.
73 Miami University Library, Ohio, OCLC Number: 1658815, Interview 8 – Deputy Head of the Village Economic and Finance Section, Microfilm – Rand Vietnam Interview Series V: Viet Cong Organizational Activities at Hamlet/Village Level (Santa Monica: RAND Corporation, 1968), p.11.
74 J.M. Carrier, & C.A.H. Thomson, *RM–4830–2–ISA/ARPA– Viet Cong Motivation and Morale: The Special Case of Chieu Hoi* (Santa Monica: RAND Corporation, 1966), pp.36–37.
75 TTU, 23970128002, Report, A Report on Counter-insurgency in Vietnam, 20 July 1962, p.2.
76 TTU, 23970128002, Report, A Report on Counter-insurgency in Vietnam, 20 July 1962, p.2.
77 TTU, 23970128002, Report, A Report on Counter-insurgency in Vietnam, 20 July 1962, p.13.
78 TTU, 23970128002, Report, A Report on Counter-insurgency in Vietnam, 20 July 1962, p.2.
79 TTU, 23970128002, Report, A Report on Counter-insurgency in Vietnam, 20 July 1962, p.2.
80 TTU, 23970128002, Report, A Report on Counter-insurgency in Vietnam, 20 July 1962, p.2.
81 TTU, 2120207002, NLF Anti-Strategic Hamlet Programme, 1962, p.39.
82 TTU, 2120207002, NLF Anti-Strategic Hamlet Programme, 1962, pp.39.
83 TTU, 2120207002, NLF Anti-Strategic Hamlet Programme, 1962, pp.33–34.
84 TTU, 23970128002, Report, A Report on Counter-insurgency in Vietnam, 20 July 1962, p.2.
85 TTU, 2390711005, A Threat to the Peace, p.11.
86 Miami University Library, Ohio, OCLC Number: 1658815, Interview 4 – Civilian Prisoner, Microfilm – Rand Vietnam Interview Series V: Viet Cong Organizational Activities at Hamlet/Village Level (Santa Monica: RAND Corporation, 1968), p.15.
87 TTU, 2390711005, A Threat to the Peace, p.11.
88 SNIE, *10–62 Communist Objectives, Capabilities, and Intentions in Southeast Asia*, 21 February 1962, p.3.
89 SNIE, *10–62 Communist Objectives, Capabilities, and Intentions in Southeast Asia*, 21 February 1962, p.3; SNIE, *10–62 Communist Objectives, Capabilities, and Intentions in Southeast Asia*, 21 February 1962, p.3.
90 Miami University Library, Ohio, OCLC Number: 1658815, Interview 9 – Village Party Committee Member, Microfilm – Rand Vietnam Interview Series V: Viet Cong Organizational Activities at Hamlet/Village Level (Santa Monica: RAND Corporation, 1968), p.11.
91 SNIE, *10–62 Communist Objectives, Capabilities, and Intentions in Southeast Asia*, 21 February 1962, p.3; Miami University Library, Ohio, OCLC Number: 1658815, Interview 9 – Village Party Committee Member, Microfilm – Rand Vietnam Interview Series V: Viet Cong Organizational Activities at Hamlet/Village Level (Santa Monica: RAND Corporation, 1968), p.11.
92 Miami University Library, Ohio, OCLC Number: 1658815, Interview 9 – Village Party Committee Member, Microfilm – Rand Vietnam Interview Series V: Viet Cong Organizational Activities at Hamlet/Village Level (Santa Monica: RAND Corporation, 1968), p.11.
93 Miami University Library, Ohio, OCLC Number: 1658815, Interview 9 – Village Party Committee Member, Microfilm – Rand Vietnam Interview Series V: Viet Cong Organizational Activities at Hamlet/Village Level (Santa Monica: RAND Corporation, 1968), p.11; SNIE, *10–62 Communist Objectives, Capabilities, and Intentions in Southeast Asia*, 21 February 1962, p.4.
94 Miami University Library, Ohio, OCLC Number: 1658815, Interview 9 – Village Party Committee Member, Microfilm – Rand Vietnam Interview Series V: Viet Cong Organizational Activities at Hamlet/Village Level (Santa Monica: RAND Corporation, 1968), p.4.
95 TTU, 0720804001, Studies of the National Liberation Front of South Vietnam, 23 April 1965, p.4.
96 SNIE, *10–62 Communist Objectives, Capabilities, and Intentions in Southeast Asia*, 21 February 1962, p.3.
97 SNIE, *10–62 Communist Objectives, Capabilities, and Intentions in Southeast Asia*, 21 February 1962, p.4; SNIE, *10–62 Communist Objectives, Capabilities, and Intentions in Southeast Asia*, 21 February 1962, p.3; SNIE, *10–62 Communist Objectives, Capabilities, and Intentions in Southeast Asia*, 21 February 1962, p.4.
98 TTU, 2390711005, A Threat to the Peace, p.17.
99 TTU, 2390711005, A Threat to the Peace, p.20.
100 SNIE, *53–63 Prospects in South Vietnam*, 17 April 1963, p.6.
101 Donnell, *14436–IBA/ARPA – Viet Cong Recruitment: Why and How Men Join*, p.31; Donnell, *14436–IBA/ARPA – Viet Cong Recruitment: Why and How Men Join*, p.31.
102 Pearce, *RM–4692–1–ARPA – Evolution of a Vietnamese Village – Part II: The Past, August 1945 to April 1965*, p.23.
103 Pearce, *RM–4692–1–ARPA – Evolution of a Vietnamese Village – Part II: The Past, August 1945 to April 1965*, p.24.
104 Donnell, *14436–IBA/ARPA – Viet Cong Recruitment: Why and How Men Join*, p.82.
105 TTU, 1490117001, Publication – My Thuan: A Mekong Delta Village in South Vietnam, 1963, Folder 17, Box 01, Michigan State University Vietnam Advisory Group Collection, p.17.
106 Donnell, *14436–IBA/ARPA – Viet Cong Recruitment: Why and How Men Join*, p.x.
107 Donnell, *14436–IBA/ARPA – Viet Cong Recruitment: Why and How Men Join*, p.x.
108 *FRUS 1961–63, Volume III: No 78. Minutes of Meeting of the Special Group for Counterinsurgency Washington, April 4, 1963, 2 p.m.*
109 JFK, RHPP–003–009, Memorandum From the Director of the Bureau of Intelligence and Research (Hilsman) and Michael V. Forrestal of the National Security Council Staff to the President, Washington, January 25, 1963, p.5.
110 JFK, RHPP–003–009, Memorandum From the Director of the Bureau of Intelligence and Research (Hilsman) and Michael V. Forrestal of the National Security Council Staff to the President, Washington, January 25, 1963, p.5.
111 Miami University Library, Ohio, OCLC Number: 1658815, Interview 9 – Village Party Committee Member, Microfilm – Rand Vietnam Interview Series V: Viet Cong Organizational Activities at Hamlet/Village Level (Santa Monica: RAND Corporation, 1968), p.30.
112 TTU, 23970128002, Report, A Report on Counter-insurgency in Vietnam, 20 July 1962, p.1.
113 TTU, 23970128002, Report, A Report on Counter-insurgency in Vietnam, 20 July 1962, p.1.
114 Miami University Library, Ohio, OCLC Number: 1658815, Interview 26 – Hamlet Cadre in self-defense Platoon, Microfilm – Rand Vietnam Interview Series V: Viet Cong Organizational Activities at Hamlet/Village Level (Santa Monica: RAND Corporation, 1968), p.3.
115 Miami University Library, Ohio, OCLC Number: 1658815, Interview 26 – Hamlet Cadre in self-defense Platoon, Microfilm – Rand Vietnam Interview Series V: Viet Cong Organizational Activities at Hamlet/Village Level (Santa Monica: RAND Corporation, 1968), p.3.
116 Donnell & Hickey, *RM–3208–ARPA – The Vietnamese 'Strategic Hamlets': A Preliminary Report*, p.16.
117 TTU, 0720406008, Studies of the National Liberation Front of South Vietnam Interviews 139, 12–14 April 1966, p.5.
118 JFK, RHPP–003–009, Memorandum From the Director of the Bureau of Intelligence and Research (Hilsman) and Michael V. Forrestal of the National Security Council Staff to the President, Washington, January 25, 1963, p.5.
119 JFK, JFKNSF–203–003, Letter From the President's Military Representative (Taylor) to the President [Appendix G] Memorandum From the Secretary of Defense's Assistant for Special Operations (Lansdale) to the President's Military Representative (Taylor) Washington, November 3, 1961, Vietnam: Subjects: Taylor Report, 3 November 1961: Rostow Working Copy. Papers of John F. Kennedy, Presidential Papers, National Security Files, Countries, Vietnam, Box 203, Appendix G, p.6.
120 Miami University Library, Ohio, OCLC Number: 1658815, Interview 8 – Deputy Head of the village Economic and Finance Section, Microfilm – Rand Vietnam Interview Series V: Viet Cong Organizational Activities at Hamlet/Village Level (Santa Monica: RAND Corporation, 1968), p.19.
121 Miami University Library, Ohio, OCLC Number: 1658815, Interview 8 – Deputy Head of the village Economic and Finance Section, Microfilm – Rand Vietnam Interview Series V: Viet Cong Organizational Activities at Hamlet/Village Level (Santa Monica: RAND Corporation, 1968), p.19.
122 Miami University Library, Ohio, OCLC Number: 1658815, Interview 8 – Deputy Head of the village Economic and Finance Section, Microfilm – Rand Vietnam Interview Series V: Viet Cong Organizational Activities at Hamlet/Village Level (Santa Monica: RAND Corporation, 1968), p.19.
123 JFK, RHPP–003–009, Memorandum From the Director of the Bureau of Intelligence and Research (Hilsman) and Michael V. Forrestal of the National Security Council Staff to the President, Washington, January 25, 1963, p.7; JFK, RHPP–003–009, Memorandum From the Director of the Bureau of Intelligence and Research (Hilsman) and Michael V. Forrestal of the National Security Council Staff to the President, Washington, January 25, 1963, p.7.
124 TTU, 23970128002, Report, A Report on Counter-insurgency in Vietnam, 20 July 1962, p.1.
125 JFK, JFKNSF–203–003, Letter From the President's Military Representative (Taylor) to the President [Appendix G] Memorandum From the Secretary of Defense's Assistant for Special Operations (Lansdale) to the President's Military Representative (Taylor) Washington, November 3, 1961, Vietnam: Subjects: Taylor Report, 3 November 1961: Rostow Working Copy. Papers of John F. Kennedy, Presidential Papers, National Security Files, Countries, Vietnam, Box 203, Appendix G, p.6.
126 Pearce, *RM–4692–1–ARPA – Evolution of a Vietnamese Village – Part II: The Past, August 1945 to April 1965*, p.28.
127 Pearce, *RM–4692–1–ARPA – Evolution of a Vietnamese Village – Part II: The Past, August 1945 to April 1965*, p.28.
128 Donnell, *14436–IBA/ARPA – Viet Cong Recruitment: Why and How Men Join*, p.32.
129 Donnell, *14436–IBA/ARPA – Viet Cong Recruitment: Why and How Men Join*, pp.80–81.

ABOUT THE AUTHOR

Dr Darren Poole is a lecturer in Military History at the University of Chester and University Centre, Shrewsbury. He specialises in counterinsurgency, the Vietnam War and general American history. Dr Poole has degrees in History, Military History, Geography and Education and he has been teaching for over 25 years. His current research examines the 'unheard voices' of conflict. These include, for example, the peasants caught in a crossfire in South Vietnam and the views of the Viet Cong themselves. Dr Poole aims to present research that complements and challenges the accepted historical narrative; in many cases his work reveals the cruelty of the 'insurgents' towards their own people and provides a 'moral' imperative for Western intervention. Dr Poole is currently working on a further book that examines the violence and terror of the Viet Cong themselves.